E-BUSINESS – APPLICATIONS AND GLOBAL ACCEPTANCE

Edited by **Princely Ifinedo**

E-Business – Applications and Global Acceptance
Edited by Princely Ifinedo

Published by InTech
Janeza Trdine 9, 51000 Rijeka, Croatia

Publishing Process Manager Alida Lesnjakovic

Technical Editor Teodora Smiljanic

Cover Designer InTech Design Team

Additional hard copies can be obtained from orders@intechopen.com

E-Business – Applications and Global Acceptance, Edited by Princely Ifinedo
p. cm.
ISBN 978-953-51-0081-2

For EU product safety concerns:
IN TECH d.o.o., Prolaz Marije Krucifikse Kozulić 3, 51000 Rijeka, Croatia,
info@intechopen.com or visit our website at intechopen.com.

Meet the editor

Dr Princely Ifinedo is an Associate Professor at the Shannon School of Business, Cape Breton University, Canada. He holds a doctoral degree (with Eximia Cum Laude Approbatur) in Information Systems Science from the University of Jyväskylä, Finland and master's degrees from the Royal Holloway University of London, UK and Tallinn University of Technology, Estonia. He has presented research at various international IS conferences (including a Best Track Paper at the 2008 AMCIS, Toronto, Canada), contributed chapters to several books/encyclopedias, and published in several reputable journals including JCIS, C&S, JSS, DATA BASE, CHB, JOCEC, JITM, IMDS, EIS, IJITDM, JITD, JITM, JGTIM, EG, JISP, and Internet Research. He has authored (and co-authored) about 90 peer-reviewed publications. Prof. Ifinedo's current research interests include, Enterprise Resource Planning (ERP) Systems Success Measurement, Job Motivation and Satisfaction of IT/IS Professionals, Adoption of IT/IS in SMEs and Healthcare, Acceptance of Social Networking Sites, IS/IT Issues in Developing Countries and Transiting Economies, Cross-cultural IS/IT Issues, E-government, E-commerce, E-business, E-learning, and Social Informatics. He is affiliated with AIS, ISACA, and CIPS.

Contents

Preface IX

Chapter 1 **Internet/E-Business Technologies Acceptance in Canada's SMEs: Focus on Organizational and Environmental Factors 3**
Princely Ifinedo

Chapter 2 **Facilitating the Intention to Expand E-business Payment Systems Use in Nigerian Small Firms: An Empirical Analysis 19**
Princely Ifinedo

Chapter 3 **Further Development of a Secured Unified E-Payment System in Nigeria: A Critical Viewpoint 41**
Charles K. Ayo and Wilfred Isioma Ukpere

Chapter 4 **Knowledge Management with Multi-Agent System in BI Systems Integration 53**
Dejan Lavbič

Chapter 5 **Web Services-Enhanced Agile Modeling and Integrating Business Processes 73**
Fatima-Zahra Belouadha, Hajar Omrana and Ounsa Roudiès

Chapter 6 **E-Business and Research Institutes: When Technologies, Platforms and Methods Converge to Meet Users' Needs 99**
Serena Pastore

Chapter 7 **A Discourse on the Construction of a Service Innovation Model: Focus on the Cultural and Creative Industry Park 119**
Rungtai Lin and Chun-Liang Chen

Preface

This edited book has been published to showcase the emergence of relevant insights, applications, and the global acceptance of electronic business (e-business). At this stage of the development of e-business, it is crucially important to monitor, report, and reflect on the progress of e-business' applications and adoption around the world. As organizations, private, public, and non-profit, of differing sizes continue to expand their use of e-business applications, practitioners and researchers in the domain should continue to devote time, energy, and effort to disseminate relevant, useful information about the e-business phenomenon. Such efforts serve to consolidate knowledge in the field. The primary objective of this book is to further strengthen the evolving knowledge in the field, as it seeks to focus on topical and timely issues regarding the acceptance of e-business applications, business processes management enhancements, integration of informational resources in e-business environments, applicability of e-business underpinnings for non-profit organizations, and the construction of a service innovation model. This book is comprised of seven chapters, representing a broad cross-section of perspectives and research on e-business.

The first chapter, "Internet/E-Business Technologies Acceptance in Canada's SMEs: Focus on Organizational and Environmental Factors" by Ifinedo examines why are Canadian small and medium size enterprises (SMEs) reticent about accepting internet and e-business technologies (IEBT) in their operations. The chapter seeks to present an understanding of the importance of key organizational and environmental factors in the context of the research setting i.e. the developed world. The author used the Technology–Organization–Environment (TOE) framework to guide his research. The results of the study indicated that perceived benefits, management commitment/support, and external pressure are significant predictors of IEBT acceptance in the sampled SMEs; his results did not show that organizational IT competence, IS vendor support, and availability of financial support positively influence IEBT acceptance in the sampled SMEs. The research study brought the attention of practitioners to the relevant factors that deserve attention in encouraging the acceptance of IEBT among SMEs in Canada.

The second chapter, "Facilitating the Intention to Expand E-business Payment Systems Use in Nigerian Small Firms: An Empirical Analysis" by Ifinedo aims to provide empirical information on the factors that influence small firms in a developing country to expand or increase their use of e-business payment solutions. The authors used a fusion of the Technology Acceptance Model (TAM) and the Technology–Organization–Environment (TOE) to conduct their research project. Their findings confirmed that the pertinence of perceived usefulness, top management support, organizational IS readiness, and IS vendor support as salient factors that could facilitate or improve a small firm's capability to expand its acceptance or use of relevant e-business payment systems or solutions in the developing world, with Nigeria as an exemple.

The third chapter, "Further Development of a Secured Unified E-Payment System in Nigeria: A Critical Viewpoint," by Ayo and Ukpere proposes the use of a unified, single smart card-based automated teller machines (ATM) card coupled with biometric-based cash dispenser for banking transactions. These authors hoped that such an application or architecture could help reducing the number of ATM cards that are currently being carried by individuals. They also believe that the biometric facility would provide an enhanced layer of security for the widely used PIN system. The authors designed a survey, which they used to evaluate the acceptability of their conceptualization and proposition among ATM users in a developing country, Nigeria. Their results support the applicability and relevance of their proposed conceptualization or model in that research setting.

The fourth chapter, "Knowledge Management with Multi-Agent System in BI Systems Integration" by Lavbič, presents information on how a novel approach can be used to integrate unstructured information on the Web and in several other internal data sources (e.g. database, datawarehouses, ERP). The author argues that there is too much information out there to digest and process, which means that there is a need to marshal the different information systems (IS) applications and tools to integrate information retrieval, classification, and presentation. The author asserts that his effort would help to minimize the gap between business users and agents deployed to perform tasks on their behalf. The researcher clamored for and went on to propose using Ontologies and Multi-Agent Systems as possible solutions to the aforementioned challenge. Importantly, the author hopes that the Ontology used in the Multi-Agent System for decision support tasks in enterprises (DSS-MAS) may permit business users to manipulate and classify informational resources in a more efficient manner.

The fifth chapter, "Web Services-Enhanced Agile Modeling and Integrating Business Processes," by Belouadha, Omrana and Roudiès is designed to enrich information on how the Internet can be employed in the management of business processes through e-business applications. In particular, the authors based their approach on extensible standards and they propose an approach that considers an agile business process as one that can be broken into independent task units in the design phase and then re-composed at the runtime. They argue that such way of designing processes would allow for the reuse of functional task units. At the same time, their conceptualization or framework has the capability to help reduce the unintended impacts on existing processes. The fact that this conceptual paper would benefit the body of work in the extant literature dealing with e-business modeling and Business Process Management (BPM) should be noted.

The sixth chapter, "E-Business and Research Institutes: When Technologies, Platforms and Methods Converge to Meet Users' Needs," is written by Pastore, who argues that research institutes and e-businesses have some mutual points that make it possible to apply similar business models to both, even though each of those may have differing missions. The author proposed a methodology that looks at the e-business environment, techniques and activities aimed at enhancing values in that area and, at the same time, seeks to find ways to apply such underpinnings for not-profit organizations and research institutes' capability to disseminate results to stakeholders. Issues dealing with Web applications and services development components are discussed in-depth in the chapter. The practical and research implications of the research's suppositions are outlined.

The seventh chapter, "A Discourse on the Construction of a Service Innovation Model: Focus on the Cultural and Creative Industry Park" by Lin and Chen aims to provide answers to the following questions: a) how do information and communication technologies (ICT) impact service innovations activities; b) what are the soft innovations in the proposed service innovation model? Their effort contributes to the literature by discussing service innovation research from the point of view of non-technological dimensions i.e. the "soft side" of service innovation. The authors identified the dimensions of service innovations that are needed for the development of the culturally induced industry, especially the ones related to a cultural creative industry park. The researchers analyzed the progress of innovation activities in such a park, as well as explored the value transformation and value repositioning from the service science perspective. They went on to propose a new cultural industrial service innovation model that examines service innovation at the firm level, using an example from a Taiwanese cultural creative industry park.

Prof. Princely Ifinedo
Cape Breton University, Sydney, NS,
Canada

1

Internet/E-Business Technologies Acceptance in Canada's SMEs: Focus on Organizational and Environmental Factors

Princely Ifinedo
Cape Breton University, Sydney, Nova Scotia, Canada

1. Introduction

Large and small business organizations around the world, including Canadian enterprises, utilize internet and e-business technologies (IEBT) to support online or electronic commerce (e-commerce) and electronic business (e-business) activities. Grandon and Pearson (2004) and Turban et al. (2010) note that IEBT enhances productivity for the adopting organization in the following ways: a) it improves efficiencies through automation of transactions, b) it reduces intermediaries in the value chain to foster greater economic advantages, c) it consolidates demand and supply through organized exchanges, d) it facilitates product improvement as well as engenders innovative ways of selling existing products and services. Against the backdrop of the popularity of IEBT, it is not surprising that several researchers have investigated and continue to study the adoption or acceptance of such technologies in differing contexts and locations (Farhoomand et al., 2000; Wymer & Regan, 2005). Studies that have focused on Canadian businesses are beginning to emerge (Raymond, 2001; Ifinedo, 2011).

This particular study is motivated by three concerns: a) it seeks to add to prior research focusing on the acceptance of IEBT and similar technologies in Canada; b) it is pays attention to small and medium-sized enterprise (SME) because of their crucial importance to economic development of countries around the world, including Canada. According to the Net Impact Study Canada (2002), Canadian SMEs deliver 60% of Canada's economic output, c) this study intends to shed light on the impact of organizational and environmental factors affecting the acceptance of IEBT in Canadian SMEs.

A research model based on the Technology-Organization-Environment (TOE) framework (Tornatzky & Fleischer, 1990), which other information systems (IS) researchers (e.g. Raymond, 2001; Scupola, 2003; Gibbs & Kraemer, 2004; Al-Qirim, 2007; Chong et al., 2009) have used in comparable studies will be used to guide the research. Such environment factors as information systems (IS) vendor support/pressure, management commitment/support, external pressure, organizational information technology (IT) competence, and the availability of financial support will be used to develop relevant hypotheses. The technological components of the framework will not be considered as several studies in the extant literature have underscored their critical relevance (Gibbs & Kraemer, 2004; Al-Qirim, 2007; Ifinedo, 2011). This research argued that our knowledge of the importance of factors related to the organization and environment when studied exclusively could enhance insight in this area of study. Moreover, the focus on the subject from the perspectives of Canadian SMEs will benefit the relevant literature.

Findings from this study showed that management commitment/support and external pressure are significant predictors of IEBT acceptance in the sampled SMEs. The results did not show that organizational IT competence, IS vendor support, availability of financial support, industry type, and firm size positively influence IEBT acceptance. Policy makers, industry leaders, and small business operators wishing to understand some of the reasons why certain SMEs in Canada lag in the adoption of IEBT and related technologies can benefit from the information provided in this study. The research also alerted the attention of local IS vendors and financial institutions to what can be done to strengthen IEBT adoption in Canadian small businesses. Global IT management as it relates to IEBT acceptance benefits from this endeavor as well.

2. Background theory and hypotheses formulation

The background theoretical framework used for this research is the Technology-Organization-Environment (TOE) model (Tornatzky & Fleischer, 1990). The TOE posits that the adoption or acceptance of innovations depends on organizational, environmental, and technological factors. Fundamentally, the TOE model is an integrative schema incorporating characteristics of the technology, contingent organizational factors, and elements from the macro-environment (Tornatzky & Fleischer, 1990; Li et al., 2010). Several studies that used the TOE framework for examining the impact of relevant organizational and environmental factors included such variables as management support, organizational IT readiness, pressures from partners, customers and competition, and so forth (Iacovou et al., 1995; Thong et al., 1996; Chwelos et al., 2001; Scupola, 2003; Gibbs & Kraemer, 2004; Hadaya, 2006; Al-Qirim, 2007; Ifinedo, 2011). As indicated above, the focus of this study will be on organizational and environmental factors.

The selected items among the organizational and environmental factors include IS vendor support and pressure, management commitment/support, external pressure, organizational IT competence, availability of financial support, firm size, and industry type. Others IS researchers have signified the pertinence of the foregoing factors in prior research (e.g. Iacovou et al., 1995; Thong et al., 1996; Chwelos et al., 2001; Scupola, 2003; Gibbs & Kraemer, 2004; Hadaya, 2006; Al-Qirim, 2007; Thong et al. 1996; Chapman et al. 2000; Jeyaraj et al., 2006; Huang et al., 2008; Li et at al. 2010; Levenburg et al., 2006; Teo, 2007). The research framework and the formulated hypothesized paths for each of the selected variables or items in the study are highlighted in Figure 1.

Past studies have shown that management commitment and support tend to favor the acceptance of technological innovations in adopting organizations, including SMEs (e.g., Iacovou et al., 1995; Premkumar & Roberts, 1999; Beatty et al., 2001; Chwelos et al., 2001; Grandon & Pearson, 2004; Al-Qirim, 2007). Jeyaraj et al. (2006) found top management support to be one of the best predictors of organizational adoption of IS innovations. This is

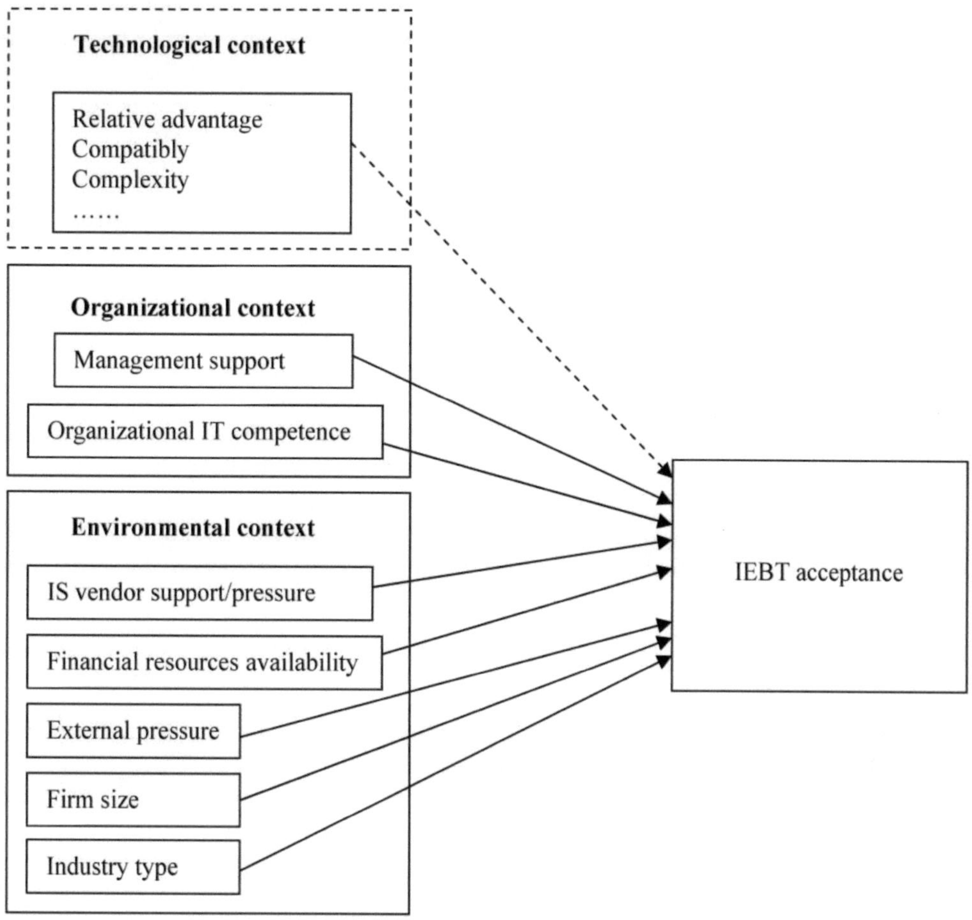

(The items in the technological contexts are not considered)

Fig. 1. The research framework.

because top managers act as change agents in the adoption process of technological innovations (Thong et al., 1996). Where such support is lacking, the acceptance of technologies such as IEBT tend to suffer (Igbaria et al., 1997; Ifinedo, 2011). Thus, it is predicted that:

H1: The greater the management commitment/support for IEBT acceptance, the greater the acceptance of such technologies.

Organizational IT competence refers to the level of technical expertise available to the organization. The more knowledge an organization has about technological innovations, the more likely it will be to adopt technological innovations (Thong & Yap, 1995; Raymond,

2001; Zhu et al., 2006). Thong and Yap (1995) found a lack of computer literacy among SME owners and a lack of knowledge regarding the benefits of IS use is an inhibitor to IS adoption in small businesses. Chircu and Kauffman (2000) found that inability to acquire skill and expertise in new technologies, and a lack of training and education form significant barriers to the adoption of IEBT. Caldeira and Ward (2002) concluded that for SMEs to successfully accept technological innovations including IEBT, their executives and employees must have a reasonable knowledge of the relevance of IS in business operations. Thus, it is predicted that:

H2: The greater the organizational IT competence available to SMEs, the greater their acceptance of such technologies.

IS vendor support refers to the support for implementing and using IT applications that a business obtains from external sources of technical expertise (Premkumar & Roberts, 1999; Rogers, 2003). IS vendors can act as change agents during the adoption of IS innovations especially for organizations lacking in such knowledge (Attewell, 1992; Rogers, 2003). In fact, it has been noted that SMEs rely on such external sources of expertise during IEBT implementations (Poon & Swatman, 1999; Al-Qirim, 2007). Additionally, IS vendors have been known to add value to the business planning of SMEs (Mcdonagh & Prothero, 2000). To that end, a lack of external technical support does inhibit the adoption of IEBT and similar technologies in small-sized businesses (Scupola, 2003; Simpson & Doherty, 2004). Thus, it is predicted that:

H3: Greater IS vendor support/pressure will lead to greater acceptance of such technologies by SMEs.

Prior studies have shown that a lack of financial resources is one of the distinguishing characteristics setting smaller businesses apart from larger enterprises (Thong et al., 1996; Chapman et al. 2000). Walczuch et al. (2000), Tan and Wu (2003), Lawson et al. (2003), and Pearson and Grandon (2004) showed that financial matters are vitally important to owners and managers and such issues often drive adoption of IS in small businesses. However, Reynolds et al. (1994) and Poon et al. (1996) implied that small-sized businesses do encounter difficulties with obtaining finance, and this unfavorable situation may set back their efforts to adopt needed IS innovations. The foregoing discussion permits the prediction that:

H4: Greater financial resource availability will lead to greater acceptance of such technologies by SMEs.

External pressure refers to the influences that an SME receives from sources external to it. The literature identifies three main sources of external pressure as follows: competitive pressure, supplier's pressure and customer's pressure (Hart & Saunders, 1998; Chau & Jim, 2002; Kula, 2003; Chong et al., 2009). It has been shown that competitive pressure impacts the adoption of IS innovations in large businesses and SMEs (Hart & Saunders, 1998; Raymond, 2001; Gatignon & Robertson, 1989; Jeyaraj et al., 2006). According to Raymond (2001), and Hadaya (2006), business partners' pressure affect the acceptance of technological innovations such as IEBT. These researchers showed that the deployment of IEBT and related technologies improves commercial transactions and relationships between businesses and their partners. With respect to customer's pressure, Hart and Saunders

(1998), Carmichael et al. (2000), Mehrtens et al. (2001), and Kula (2003) the key driver for SMEs to accept IEBT and other innovations is customer feedback, demand, and pressure. Thus, it is predicted that:

H5: Greater external pressure to adopt IEBT will lead to greater acceptance of such technologies by SMEs.

Firm size has been found to positively predict the adoption of IS (Jeyaraj et al., 2006; Al-Qirim, 2007; Teo, 2007; Huang et al., 2008; Li et at al. 2010); at the same time, others did not confirm this relationship for IS adoption (e.g., Goode & Stevens, 2000; Gibbs & Kraemer, 2004) and IEBT (Ifinedo, 2011). Similarly, the industry type or sector in which a business operates may influence its ability to adopt IS innovations (Drew, 2003; Levenburg et al., 2006; Jeyaraj et al., 2006; Li et at al. 2010); however, the study by Chatterjee et al. (2002) and Teo (2007) did not affirm this viewpoint. Evidence suggests that service businesses are more predisposed towards using the internet for business activities than manufacturing enterprises (Drew, 2003; Goode and Stevens, 2000).

H6: Firm size will be positively related to the acceptance of such technologies by SMEs.

H7: Industry type will be positively related to the acceptance of such technologies by SMEs.

3. Research methodology

Data collection

The survey method was used for data collection. The sampled firms came from four Atlantic Provinces: Nova Scotia, Newfoundland and Labrador, Prince Edward Island, and New Brunswick. The study considered a wide range of industries for inclusion. Data collection took place between November 2007 and March 2008. 2200 questionnaires were mailed out. Key informants including senior organizational managers and owners of SMEs were contacted. Each received a packet containing a cover letter, a questionnaire, and a self-addressed, stamped envelope. Respondents were assured that their individual responses would be treated with anonymity and confidentiality. Above all, participation in the study was voluntary.

The majority of the measures used in the study were taken from previously validated sources (e.g. Iacovou et al., 1995; Igbaria et al., 1997; Premkumar & Roberts, 1999; Grandon & Pearson, 2004; Chong & Pervan, 2007) and a few adapted from the literature. The measurement items were anchored on a 7-point Likert scale ranging from "strongly disagree" (1) to "strongly agree" (7) in which participants were asked to indicate an appropriate response. Table 1 highlights the constructs' descriptive statistics. A full list of the measures used is provided in the Appendix. Firm size was measured by annual sales revenue and industry sector was delineated as manufacturing, services, and others (e.g. not-for-profit).

The Cronbach alpha and composite reliability for each dimension exceeds the 0.7 limit, recommended by Nunnally (1978) to indicate a reasonably high reliability of the research measures and constructs. As well, the factor loading of each measurement item is adequate in line with recommended threshold values (Nunnally, 1978; Hair et al., 1998).

Construct	Items	Mean	SD	Factor loading	Composite reliability	AVE
Management commitment/support	MT1	4.46	1.61	0.859	0.90	0.69
	MT2	4.49	1.68	0.841		
	MT3	4.06	1.63	0.795		
	MT4	4.02	1.69	0.829		
Organizational IT competence	OR1	4.37	1.50	0.907	0.94	0.74
	OR2	4.39	1.44	0.949		
	OR3	4.08	1.52	0.876		
	OR4	4.32	1.61	0.804		
External pressure	EX1	4.03	1.47	0.825	0.92	0.66
	EX2	3.72	1.36	0.839		
	EX3	3.00	1.57	0.725		
	EX4	3.56	1.47	0.739		
	EX5	3.92	1.53	0.853		
	EX6	3.11	1.55	0.889		
IS vendor support/pressure	IV1	2.62	1.51	0.973	0.97	0.96
	IV2	2.63	1.55	0.969		
	IV3	2.71	1.52	0.997		
Financial support availability	FN1	2.26	1.58	0.654	0.87	0.69
	FN2	3.31	1.53	0.817		
	FN3	3.04	1.14	0.992		
Firm size	SIZ	NA	NA	1.00	1.00	1.00
Industry type	TYP	NA	NA	1.00	1.00	1.00
IEBT acceptance	IA1	5.36	1.34	0.774	0.86	0.61
	IA2	5.37	1.28	0.803		
	IA3	3.92	1.47	0.732		
	IA4	4.00	1.41	0.819		

NA = Not applicable

Table 1. The constructs with their descriptive statistics and reliability values.

Survey results

Of the 2200 questionnaires mailed out, 192 questionnaires were undelivered. 237 responses were received, of which, 214 were considered valid; this represents an effective response rate of 11.8%. Table 2 shows the participants' demographics. The participants' average work experience was 13.4 years (s.d. = 11.01). The other profiles of the responding SMEs are highlighted in Table 3.

Profile	Frequency	Percentage (%)
Gender		
Male	125	58.4
Female	85	39.7
Missing	4	1.9
Age		
Less than 20 years	4	1.9
21-30	26	12.1
31-40	30	14.0
41-50	78	36.4
51-60	57	26.6
60 years and above	19	8.9
Education		
Primary education	7	3.3
Secondary education	40	18.7
College/Bachelor's education	115	53.7
Post-graduate degree	44	20.6
Other	8	3.7
Job title		
Owner/Proprietor	84	39.3
VP, Director	41	19.2
Business Manager, Accountant	67	31.3
Other	22	10.2

Table 2. Demographics of the respondents.

Profile	Frequency	Percentage (%)
Business type		
Adverting, Marketing	19	8.9
Manufacturing	41	19.2
Retail, Wholesale	35	16.4
Auto Dealership, Auto repairs	14	6.5
Construction	6	2.8
Design outfit, Decorator	8	3.7
Education, Driving School	5	2.3
Hotel, Hospitality	10	4.7
Insurance, Accounting firms	21	9.8
Real estate, Legal firm	12	5.6
Other (e.g. not-for-profit)	43	20.1

Profile	Frequency	Percentage (%)
Annual sales revenues Canadian (C$)		
Less C$500,000	102	47.7
C$500,000 - C$ 1.0 million	48	22.4
C$ 1.1 - C$5.0 million	38	17.8
C$ 5.1 - C$ 10.0 million	9	4.2
C$ 10.1 - C$ 20.0 million	11	5.1
C$ 20.1 - C$50.0 million	6	2.8
Workforce		
Less 50 employees	175	81.8
51 - 99 employees	23	10.7
100 - 500 employees	11	5.1
Missing data	5	2.3

C$ = Canadian dollar

Table 3. Profile of the participating SMEs

4. Data analysis

The Partial Least Squares (PLS) technique of structural equation modeling was used for analysis. The specific tool used was SmartPLS 2.0, which was created by Ringle et al. (2005). The PLS supports two measurement models: (a) the assessment of the measurement model and (b) the assessment of the structural model.

Assessment of the measurement model

The psychometric properties of the research model were examined by the following indicators: internal consistency, convergent, and discriminant validities. Hair et al. (1998) suggest that item loadings of 0.5 are adequate; those with values lower than 0.5 were deleted from the scales accordingly. The composite reliabilities for each of the study's constructs were all above the recommended 0.7 level to indicate internal consistency of the data (Hair et al., 1998; Chin, 1998). Fornell and Larcker (1981) recommend that the average variance extracted (AVE) criterion be followed in assessing the convergent validity. These researchers suggested that an AVE value of 0.50 is ideally acceptable as it indicates that a latent variable is able to explain more than half of the variance of its indicators on average. The discriminant validity is assured when the following two conditions are met: (a) the value of the AVE is above the threshold value of 0.50; (b) the square root of the AVEs is larger than all other cross-correlations. Table 4 shows that the AVE ranged from 0.61 to 0.96 (excluding the single-item variables). In no case was any correlation between the constructs greater than the squared root of AVE (the principal diagonal element). Overall, the results showed the study's measures were psychometrically adequate for this study.

Assessment of the structural model

The structural model provides information related to the path significance of hypothesized relationships using the path coefficients (β) and the squared R (R^2). The strength of the

Construct	1	2	3	4	5	6	7.	8
1: Managsupp	**0.831**							
2: OrgITcomp	0.687	**0.860**						
3: ISVSP	0.259	0.206	**0.980**					
4: FinAva	0.330	0.294	0.472	**0.831**				
5: Exttpr	0.476	0.495	0.575	0.357	**0.812**			
6: FrmSZ	0.282	0.335	0.130	0.132	0.288	**1.00**		
7: Indstyp	0.102	0.130	0.069	0.161	0.089	0.129	**1.00**	
8: IEBT	0.476	0.495	0.575	0.357	0.582	0.288	0.093	**0.781**

Note: a) The bold fonts in the leading diagonals are the square root of AVEs.
b) Off-diagonal elements are correlations among constructs.
c) Exttpr = External pressure, FinAva = Financial support availability, Managsupp = Management commitment and support, OrgITcomp = Organizational IT competence, PercdBen = Perceived benefits, ISVSP = IS vendor support, FrmSZ = Firm size, Indstyp =Industry type, IEBT= IEBT acceptance

Table 4. Inter-construct correlations and the square root of AVE.

relationship is indicated by the β (Chin, 1998). The SmartPLS 2.0 results for the βs and the R^2 are shown in Figure 2. The path significance levels (t-values) are estimated by the bootstrapping method.

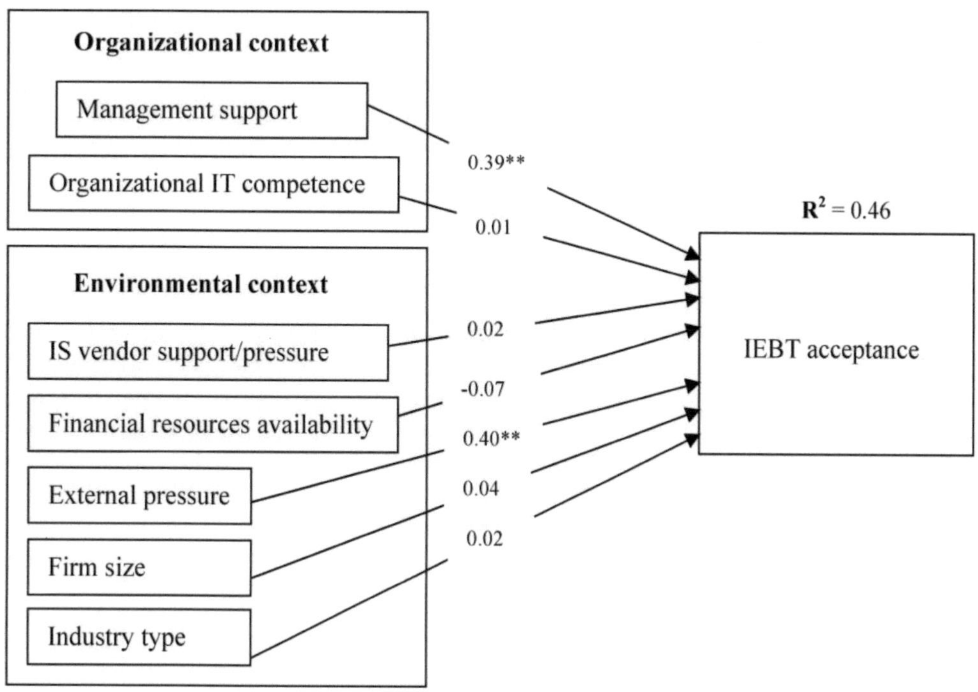

** = significant at $p < 0.001$

Fig. 2. The SmartPLS 2.0 results of the structural model.

Surprisingly, only two out of the seven hypotheses were supported. Hypothesis (H1) was confirmed to show that that management support/commitment is crucial in encouraging IEBT acceptance in Canadian SMEs. Also, the data analysis supported hypothesis (H5), which predicted that external pressure enhances IEBT acceptance. The data did not provide support for the rest of the hypotheses. All the variables together explain 46% of the variance in the dependent construct. This indicates that the proposed research conceptualization possess adequate predictive power and is useful in explaining the acceptance of IEBT for the sampled SMEs. Further discussion on the results is presented in the next section.

5. Discussions

This research project used a modified version of the TOE framework to investigate factors influencing the acceptance of IEBT in SMEs based in Atlantic Canada. The data analysis confirmed the significance of management support/commitment and external market pressure in the adoption process. To the extent that management support/commitment is considered crucial for the successful acceptance of IEBT by Canadian SMEs, this study's finding provides empirical support for such a claim. SMEs in Atlantic Canada indicated that the levels of IEBT acceptance were higher where management support/commitment was relatively high. This finding lends credence to the body of work indicating that management support/commitment is positively associated with the successful acceptance of technological innovations such as IEBT in small businesses (Thong et al., 1996; Igbaria et al., 1997; Teo et al., 1997; Premkumar & Roberts, 1999).

External pressure was also found to be an important factor positively influencing the acceptance of IEBT in the sampled SMEs. The data is indicating that as the use of IEBT gain in popularity, it is to be expected that SMEs will succumb to the pressure from their customers, partners, and competitors to adopt such innovations. Other previous studies have highlighted the pertinence of such influences in the adoption of technological innovations, inclusion IEBT in SMEs (Hart & Saunders, 1998; Raymond, 2001; Hadaya, 2006; Carmichael et al., 2000; Kula et al., 2003; Cragg & King, 1993; Premkumar & Roberts, 1999; Mehrtens et al., 2001; Grandon & Pearson, 2004). Thus, the finding consolidates the body of knowledge in the area.

The other variables or items used in this research produced results inconsistent with the stated predictions. The organizational IT competence of the sampled SMEs was not adequate enough to influence their acceptance of IEBT. To some degree, this result corroborates the viewpoint suggesting that the levels of technical expertise available to Canadian small businesses are not adequate (Annis et al. 2005; Noce & Peters, 2006; Martin & Milway, 2007). As well, the environmental factors of firm size and industry type did not appear to have any meaningful relationships with IEBT acceptance to support the views espoused by other IS researchers (Goode & Stevens, 2000; Gibbs & Kraemer, 2004; Chatterjee et al., 2002; Teo, 2007).

Although prior studies have shown that external support from IS vendors boded well for the adoption of technological innovations, including IEBT in small organizations (Gatignon & Robertson, 1989; Doolin et al., 2003; Thong et al., 1996; Poon & Swatman, 1999; Al-Qirim, 2007), the study's finding did not provide support for the claim. It is possible that the measurement items used in this study did go as far as capturing the depth of services provided by IS vendors. Further to this, contextual factors could also account for the result obtained herein. It is also possible that the sampled SMEs may not have a favorable view of IS vendors in their contexts. It is also plausible that local IS vendors may be having difficulties in meeting the specific needs of SMEs in their contexts.

This research did not confirm the availability of financial resources as an important factor needed to enhance IEBT acceptance among the sampled SMEs in Canada. This finding may have extraneous underpinnings. For example, the head of Canadian Bankers Association disproved the notion suggesting that banks in the country "don't serve the small business market in Canada" well enough. On other hand, a report from the Canadian Federation of Independent Business raises "questions as to whether [some major financial institutions in the country] have intentionally adopted a domestic strategy that focuses less importance on the SME market" (Lam, 2010). The discordance between the two parties, to some degree, lends support to the viewpoint among some practitioners in Canada who are of the opinion that SMEs may not be receiving adequate financial support from banks to accept IEBT. The finding in this study may be highlighting the state of affairs in the country on this matter.

Overall, the foregoing results (affirmed and rejected) support the viewpoint suggesting that factors related to management support/commitment and external pressure may be possible *enablers* of IEBT acceptance for SMEs based in Canada. On the other hand, the variables related to organizational IT competence, IS vendor support/pressure, and financial resource availability could be classified as possible *inhibitors* to the process (Gibbs & Kraemer, 2004). Firm size and industry type are wider environmental factors deserving of further examination. The diagrammatic illustration provided in Figure 4 indicates that more efforts may be required to push the items or variables identified as *inhibitors* to improve the accentuate of IEBT in the sampled SMEs in Canada while the *enablers* may require little or no attention.

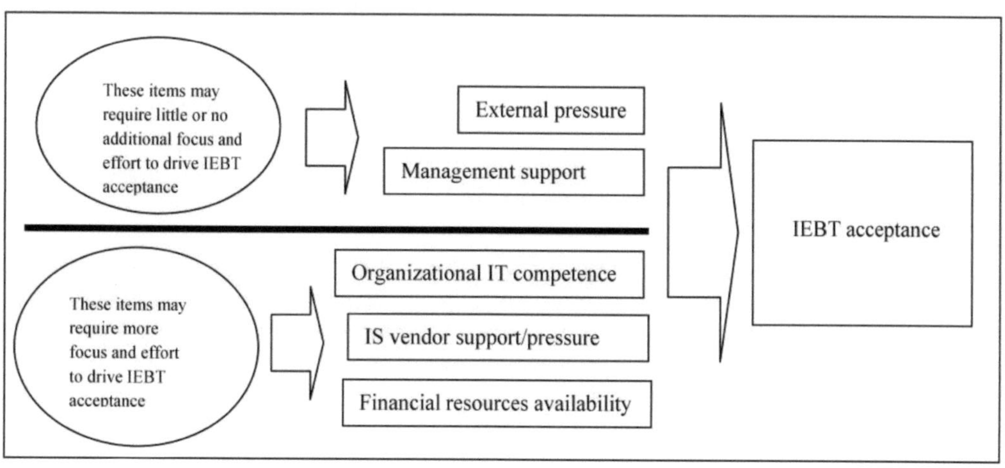

Fig. 3. Inhibitors and enablers of IEBT acceptance by SMEs.

Implications for research and practice

To facilitate greater acceptance of IEBT and related technologies in the Atlantic region of Canada, the government could consider committing resources towards sensitizing SMEs' owners and their employees about the pertinence of such innovations in enhancing business operations. For the same reasoning, the need for e-business mentoring, coaching, and training (Simpson & Doherty, 2004) becomes more cogent. Awareness campaigns tailored for SMEs' owners would be useful in increasing their knowledge of how an IS can be used in business operations. The information provided in this study may benefit IS local vendors and financial institutions regarding areas where efforts could be expended as concerted attempts are made to strengthen Canada's e-economy aspirations.

With respect to research, this research broadly lends credence to findings and observations regarding the salient factors i.e. management support/commitment and external pressure that influence the adoption and acceptance of IEBT in SMEs. To that end, this research effort provides support to prior studies that had highlighted significant of such factors in comparable research (Gatignon & Robertson, 1989; Jeyaraj et al., 2006; Chong & Pervan, 2007; Huang et al., 2008). Specifically, this current study affirms the views indicating that external pressure and management support are important predictors of innovations adoption in Canada's small businesses. This study's finding related to the pertinence of management support concurs with results in Raymond and Bergeron (1996) and de Guinea et al. (2005) that signifies their importance for achieving IS success in Canadian's SMEs. The inadequate levels of IT expertise, and overall lack of awareness of IS products/issues in Canada (Warda, 2005; Noce & Peters, 2006) is supported by this study's findings.

This current work complements the emerging desire among some researchers to specifically focus on and bring into the limelight issues related to the adoption of IEBT and similar technologies in less endowed regions of advanced countries. For example, the studies by Premkumar and Roberts (1999), Scupola (2003), Grandon and Pearson (2004), and Simpson and Doherty (2004) focused on rural USA, Southern Italy, the Yorkshire region of the UK, and Mid West region of the US, respectively. Additionally, the dependent variable, i.e. acceptance as used in this research departs from prior research efforts that tend to operationalize such constructs with a single item of Use (Usage) or Intention to use. The utilization of such singular items may obfuscate reality and has, in fact, been criticized for limiting insight (Legris et al., 2003). In that respect, the measures used to operationalize acceptance in this study may be beneficial to others wishing to investigate comparable issues.

Limitations and future research

Asking only one respondent to present a view on behalf of their organization may be problematic. The foregoing fact might have negatively impacted the results obtained and discussed in this research. The research project included a variety of IEBT, the possible levels of complexity in the use of such technologies were not controlled in this study; this may be limiting. For example, perceptions of email use and e-ERP use in the sampled SMEs may not be similar. Thus, the inclusion of both types of technologies might negative influence the result. What was discussed here applies to sampled SMEs in a region of Canada; it is not advised that the study's findings be generalized to the whole country's small businesses. Caution should be taken in interpreting the results presented herein.

This study has opened opportunity for future research. Some of the aforementioned limitations could be addressed in subsequent studies. This research can be replicated in other regions of Canada to reify or debunk claims presented in this study. The data used in this study is cross-sectional in nature; future efforts could consider using longitudinal data to facilitate more insight. It is possible that other factors not included in this study could be identified to enhance insight. The research framework could be further reinforced with the identification of other relevant organizational and environmental factors such as government support not considered in this study. Future research using meta-analytic approaches could examine the enablers and inhibitors of IEBT adoption in SMEs in comparable parts of the developed world. Knowledge from such efforts stands to consolidate theories related to the acceptance of IEBT and related technologies in SMEs.

6. Conclusion

This research, to some extent, drew from the TOE framework in investigating the acceptance of IEBT in SMEs based in Atlantic region of Canada. The study's findings indicated that management support/commitment and external pressure are significant predictors of the acceptance of IEBT in the study's setting. The factors of organizational IT competence, financial resource availability, IS vendor support/pressure, firm size, and industry type were found to be insignificant in the acceptance process of IEBT by the sampled SMEs. The foregoing results permitted the identification of possible *enablers* and *inhibitors* of IEBT acceptance in the sampled Canadian SMEs. It is hoped that the discussions and conclusion provided in this study would benefit practitioners and policy makers in the country and elsewhere. The study has offered some useful contributions to the growing body of works researching the factors influencing IEBT acceptance in SMEs across regional contexts, and it seeks to complement past research efforts in Canada.

7. Appendix

The constructs and items used in the questionnaires.

Management commitment & support
Management is interested in the use of internet/e-business technologies in our operations.
Management is supportive of the use of internet/e-business technologies in our operations.
Our business has a clear vision regarding the use of internet/e-business technologies.
Management communicates the need for internet/e-business technologies usage in the firm.
Organizational IT competence
Our firm knows how information technology (IT) can be used to support our operations.
Our firm has a good understanding of how internet/e-business technologies can be used in our business.
We have the necessary technical, managerial and other skills to implement IEBT.
Our business values and norms would not prevent us from adopting IEBT in our operations.
External pressure
Some of our competitors have already started using internet/e-business technologies.

Our competitors know the importance of IEBT and are using them for operations.
We know our customers are ready to do business over the Internet.
Our customers are demanding the use of IEBT in doing business with them.
Our partners are demanding the use of IEBT in doing business with them.
We know our suppliers and partners are ready to do business over the Internet.
IS vendor support/pressure
IS vendors in the region are actively promoting IEBT and other technologies by providing incentives for adoption.
IS vendors are encouraging our business to adopt IEBT by providing us with free training sessions.
We can obtain support easily from local IS vendors as we implement IEBT.
Financial resource availability
Supporting institutions e.g. banks provide financial assistance for SMEs wishing to adopt e-business technologies.
Our own business will take e-business more seriously if we receive adequate financial support from local banks.
We believe that financial support for e-business engagements can be obtained easily from banks and other financial institutions.
Acceptance of IEBT
Our company makes use of IEBT, very often.
Our company uses IEB e-commerce/e-payment, at all times, for its transactions.
Our company uses IEB its critical operations.
The number of business operations and activities in my company that requires IEBT is high.

8. Acknowledgement

This research project was sponsored by Grant (#8271) received from Cape Breton University, NS, Canada.

The author is grateful to all the study's participants. Comments received from colleagues and the efforts of the study's Research Assistants are valued.

9. References

Al-Qirim, N. (2007). The adoption of ecommerce communications and applications technologies in small businesses in New Zealand. Electronic Commerce Research and Applications, 6(4), 462-473.

Annis, R.C., McNiven, J., & Curri, M. (2005). Industry Canada Broadband Impact Study Final Report. Brandon, Manitoba: Rural Development Institute, Brandon University.

Attewell, P., 1992. Technology diffusion and organizational learning: The case of business computing. Organization Science, 3(1), 1-19.

Beatty, R.C., Shim, J.P., & Jones, M.C. (2001). Factors influencing corporate web site adoption: A time based assessment. Information and Management, 38(6), 337–354.

Caldeira, M.M., & Ward, J.M. (2002). Understanding the successful adoption and use of IS/IT in SMEs: An explanation from Portuguese manufacturing industries. Information Systems Journal, 12(2), 121-152.

Carmichael, C., Turgoose, C., Gary, M.O., & Todd, C. (2000). Innovation and SMEs the case of Yorkshire, UK. Journal of Industry and Higher Education, 14(4), 244-248.

Chapman, P., James-Moore, J., Szczygiel, M., & Thompson, D. (2000). Building Internet Capabilities in SME's. Logistics Information Management, 13(6), 353-361.

Chatterjee, D., Grewal, R., & Sambamurthy, V. (2002). Shaping up for e-commerce: Institutional enablers of the organizational assimilation of web technologies. MIS Quarterly, 26(2), 65-89.

Chau, Y. K., & Jim, C.F. (2002). Adoption of electronic data interchange in small and medium enterprises. Journal of Global Information Management, 10(4), 61-85.

Chin, W. (1998). Issues and opinion on structural equation modeling. MIS Quarterly, 22(1), vii-xvi.

Chircu, A.M., & Kauffman, R.J. (2000). Limits to value in electronic commerce-related IT investments. Journal of Management Information Systems, 17(2), 59–80.

Chong, S., & Pervan, G. (2007). Factors influencing the extent of deployment of electronic commerce for small and medium-sized enterprises. Journal of Electronic Commerce in Organizations, 5(1), 1-29.

Chong, A. Y-L., Ooi, K-B., Lin, B., Tang, S.Y. (2009). Influence of interorganizational relationships on SMEs' e-business adoption. Internet Research, 19(3), 313-331.

Chwelos, P., Benbasat, I., & Dexter, A.S. (2001). Empirical test of an EDI adoption model. Information Systems Research, 12(3), 304–321.

Cragg, P., & King, M. (1993). Small-firm computing: Motivators and inhibitors. MIS Quarterly, 17(1), 47-60.

de Guinea, O.A., Kelley, H., & Hunter, M.G. (2005). Information systems effectiveness: Extending a Singapore model in Canada. Journal of Global Information Management, 13(2), 55-79.

Doolin, D., Mcleod, L., McQueen, B., & Watton, M. (2003). Internet strategies for establishing retailers: four New Zealand case studies. Journal of Information Technology Cases and Applications, 5(4), 3–19.

Drew, S. (2003). Strategic uses of e-Commerce by SMEs in the East of England. European Management Journal, 21(1), 79-88.

Farhoomand, A.F., Tuunainen, V.K., & Yee, L.W. (2000). Barriers to global electronic commerce: A cross-country study of Hong Kong and Finland. Journal of Organizational
Computing and Electronic Commerce, 10(1), 23-48.

Fornell, C., & Larcker, D.F. (1981). Evaluating structural equations models with unobservable variables and measurement error. Journal of Marketing Research, 8(1), 39-50.

Gatignon H., & Robertson T.S. (1989). Technology diffusion: An empirical test of competitive effects. Journal of Marketing, 53(1), 35–49.

Gibbs, J.L., & Kraemer, K.L. (2004). A cross-country investigation of the determinants of scope of e-commerce use: An institutional approach. Electronic Markets, 14(2), 124-137.

Goode, S. & Stevens, K. (2000). An analysis of the business characteristics of adopters and non-adopters of World Wide Web technology. Information Technology and Management, 1 (1/2), 129-154.

Grandon, E.E., & Pearson, J. (2004). Electronic commerce adoption: An empirical study of small and medium US Businesses. Information and Management, 42(1), 197-216.

Hair, J.F. Jr., Anderson, R.E., Thatham, R.L., & Black, W.C. (1998). Multivariate data analysis. Upper Saddle River, NJ: Prentice-Hall International, Inc.

Hart, P.J., & Saunders, C.S. (1998). Emerging electronic partnerships: Antecedents and dimensions of EDI use from the supplier's perspective. Journal of Management Information Systems, 14(4), 87–111.

Hadaya, P. (2006), Determinants of the future level of use of electronic marketplaces: The case of Canadian firms. Electronic Commerce Research, 6(2), 173-185.

Huang, Z., Janz, B.D. & Frolick, M.N. (2008). A comprehensive examination of Internet-EDI adoption. Information Systems Management, 25(3), 273–286.

Iacovou, C.L., Benbasat, I., & Dexter, A.S. (1995). Electronic data interchange and small organizations: adoption and impact of technology. MIS Quarterly, 19(4), 465–485.

Ifinedo, P. (2011). An empirical analysis of factors influencing Internet/e-business technologies adoption by SMEs in Canada. International Journal of Information Technology & Decision Making, 10(4), 731–766

Igbaria, M., Zinatelli, N., Cragg, P., & Cavaye, A.L.M. (1997). Personal computing acceptance factors in small firms: A structural equation model. MIS Quarterly, 21(3), 279-305.

Industry Canada (2001). Micro-enterprises Survey 2000: A Progress Report Small Business Policy. Available at <hhttp://www.ic.gc.ca/epic/site/sbrp-rppe.nsf/en/rd01992e.html., 2001>. Accessed April 13, 2008.

Jeyaraj, A., Rottman, J. W., & Lacity, M.C. (2006). A review of the predictors, linkages, and biases in IT innovation adoption research. Journal of Information Technology, 21(1), 1-23.

Kula, V., & Tatoglu, E. (2003). An exploratory study of Internet adoption by SMEs in an emerging market economy. European Business Review, 15(5), 324-333.

Lam, E. (2010). CIBC 'far and away the worst bank' for smaller businesses: report. Available at < http://www.canada.com/business/CIBC+away+worst+bank+smaller+businesses+report/2877729/story.html >. Accessed August 3 2010.

Lawson, R., Alcock, C., Cooper, J., & Burgess, L. (2003). Factors affecting adoption of electronic commerce technologies by SMEs: an Australian study, The Electronic Journal on Information Systems in Developing Countries, 14(1), 1-9.

Legris, P. Ingham, J., & Collerette, P. (2003). Why do people use information technology?: A critical review of the technology acceptance model. Information and Management, 40(3), 191-204.

Levenburg, N., Magal, S.R., & Kosalge, P. (2006). An exploratory investigation of organizational factors and e-business motivations among SMEs in the US. Electronic Markets, 16(1), 70-84.

Li, D., Lai, F., & Wang, J. (2010). E-business assimilation in China's International trade firms: The technology-organization-environment framework. Journal of Global Information Management, 18(1), 39-65.

Martin, R.L., & Milway, J.B. (2007). Enhancing the Productivity of Small and Medium Enterprises through the Greater Adoption of Information and Communication Technology, Information and Communication Technology Council Report. Available at < http://www.ictc-ctic.ca/en/ > Accessed 14 June 2008.

Mcdonagh, P., & Prothero, A. (2000). Euroclicking and the Irish SME: Prepared for e-commerce and the single currency. *Irish Marketing Review*, 13(1), 21-33.

Net Impact Study Canada (2002). The SME Experience - A Preliminary Report - November 2002 - Canadian e-Business Initiative. Available at < http://www.cebi.ca/epic/site/ecic-ceac.nsf/vwapj/NI_SME-e.pdf/$file/ NI_SME-e.pdf > Accessed 20 April 2009.

Nunnaly, J.C. (1978). Psychometric theory. New York, NY: McGraw-Hill.

Pearson, M. & Grandon, E. (2004). E-commerce adoption: perceptions of managers/owners of small and medium sized firms in Chile. Communications of the Association for Information Systems, 13, 81-102.

Poon, S., Swatman, P.M.C., & Vitale, M. (1996). Electronic networking among small business in Australia-An exploratory study. In *proceedings of the 9th International Conference on EDIIOS*, Bled, Slovenia, June 10-12.

Poon, S., & Swatman, P. (1999). An exploratory study of small business Internet commerce issues. Information and Management, 35 (1), 9-18.

Premkumar, G., & Roberts, M. (1999). Adoption of new information technologies in rural small businesses. Omega: International Journal of Management Science, 27(4), 467-484.

Raymond, L., & Bergeron, F. (1996). EDI success in small and medium-sized enterprises: A field study. Journal of Organizational Computing & Electronic Commerce, 6(2), 161-172.

Raymond, L. (2001). Determinants of web site implementation in small businesses. Internet Research, 11(5), 411- 422.

Reynolds, W., Savage, W., & Williams, A. (1994). Your own business: a practical guide to success. Nelson Australia, South Melbourne, Victoria, Australia.

Ringle, C.M., Wende, S., & Will, A. (2005). SmartPLS 2.0 (M3) beta, Hamburg: http://www.smartpls.de.

Scupola, A. (2003). The adoption of Internet commerce by SMEs in the South of Italy: An environmental, technological and organizational perspective. Journal of Global Information Technology Management, 6(1), 52-71.

Tan, Z., & Wu, Q. (2003). Globalization and e-commerce I: Factors affecting e-commerce diffusion in China. Communications of the Association for Information Systems, 10(2), 25-35.

Teo, H.H., Tan, B.C.Y., & Wei, K.K. (1997). Organizational transformation using Electronic Data Interchange: The case of TradeNet in Singapore. Journal of Management Information Systems, 13(4), 139-166.

Teo, T.S.H. (2007). Organizational Characteristics, Modes of Internet Adoption and Their Impact: A Singapore Perspective. Journal of Global Information Management, 15(2), 91-117.

Thong, J., & Yap, C. (1995). CEO characteristics, organisational, characteristics and information technology adoption in small business. Omega: International Journal of Management Sciences, 23(4), 429-442.

Thong, J.Y.L., Yap, C.S., & Raman, K.S. (1996). Top management support, external expertise and information systems implementation in small business. Information Systems Research, 7(2), 248-267.

Tornatzky, L.G., & Fleischer, M. (1990). The processes of technological innovation. Lexington, MA: Lexington Books.

Turban, E., King, D., & Lang, J. (2010). Introduction to electronic commerce. New York, NY: Prentice Hall, NY.

Warda, J. (2005). Incentive for ICYT adoption: Canada and Major Competitor. Available at < http://www.itac.ca/uploads/research/05july.pdf >. Accessed July 20 2010.

Wymer, S. & Regan, E. (2005). Factors influencing e-commerce adoption and use by small and medium businesses. *Electronic Markets*, 15(4), 438-453.

Zhu, K., Kraemer, K.L., & Xu, S. (2006). The process of innovation assimilation by firms in different countries: A technology diffusion perspective on e-business. Management Science, 52(10), 1557-1576.

2

Facilitating the Intention to Expand E-business Payment Systems Use in Nigerian Small Firms: An Empirical Analysis

Princely Ifinedo
Cape Breton University, Sydney, Nova Scotia, Canada

1. Introduction

Electronic business (e-business) refers to the utilization of information and communication technologies (ICT) to support of all aspects of business (Turban et al., 2010). The term was first used by IBM's marketing and Internet teams in 1996 (Amor, 1999). E-business payment systems or solutions refer to the various innovative applications and approaches including the use of credit cards, magnetic ink character recognition (MICR) checks, automated teller machines (ATMs), electronic cash (E-cash), electronic funds transfer (EFT), amongst others that are used to facilitate the customer's decision to pay for a product or services (Vassiliou, 2004). Gholami et al. (2010, 53) while citing Andam (2003, 22) describe e-payment systems as "the use of pre-loaded, debit and credit cards on the Internet or other electronic devices to perform daily transactions which include paying for goods and services, transfers and bill payments at any time of the day." These researchers added that e-payments are part of a larger electronic payment systems (EPS), which includes a system of financial exchange between buyers and sellers in the online environment through the use of such digital financial instruments as credit cards, electronic checks, and digital cash.

With e-business payment systems, individuals and organizations have the opportunity to pay for goods and services over the counter or online without using cash (Gholami et al., 2010). The role of e-payment systems is paramount to the growth of e-business itself (Vassiliou, 2004) and the emergence of such methods of payment has had a significant impact of global e-business (Leadpile, 2006; EIU, 2011). A recent report by Leadpile (2006) predicted that e-business around the world will likely surpass the $1 trillion mark by 2012. The level of commercial activities and transactions generated through e-business in a country does have a positive correlation with the nation's overall economic growth and well-being (EIU, 2010; WEF, 2011). By the same token, parts of the world especially those in developing societies where the expansion of e-business has been slow to develop, run the risk of being marginalized in the emerging digital or network economy (Ifinedo, 2005a; EIU, 2011; WEF, 2011). While previous research efforts in the relevant literature have discussed factors impacting the adoption and diffusion of e-business and e-payments systems in the developed world (Vassiliou, 2004; Zhu et al., 2003; Ifinedo, 2011a, b; Laukkanen & Pasanen, 2008; Lee, 2009), focus on issues in the developing world has not been adequately researched (Mbarika et al., 2005; Ayo, 2006; Ayo et al., 2011).

It is vitally important to examine the antecedents of e-business payment systems use in developing countries such as Nigeria. It is worth pointing out that Nigeria is largely a cash-based country in which a high percentage of its economic transactions are conducted with cash (Gholami et al., 2010; Ayo et al., 2011). This is partly due to the country's socio-cultural imperatives (Ifinedo, 2005b) and the embryonic development of e-business payment systems acceptance among businesses and the population. The Central Bank of Nigeria (CBN) realizing the need to improve the economic transactions climate in the country is clamoring for a paradigm change from a cash-based economy to a cashless one. According to Gholami et al. (2010, p.52), "for instance, a national payment system has been set in force [in Nigeria] to encourage e-payment adoption. The banks and electronic switching companies have also rolled out infrastructure to facilitate the use of e-payments." In spite of such various efforts and commitments, banking reports and academic studies indicated that the adoption of e-business payment systems in Nigeria continue to be low and unimpressive (Babalakin & Co; 2002, Agbada, 2008; Akpan, 2008; Gholami et al., 2010; Ayo et al., 2011). The question then arises: *what can be done to facilitate the intention to expand e-business payment systems use in Nigerian small firms and outfits*?

Some prior work has been done in the area. For example, Ayo (2006) investigated the prospects of e-business growth in Nigeria using the ability, motivation and opportunities (AMO) model; he found that a good number of Nigerian companies have some sorts of online presence, which is encouraging as the country aims to fully integrated into the network economy (Ifinedo, 2005a). Ayo (2006) asserted that the motivation and opportunities for e-business was low mainly due to lack of e-payment infrastructure and access to ICT facilities. Likewise, Gholami et al.'s (2010) findings showed that perceived benefits, effort expectancy, social influence, trust, awareness, and demographic variables affected individuals' intention to adopt e-payment systems in Nigeria. Recently, Ayo et al. (2011) using an extended technology acceptance model (TAM) found that perceived ease of use and perceived usefulness were not only antecedents of e-business payment and banking acceptance in Nigeria, these factors also mattered in promoting continued usage of such innovations among businesses and the Nigerian populace. Additionally, foregoing researchers revealed that organizational reputation, perceived risk, and trust are major influences in the continued usage of such systems.

This chapter aims at contributing to the emerging body of work in this area of interest. I intend to build upon the insight suggesting that it is worthwhile to focus attention on the issues at the micro level or at the boundary of the firm. I concur with Molla and Licker (2005) who argue that issues such as government support for firms to adopt needed technologies, information systems (IS) vendor support, top management support, and organizational readiness are worthwhile when discussing factors that may encourage or discourage the adoption of ICT-enabled initiatives such as e-business payment systems in the developing world. Specifically, this chapter will draw from relevant constructs from the TAM (Davis, 1989), which will be fused into the technology-organization-environment (TOE) framework (Tornatzky & Fleischer, 1990) to enhance knowledge.

Nigeria was selected because of its paramount socio-economic, technological, and political standing in the sub-Saharan Africa (SSA) region (WEF, 2011; ITU, 2011; Internetworldstats, 2011). It is not claimed herein that Nigeria is a perfect representative of all the countries in SSA; however, its business environment vis-à-vis e-business payment technologies usage may mirror those in comparable countries in the region. I intend to focus attention on small firms in Nigeria as the adoption of e-payment systems in larger firms is more likely to be at advanced stages. Moreover, small firms - usually with fewer than 500 employees - play crucial role in the national economic development of most countries around the world, including Nigeria (Ifinedo, 2005b, Ifinedo, 2011a)

This research is important for the literature as it seeks to add to the discourse of e-business payment systems adoption with information from a region of the world, that is, SSA that has not been adequately researched (Mbarika et al., 2005). In fact, others (Farhoomand et al., 2000; Tan et al., 2007) have suggested that the diffusion of e-business and related innovations in organizations in developing and developed countries differs significantly. Thus, by focusing on e-business payment systems use intentions among Nigerian firms, our knowledge of pertinent factors in the context of developing countries will be enhanced. In particular, the intention to expand e-payment use in this study refers to an ideal situation in which a firm indicates that it uses all the possible e-payment solutions for its business transactions.

2. Background information on Nigeria

Nigeria is the most populous country both in SSA and Africa with a population of about 155 million people in 2010 (CIA WorldFact, 2011). Its Gross Domestic Product (GDP) purchasing power parity and GDP per capita in 2010 were US$369.8 billion and $2400, respectively. Although businesses and individuals in Nigeria have been adopting modern ICTs (Anandarajan et al., 2002) for some time now, the overall ICT adoption and usage levels in the country has been slow compared to those of advanced Western countries (Ifinedo, 2005a; WEF, 2011; ITU, 2011). Recently, the Nigerian IT Development Agency (NITDA) was mandated to improve the nation's capability to use ICT for development purposes. One of its objectives is to "promote electronic trade, business and commerce in the country". In spite of efforts to encourage the spread of e-business in Nigeria, evidence suggests that the growth and use of e-payment systems is still very slow to consolidate in the country (Ayo et. al., 2008; Eze, 2008).

With regard to the use of ICT products for development (i.e. e-readiness index), Nigeria has not fared well on this index. It ranked 61st out of 70 countries on a ranking of e-readiness produced by the Economist Intelligence Unit (EIU, 2011). Similarly, Nigeria ranked 99th out of 133 countries on the networked readiness index for 2009-2010 that was produced by World Economic Forum (WEF, 2011). The Economist Intelligence Unit's (EIU, 2007) study of government e-payment adoption globally indicated that Nigeria ranked 42nd among the 43 countries that were investigated in that study. These indicators and indices clearly show that Nigeria is not fully prepared for the digital or network economy. Nonetheless, some notable changes and progress have surfaced in Nigeria since 2001. The Nigeria's telecommunication sector, which was perennially underdeveloped and unreliable has been deregulated and liberalized (Ifinedo, 2005b; 2008; ITU, 2011). Four GSM networks were licensed by 2002. Also, more than 400 ISPs and a number of data carriers, Internet exchange and gateway operators have been licensed in the country (Internetworldstats, 2011). These apparent developments make Nigeria one of the fastest growing ICT markets in SSA after South Africa (Internetworldstats, 2011).

In 2001, there were only 200,000 Internet users in Nigeria (0.1% of the population); this has jumped to 43,982,200 (28.9% of the population) in 2010 (Internetworldstats, 2011). Nigeria has introduced lower tariffs for ICT imports and a number of local personal computers (PC) manufactures have started producing PCs in the country (Ifinedo, 2008). With such marked improvements in the technological infrastructure of the country, it comes as no surprise that e-business is beginning to take hold among business organizations in Nigeria (Ifinedo, 2008; Ayo et. al., 2008; Chiemeke et al., 2006; Eze, 2008).

3. E-business payment solutions in Nigeria

The Central Bank of Nigeria (CBN) is concerned about the risks involved in issuing, storing, processing, distributing, and transporting cash in the country (Babalakin & Co, 2002; Gholami et al., 2010). The CBN laments the slow pace of e-business payment systems adoption in the country and is actively promoting the use of such systems in the country (Akpan, 2008; Emordi, 2007). A report indicated that the value of electronic payment and commerce in the country in 2006 stood at 360 billion naira (about US$2.81 billion) (Ayo et. al., 2008). In contrast, e-commerce trend in developed countries such as Canada, in the same year was valued at US$49.9 billion (Grau, 2008). Despite the slow progress of e-business payment systems adoption in the country, recent studies have shown that Nigerian businesses and the population are familiar with the benefits of such payments systems and may be interested in continuing the use of such solutions if the right facilitating conditions are provided (Chiemeke et al., 2006; Akpan, 2008; Adesina et al., 2008). Some of the noted benefits include convenience, efficiency, and the ease of use associated with such payment platforms (Akpan, 2008; Gholami et al., 2010).

The development of e-payment solutions in Nigeria has been progressing with time (Akpan, 2008). The introduction of MICR checks revolutionized e-payment systems solutions in the country (Adesina et al. 2008). This was followed by the introduction of the ATMs for dispensing cash, checking of account balance, and for paying utility bills in the early 1990s. By 1993, smart cards payment system was introduced by the CBN to deal with financial transactions (Agbada, 2008; Akpan, 2008). Debit cards (VISA, MasterCards, Euro cards, American Express, Valucard, EasyCash, and Smart pay) were later introduced in the country. The first credit card in Nigeria was introduced in 2004 by Master Card in conjunction with Cards Technology Limited and Ecobank (one of the country's local banks). This allowed card holders to make purchases or withdraw cash up to certain limits. By the end of 2007, the number of cards issued in Nigeria increased by 200% (i.e. from four million to twelve million cards) (Emordi, 2007). The impact of the foregoing e-payments had positive effects in moving Nigeria toward a cashless society. Table 1 shows the Economic Report of the CBN for the first half of 2008 with a summary of the value and volume of e-payment systems as a percentage of total transactions in Nigeria (Emordi, 2007).

Channel of transaction	Volume in Percentage (%)	Value in Percentage (%)
ATM	87	90.8
Mobile	7.3	0.10
Web (Internet)	3.2	4.8
POS (Point of sales systems)	2.5	4.3

Table 1. Percentage value and volume of e-payment in Nigeria

Notwithstanding the reported growth in the acceptance of e-payment solutions in Nigeria, researchers (Ezeoha, 2005; Chiemeke et al, 2006; Agbada, 2008; Adesina et al, 2008; Gholami et al., 2010; Ayo et al., 2011) have shown that there are still problems with respect to the behavioral intentions of small business in using and accepting e-business payment solutions in Nigeria. Examples of inhibiting factors noted in such prior studies include insecurity, fraud, lack of standardization of channels, illiteracy, age differences, and inadequate operational facilities such as telecommunication and electricity supply. As already indicated above, this current research seeks to add to the discourse of factors affecting the intention to use e-business payment systems in Nigeria with an examination of the influences of perceived usefulness, perceived ease of use, management support, organizational readiness, IS vendor support, government support, and financial resources support. I hope the study's insight will provide new useful insights to both the practitioners' and researchers' communities.

4. Theoretical underpinnings

The technology acceptance model (TAM) is regarded as the most widely used theoretical framework for assessing the acceptance of technologies in the literature (Legris et al., 2003). The TAM was developed by Davis (1989); it posits that users' acceptance or adoption of technological innovations can be predicted by the users' views of the perceptions related to ease of use and usefulness of the system (Davis, 1989).

The perceived ease of use describes "the degree to which a person believes that using a particular system would be free of effort" (Davis, 1989, 320). Perceived usefulness describes the user's perceptions of the expected benefits derived from using a particular IS system (Davis, 1989). In this research, the dependent variable is intention to expand use. The constructs from the TAM, which were essentially technology-related factors, were integrated into the technology-organization-environment (TOE) framework. The TOE framework posits that the adoption of innovations depends on organizational, environmental as well as technological factors (Tornatzky & Fleischer, 1990). In general, the TOE model is an integrative schema that incorporates the characteristics of the technology, contingent organizational factors, and other elements from the macro-environment. Prior studies (e.g. Ifinedo, 2011a, b) that used the TOE framework to examine the antecedents of factors on e-business usage and acceptance in small firms elsewhere included such variables as top management support, organizational readiness, IS vendor support, government support, and financial resources availability.

5. Hypotheses formulation

This study' research framework highlighting factors identified as being pertinent to the intention to expand the use of e-business payment solutions among Nigerian small firms are presented in Figure 1. Previous studies (e.g. Al-Ghait et al., 2010; Gholami et al., 2010) indicated that the adoption and usage of online services and e-payment systems can be impacted by such factors as gender, age, education, organizational size, and revenues. To that end, these variables were incorporated into the research model to increase insight.

With regard to IS acceptance, Davis (1989) demonstrated that perceived ease of use and perceive usefulness have positive effects on use or adoption of an IS. Evidence from the

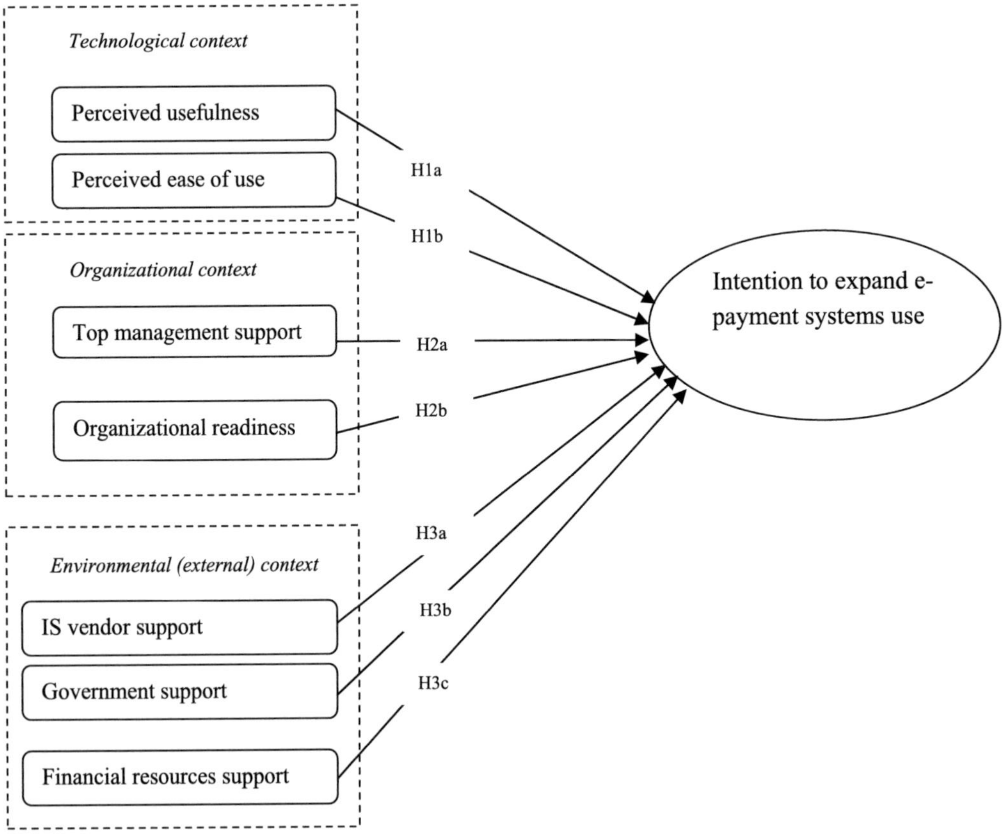

Fig. 1. The research model

extant literature has supported the importance of the TAM's constructs in determining IS use (Legris et al., 2003). Lee (2009) showed that perceived usefulness and perceived ease of use have positive impacts on the adoption of internet banking with the variable of attitude toward use serving as a mediator. Others including Reid and Levy (2008) and Ayo et al. (2011) found that perceived usefulness and perceived ease of use influence customers' acceptance of e-banking, which is a larger concept that includes EPS. Ramaya et al. (2005) found both perceived usefulness and perceived ease of use to be significant determinants of intention to use an online bill payment system for graduate students. Ozkan's (2010) study of the factors facilitating the adoption of e-payment systems indicated that perceived advantage (perceived usefulness, in this instance) was a significant variable in the relationship. Thus, it is predicted that:

H1a: Perceived usefulness positively influences the intention to expand e-business payment systems use in Nigerian small firms

H1b: Perceived ease of use positively influences the intention to expand e-business payment systems use in Nigerian small firms

Thong et al. (1996, p253) describe top management support as the "active engagement of top management with IS implementation." Prior research has shown that top management support and commitment generally boded well for the acceptance of technological innovations in small businesses (Iacovou et al., 1995; Premkumar & Roberts, 1999; Al-Qirim, 2007). This is because top managers act as change agents in the adoption process of technological innovations (Igbaria et al., 1997). When top managers understand the importance of technological innovations such as e-payment systems in their organizations, they tend to play a crucial role in influencing other organizational members to accept the use of such innovations. Chatterjee et al. (2002) found lack of top management support to be a hindrance to e-business adoption in organizations. In the context of SSA, Eze (2007) and Cloete et al. (2002) found support for the relevance of this factor in the successful adoption of e-business in the region. Thus, it is predicted that:

H2a: Top management support positively influences the intention to expand e-business payment systems use in Nigerian small firms

Organizational readiness is defined by Iacovou et al. (1995, 467) as "the availability of the needed organizational resources for adoption." Organizational readiness of businesses is critically important for IS adoption and it encompasses not only physical assets, but also human knowledge of IS (Mehrtens et al., 2001; Zhu et al., 2003). Chircu and Kauffman (2000) revealed that lack of computer literacy among owners of small businesses and a lack of knowledge of the benefits of IS use is an inhibitor to IS adoption in small firms. In SSA, Saffu et al. (2007) indicated that e-business thrives better where operators of business have an understanding of e-business concepts in their setups. Thus, it is predicted that:

H2b: Organizational readiness positively influences the intention to expand e-business payment systems use in Nigerian small firms

In this study, IS vendor support refers to the support for implementing and using technological innovations that a business obtains from external sources of technical expertise (Attewell, 1992; Thong et al., 1996; Premkumar & Roberts, 1999). According to Attewell (1992), business organizations tend to postpone technology adoption due to lack of expertise and knowledge. Importantly, the availability of external IS support can help businesses to bridge knowledge gaps related to IS innovation acquisition. I argue that small firms in Nigeria that have access to needed external sources of expertise related to the use of e-payment systems will be better served in their quests to expand their use of such innovations compared to counterparts lacking such assistance. It is worth noting that low levels of ICT skills is among the major barriers of e-business expansion in SSA (Ifinedo, 2005a, b; 2008); thus, the availability of IS vendor support can mitigate this shortcoming. Researchers elsewhere have found this factor to be an important factor in the adoption and usage of e-business and related technologies (Doolin et al., 2003; Scupola, 2003). Thus, it is predicted that:

H3a: IS vendor support positively influences the intention to expand e-business payment systems use in Nigerian small firms

Here, government support refers to the assistance provided by the authority to encourage the spread of IS innovations such as e-business payment systems in its context. Some studies suggested that government support is required for the spread of technological innovations such as e-business within a country (Teo et al., 1997; Chau & Jim, 2002) while others (e.g. Ifinedo, 2011a) did not find support such a relationship. The government in Nigeria through the CBN has realized the pertinence of e-payment solutions in the country's economic growth. To that end, when concerted efforts are directed toward promoting such innovations among small firms in the country, it is to be expected that the use of such systems will be positively encouraged in the country. Thus, it is predicted that:

H3b: Government support positively influences the intention to expand e-business payment systems use in Nigerian small firms

The apparent lack or financial resources in small firms and their resistance to invest in complex IS have been reported as major barriers in some studies (Tuunainen, 1998; Chapman et al., 2000; Love et al., 2001). Research has also shown that small firms do encounter difficulties with respect to obtaining finance, and this unfavorable situation often set back their efforts to adopt needed IS innovations (Tuunainen, 1998; Chapman et al., 2000; Love et al., 2001). Tan and Wu (2003) and Pearson and Grandon (2004) showed that financial matters are vitally important to owners and managers and such issues often influence the adoption of IS in small businesses. However, others (e.g. Dongen et al., 2002; Simpson & Doherty, 2004) found that a lack of financial resources was not a sufficient factor to set back e-business adoption in small firms. Perhaps due to economic reality, Nigerian small firms lack required financial resources to enable them procure and adopt useful and relevant business tools (Ifinedo, 2005b; 2008). To that end, where such resources exist, it is to be expected that the intention to expand the use of e-payment solution will be relatively higher. Thus, it is predicted that:

H3c. Financial resources support positively influences the intention to expand e-business payment systems use in Nigerian small firms

6. Research methodology

Data collection

This work is a part of a major research conducted by the researcher and his associates in Nigeria. This study's data was collected in Lagos and environs; the city is the largest commercial city in Nigeria (and in SSA) (Eze, 2007). I believe that the search of small firms with knowledge of e-business payments will be easier in such a place. The targeted population comes from the list of business contacts held by a local university in the city. This approach is akin to judgmental sampling (Iacobucci & Churchill, 2009) because the researcher selects respondents based on his/her knowledge of the suitability of the participants. Other prior studies in Nigeria have used a similar method for data collection (Anandarajan et al., 2002; Ayo et al., 2008, Ifinedo, 2008). The identified participants, who were mainly middle-level managers, came from a wide range of industries. As the unit of analysis of this study was at the level of the organization, the inclusion of such organizational informants would ensure that useful insights are provided.

To ensure content validity, six (6) knowledgeable individuals, including business managers and IS faculty members participated in a pilot test with an initial draft of the questionnaire. The comments and suggestions received from these individuals helped to improve the quality of the final questionnaire. The research effort identified 300 possible respondents from the contacts list and each received a copy of the questionnaire in person. Each package contained a cover letter explaining the purpose of the study. Participation in the study was voluntary. Respondents were assured that their individual responses would be treated as confidential. The participants were also motivated with a promise of receiving a summary of the results.

The majority of the measures used in the study were taken from previously validated sources (Davis, 1989; Iacovou et al., 1995; Igbaria et al. 1997; Thong et al., 1996; Premkumar & Roberts, 1999; Ifinedo, 20011a, b). Please see the Appendix for a list of the measures used in the study. The measurement items were anchored on a 7-point Likert scale ranging from "strongly disagree" (1) to "strongly agree" (7) in which participants were asked to indicate an appropriate response. Table 1 highlights the construct's sources and their descriptive statistics. The composite reliability scores for each factor exceeded the recommended 0.7 threshold to indicate a reasonably high reliability of the research measures and constructs (Nunnally, 1978).

Construct	Items	Mean	SD	Factor loading	Composite reliability	Sources
Perceived usefulness						Davis (1989)
	PUSS1	4.60	1.39	0.771		
	PUSS2	4.30	1.69	0.837		
	PUSS3	4.11	1.76	0.771	0.874	
	PUSS4	4.30	1.67	0.840		
	PUSS5	2.95	2.37	0.579		
Perceived ease of use						Davis (1989)
	PEOU1	4.35	1.45	0.776		
	PEOU1	4.44	1.28	0.771		
	PEOU1	4.46	1.23	0.836	0.884	
	PEOU1	4.42	1.39	0.861		
Top management support						Thong et al. (1996) ; Igbaria et al. (1997)
	MGT1	4.63	1.43	0.867		
	MGT2	4.61	1.46	0.826	0.903	
	MGT3	4.52	1.47	0.884		
	MGT4	4.30	1.60	0.767		
Organizational readiness	ORG1	4.80	1.18	0.807		Iacovou et al. (1995)
	ORG2	4.82	1.21	0.815		

	ORG3	4.46	1.53	0.743	0.870	
	ORG4	4.55	1.52	0.694		
Government support						Ifinedo (2011a)
	GOVT1	3.57	1.91	0.676		
	GOVT2	3.34	1.92	0.796		
	GOVT3	3.34	1.72	0.910	0.892	
	GOVT4	3.42	1.89	0.770		
IS vendor support	ISV1	3.94	1.66	0.865		Premkumar & Roberts (1999)
	ISV2	3.47	1.71	0.856	0.918	
	ISV3	4.02	1.38	0.942		
Financial resources support						Ifinedo (2011a)
	FINS1	3.57	1.79	0.837	0.839	
	FINS2	3.66	1.81	0.863		
Intention to use e-payment						Davis (1989)
	INT1	5.60	2.25	0.958		
	INT2	5.56	2.24	0.935	0.974	
	INT3	5.61	2.26	0.951		
	INT4	5.81	1.93	0.956		

SD = Standard deviations

Table 1. The constructs' descriptive statistics and their reliability values

7. Survey results

One hundred and fifty six (156) responses were received from the administered 300 questionnaires, which gives an effective response rate of 52% for this study. However, 22 responses were not considered valid for this research; these included responses from the public sector, those with a high percentage of missing entries, and those indicating non-adoption of any e-payment solutions in their business operations. The data showed that 64%, 75%, 43%, and 40% of the respondents indicated using credit cards, automated teller machines (ATMs), electronic cash (E-cash), and electronic funds transfer (EFT), respectively in their organizational business transactions.

Table 2 summarizes the profile of respondents. The participants' average work experience was 3.94 years (s.d. = 1.22). The respondents included 64% middle-level managers and 26% top managers. Seventy-two percent (74%) of the sample had at least a university degree. The average age of the respondents was 32.3 years. The employees in the sampled firms ranged from 1 to 500 employees with a median of 6 employees. The other profiles of the responding businesses are highlighted in Table 3.

Profile	Frequency	Percentage (%)
Gender		
Male	94	70.1
Female	40	29.9
Age		
Less than 20 years	2	1.5
21-30	37	27.6
31-40	67	50.0
41-50	23	17.2
51-60	5	3.7
Education		
Primary education	1	0.7
Secondary education	4	3.0
College/Bachelor's education	74	55.2
Post-graduate degree	53	39.6
Other	2	1.5
Job title		
CEO	9	6.7
Director (e.g. Operations, Sales)	11	8.2
Manager (Admin, IT, Project, etc.)	74	55.2
Engineer	8	6
Assistant/Office Executive	18	13.4
Other (e.g. Surveyor, Lab	12	9
Technician)	2	1.5
Missing		

Table 2. The profile of the respondents

The problem of common method bias exists for studies that used single informants such as this one. I followed the procedural remedies for controlling common method biases. First, to increase the study's validity, I used clear and concise questions in the questionnaire. Second, to reduce apprehension, I assured the respondents that their data will be treated with anonymity. Third, I used a statistical procedure i.e. the Harmon one-factor test (Podsakoff et al., 2003) to assess if such biases were a problem in the collected data. The test results showed that several factors with eigenvalues greater than one are present in the collected data. Accordingly, the most covariance explained by one factor in the data is 26.5% to indicate that common method variance is not a problem for the data.

Profile	Frequency	Percentage (%)
Business type		
Adverting, Marketing, Sales	10	7.5
Manufacturing	18	13.4
Retail, Wholesale	19	14.2
Financial services	35	26.1
Pharmaceutical/Chemical	6	4.5
Information Technology (IT) and Telecoms	23	17.2
Oil and Gas Services	8	6.0
Hospitality	6	4.5
Other (e.g. Aviation, Surveying)	7	5.2
Missing data	2	1.5
Annual sales revenues		
Less 500,000 naira	3	2.2
500,001 - 1.0 million naira	9	6.7
1.1 - 5.0 million naira	7	5.2
5.1 - 10.0 million naira	8	6.0
10.1 - 20.0 million naira	15	11.2
20.1 - 50.0 million naira	81	60.4
Missing data	11	8.2
Workforce		
1-25 employees	27	20.1
26-50 employees	12	9.0
51 - 75employees	6	4.5
76 -100 employees	8	6.0
Above 100 employees	78	58.2
Missing data	3	2.2

Note: The exchange rate of the naira per US dollar is 150.48 in year 2009.
Table3. Profile of the participating businesses

In testing for nonresponse bias, I divided the collected data into two parts i.e. early and late respondents. The mean values of selected items for early and late respondents in a survey were then compared (Iacobucci & Churchill, 2009). Chi-square ($\chi 2$) test was used to compare the sampled firm size, annual revenue, and industry type. The results of the Chi-square tests (significant at $p < 0.05$) showed there were no significant differences in the chosen characteristics.

8. Data analysis

I used the Partial Least Squares (PLS) technique for data analysis. The PLS approach is suitable for validating predictive models (Chin, 1998), and the approach permits information about the measurement and structural models to be presented. The specific tool used in this study was SmartPLS 2.0 that was developed by Ringle et al. (2005).

9. The measurement model

The measurement model assesses the reliability, convergent, and discriminant validities of the data. The internal consistency of the data measures is assured when the reliability of each measure in a scale is above 0.7 (Nunnally, 1978). Composite reality scores of 0.7 and above is also considered adequate to assure reliability (Nunnally, 1978; Hair et al., 1998). The convergent validity of the data is assured when each item has an item loading that is greater than 0.5 on its associated construct. Fornell and Larcker (1981) recommend that the following conditions be met for adequate discriminant validity to be assured: a) the square root of the average variance extracted (AVE) of all constructs should be larger than all other cross-correlations; b) the value of the AVE should be of the threshold value 0.50. Table 4 shows that the AVE ranged from 0.59 to 0.90, and in no case was any correlation between the constructs greater than the squared root of AVE (the principal diagonal element). Thus, the measurement items used for this study demonstrate good psychometric properties.

	AVE	1	2	3	4	5	6	7	8
1:Perceived usefulness	0.59	**0.768**							
2:Perceived ease of use	0.66	0.514	**0.812**						
3:Top management support	0.70	0.656	0.513	**0.837**					
4:Organizational readiness	0.63	0.567	0.392	0.598	**0.793**				
5:Government support	0.67	0.521	0.454	0.353	0.367	**0.819**			
6: IS vendor support	0.79	0.356	0.650	0.346	0.416	0.514	**0.889**		
7:Financial resources support	0.72	0.289	0.486	0.377	0.352	0.521	0.650	**0.849**	
8:Intention to expand e-payment system use	0.90	0.288	0.173	0.317	0.298	0.200	0.292	0.197	**0.949**

Note: a) The bold fonts in the leading diagonals are the square root of AVEs, b) off-diagonal elements are correlations among constructs

Table 4. Inter-construct correlations, AVE, and the square root of AVE

10. The structural model

The structural model in PLS presents information related to the path coefficients (β) and the squared R (R^2). The strength of the relationship is indicated by the β and the R^2 shows the percentage of variance in the model to give an indication of its predictive power. The path significance levels (t-values) are estimated by the bootstrapping method. The SmartPLS 2.0 results for the βs and the R^2 are shown in Figure 2.

Four out of the seven hypotheses were supported; hypothesis (H1a) was confirmed to show that perceived usefulness of e-business payment systems positively influences the intention to expand e-business payment systems use in Nigerian small firms. Hypothesis (H1b) was unsupported by the data. Hypothesis (H2a) was supported to affirm the view that top management support is crucially important in facilitating the intention to expand the use of e-business payment systems in Nigerian small firms. The data did not provide support for hypothesis (H2b). The result also demonstrated significant, statistical support for hypothesis (H3a) which predicted that IS vendor support would positively influence the intention to expand e-business payment systems use in Nigerian small firms.

Contrary to the hypotheses formulated in H3b and H3c, government support and financial resources support did not positively influence the intention to expand e-business payment systems use in Nigerian small firms. It is worth noting that the nature of the relationships appeared to be negative. None of the control variables used in this study had any significant impact of the dependent variable to assure me that such factors had little impact in my research conceptualization. Together, all the variables explained 21% of the variance in the dependent construct. The foregoing information suggests that the proposed research conceptualization possess adequate predictive power to permit an understanding with regard to the intention to expand e-business payment systems use in Nigerian small firms. Further discussion on the results is presented in the next section.

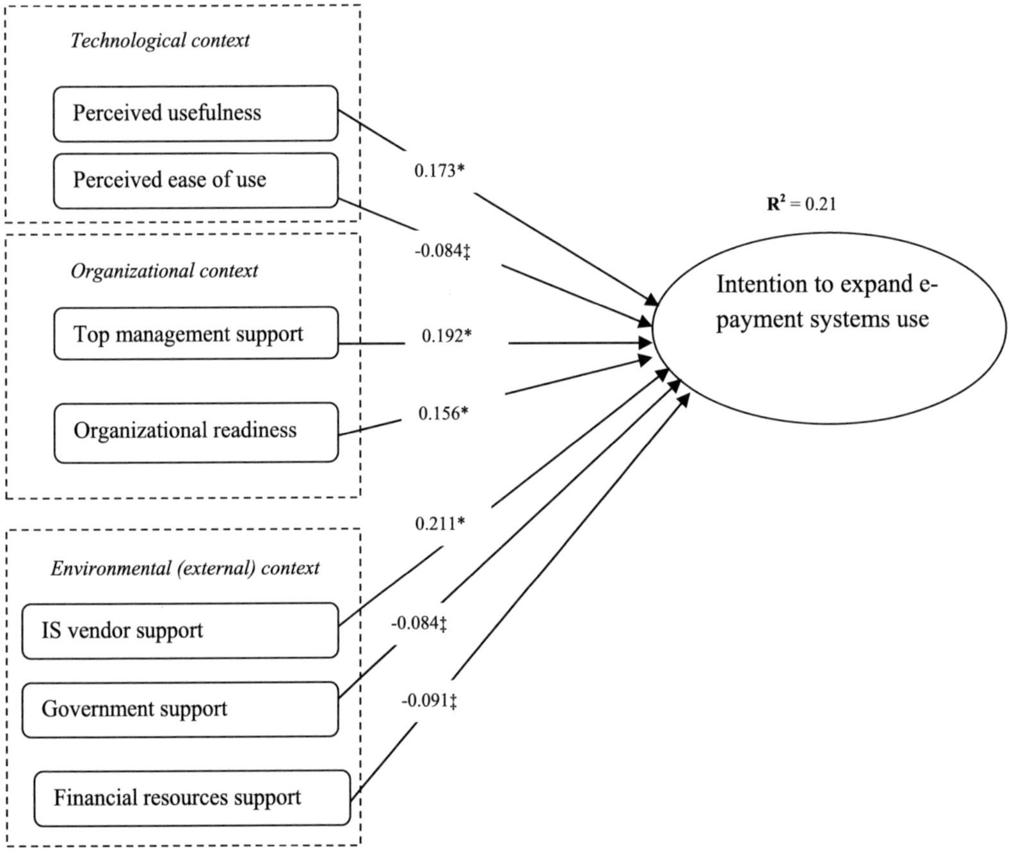

* Denotes significance at the $p < 0.05$ level, ‡ = Not significant
Fig. 2. The SmartPLS results for the research model

11. Discussions

The findings of this research confirmed a number of factors that positively influence the intention to expand e-business payment systems use in Nigerian small firms. The hypotheses formulated to determine the importance of perceived usefulness, top management support, organizational readiness, and IS vendor support in the research model were all confirmed, the other factors were not supported by the collected data. While perceived usefulness was found to be an important factor for the firms sampled in this study, perceived ease of use did not have any meaningful influence on small firm's intention to expand e-business payment systems use. The finding with respect to the variable of perceived usefulness is consistent with the results of other studies (e.g. Ramaya et al. 2005; Ozkan, 2010; Ayo et al., 2011). It is surprising to notice that perceived ease of use is not a significant factor in the research model. This result might be suggesting that small firms in Nigeria may be finding the use of such systems to be complex.

Consistent with past studies (e.g. Thong et al., 1996; Ozkan, 2010; Ifinedo, 2011a), both top management support and organizational readiness were found to have positive influences on the intention to expand e-business payment systems use in Nigerian small firms. These results indicated that small firms in Nigeria that have higher levels of top management support and the required organizational readiness in their setups are more inclined to expand their use intentions of e-business payment solutions. The results of this study confirmed that the availability of IS vendor support augured well for intention to expand the use of e-payment in Nigerian small firms; this positive relationship is consistent with the results of similar prior research (Thong et al., 1996; Premkumar & Roberts, 1999; Ifinedo, 2011a). The variables of government support and financial resource support did not positively influence the intention to expand e-business payment systems use in Nigerian small firms. Two plausible reasons are offered for the lack of support these foregoing hypotheses: a) the result might have been impacted by extraneous factors i.e. the respondents may believe that government agencies and financial organizations in Nigeria are not providing needed assistance to small firms wishing to adopt such innovations, b) it is also possible that measuring items used to operationalize these items may be limited in scope or lack adequate validity.

12. Implication for research and practice

This research has implications for future study. First, the use of the TOE framework in this current study has engendered deeper insight at the micro level regarding possible factors that positively influence the intention to expand e-business payment systems use in Nigerian small firms. This chapter expanded the body of knowledge in the area with its perspectives and insights; others may be enticed to continue research in the area. Second, the dependent variable, i.e. intention to expand e-business payment systems use that was used departs from prior research efforts that tend to operationalize such constructs with a single item of Use (Usage) or Intention to use. The utilization of such singular items may obfuscate reality and has, in fact, been criticized for limiting insight (Legris et al., 2003). Third, this research generally affirms findings and observations regarding the factors influencing the adoption of e-business in small organizations both in SSA and elsewhere. It also underscores factors or issues that may have little or no relevance to such discourse.

The attention being paid to issues in a developing part of the world i.e. Nigeria in the SSA could positively serve theory consolidation and development, which goes to enrich the literature. As well, policy makers, industry leaders, and business executives wishing to understand some of the reasons why the use of e-payment has been sluggish in Nigeria may benefit from the information provided in this study. Given that the respondents from small firms in Nigeria indicated that the perceived usefulness of e-payment, their organizational readiness, top management and IS vendor support can positively influence their intention to increase their use of e-business payment solutions, I recommends that such factors should be continually monitored when decision related to the continued use of such systems are being proposed in adopting firms. Similarly, more concerted efforts need to be undertaken to sensitize business owners and their employees or increase awareness of such innovations. The need for e-business payment systems coaching and training is deserving of attention (Simpson & Doherty, 2004).

In light of the fact that government support was not found to positively influence the intention to expand e-business payment systems use in Nigerian firms, it is reasonable to suggest that by increasing assistance in this area, many more small firms in the country may be encouraged to increase their use of such e-payment technologies. To that end, relevant government agencies and other local sources of expertise in Nigeria can be marshaled towards providing needed awareness and coaching programs aimed at encouraging positive outcomes in e-payment use in small firms in the country. With such sorts support on board, it is to be expected that more and more small firms in Nigeria will see they need to expand their use of such e-payment platforms. Small loans from local financial houses should be actively promoted to enable small firms needing such to procure needed e-payment infrastructure.

13. Limitations and avenues for future research

This exploratory research has its share of limitations. First, despite the fact that common method bias was not seen to pose a problem for this study's data, it is still possible that respondents may be subject to a halo effect. I accept that asking only one respondent to present a view on behalf of their organization may be problematic. Second, the results from this endeavor should not be generalized for the whole of Nigeria as only a small part of the country was included in this study. Data from other parts of the country may be different from what is reported and discussed herein. Third, the research included the views of both owners and employees in the sampled organizations. It is possible that the views of both cohorts may differ somewhat on certain issues presented in the questionnaire. I did not control for this possibility of such happening in this study.

Future research can build upon this current research's conceptualization. Whenever possible, some of the aforementioned limitations could be addressed in subsequent studies. The amount variance explained by the factors considered in this study, which is 21% implies that other relevant factors and issues can be incorporated into the research model to increase its predictive power. The effects of security, perceived trust, and perceived risks could be investigated. This research effort can be replicated in other SSA countries to reify or debunk claims presented in this study. The data used in this study is cross-sectional in nature; future efforts could consider using longitudinal data to facilitate more insight. Industry specific studies could also be commissioned to further enhance insight. Future research using meta-analytic approaches could examine the enablers and inhibitors of e-business payment systems use intentions in the country (and region). Knowledge from such efforts stands to consolidate theories related to the acceptance of e-business payment systems use in SSA.

14. Conclusion

This chapter focused on the factors positively influencing the intention to expand the use e-business payment systems in Nigerian firms. A research model fusing the TAM into the TOE was used to guide the discourse. Factors including perceived usefulness, perceived ease of use, organizational readiness, top management support, IS vendor support, and government support were considered in this study. This current study's findings lend credence to results obtained elsewhere and it provides support for the relevance of the TAM and TOE as useful models for examining the use intentions of technological innovations. Perceived usefulness, organizational readiness, top management support, and IS vendor support were all found to positively influence the intention to expand the use of e-business payment systems in Nigerian firms. Accordingly, more progress can be sustained and assured when adequate attention is accorded the foregoing significant factors vis-à-vis facilitating an increase in the use behaviors of e-payment systems in Nigerian small firms. The relevant literature and practitioners stand to benefit from the information provided in this study, and it is hoped that future research will build upon the findings reported herein as efforts are made to understand technology diffusion in developing countries such as Nigeria.

15. Appendix: The measurement items and scales

Perceived Usefulness

- Using e-payment solutions would make work easier for our employees and managers
- Using e-payment solutions would increase employees' and managers' productivity
- Using e-payment solutions would increase the performance of our employees.
- Our employees and managers would find e-payment solutions useful in their jobs
- Using e-payment solutions would provide information for strategic decisions

Perceived ease of use

- The use of e-payment solutions would be clear and understandable for us
- Learning to use e-payment solutions would be easy for our employees
- Overall, e-payment solutions would be easy to use in our organization
- It would be easy to become skilful at using e-payment solutions in our firm

Top management support

- Management is interested in the use of e-payment solutions in our operations
- Management is supportive of the use of e-payment solutions in our operations
- Our business has a clear vision regarding the use of e-payment solutions
- Management clearly communicates the need for e-payment solutions usage in the firm

Organizational readiness

- Our firm knows how information technology (IT) can be used to support our operations
- Our firm has a good understanding of how e-payment solutions can be used in our business

- We have the necessary technical, managerial and other skills to implement e-payment solutions in our firm
- Our business values and norms would not prevent us from adopting e-payment solutions in our operations

Government support

- We believe the government is championing the cause of e-business in the country
- We believe the government is investing in the necessary infrastructure to support the emergence of e-business payment solutions.
- Government policies and guidelines towards e-business (e-payment solutions) are commendable
- We are of the view that the government adequately supports e-business and related concepts in the country

IS vendor support

- IS vendors in the region are actively promoting e-business systems and other technologies by providing incentives for adoption
- IS vendors are encouraging our business to adopt e-business systems by providing us with free training sessions
- We can easily obtain support from local IS vendors as we implement e-business systems

Financial resource support

- Supporting institutions in Nigeria e.g. banks provide financial assistance for small firms wishing to adopt e-business and e-payment solutions
- Our company could easily procure financial support from financial institutions to enable us implement e-payment/e-business solutions in our business

Intention to expand e-business e-payment systems

- My company will use e-payment solutions on a regular basis, in the future
- My company intends to expand its use of e-payment systems rather than discontinue their use
- My company's intensions are to use a lot more e-payment solutions in the future
- There is likelihood that my company will expand its use of e-payment options in the future rather than use alternative means

16. Acknowledgment

The author is indebted to Prof C.K. Ayo (Covenant University, Ota, Nigeria) and Mrs Uyinomen O. Ekong (University of Uyo, Uyo, Nigeria) for their assistance in this research project. The author is grateful to C. M. Ringle, S. Wende, and A.Will for the use of their software, SmartPLS 2.0.

17. References

Adesina, A.A., Ayo, C.K. & Ekong, U.O. (2008). An empirical investigation of the level of users' acceptance of e-banking in Nigeria: based on technology acceptance model. In *Proc. of 1st Int'l Conf. on Mobile e-Services*. LAUTECH, Ogbomosho, Nigeria.

Agbada, A.O. (2008). E-banking in Nigeria, problems and prospects from customer's perspective. *CBN Bullion Magazine,* 32(4), October-December 2008 edition.

Akpan, N., (2008). E-payment solutions: are banks getting it right?" Business day Newspaper, Wednesday February 27th 2008.

Al-Ghait, W., Sanzogni, and Sandh, K. (2010). Factors influencing the adoption and usage of online services in Saudi Arabia, The Electronic Journal on Information Systems in Developing Countries, 40(1), 1-32.

Al-Qirim, N. (2007). The adoption of ecommerce communications and applications technologies in small businesses in New Zealand. Electronic Commerce Research and Applications, 6(4), 462-473.

Amor, D. (1999). The e-business (r)evolution. Upper Saddle River, N.Y.: Prentice Hall.

Anandarajan, M., Igbaria, M., & Anakwe, U. (2002). IT acceptance in a less-developed country: a motivational factor perspective. International Journal of Information Management, 22(1), 47-65.

Andam, Z. R. (2003). E-commerce and e-business, e-primer for the information economy, Society and Polity Series, UNDP-APDIP and e-ASEAN Task Force.

Attewell, P. (1992). Technology diffusion and organizational learning: The case of business computing. *Organization Science, 3(1)*, 1-19.

Ayo, C. K. (2006). The Prospects of E-commerce in Nigeria. Journal of Internet Banking and Commerce, 11(3), 20–35.

Ayo, C.K., Adebiyi, A., Fatudimu, I.T., & Ekong, U.O. (2008). A framework for e-commerce implementation: Nigeria a case study. *Journal of Internet Banking and Commerce, 13(2),* 1-12.

Ayo, C. K., Adewoye, J. O, & Oni, A. A. (2011). The state of e-banking implementation in Nigeria: A post-consolidation review, Journal of Emerging Trends in Economics and Management Sciences, 1(1), 37-45.

Babalakin & Co. (2002). Cybernetic banking (changing the banking landscape in Nigeria) Central Bank of Nigeria Website. Retrieved from http://www. cenbank.org/Paymentsystem/evolution.asp.

Chapman, P., James-Moore, J., Szczygiel, M., & Thompson, D. (2000). Building Internet Capabilities in SME's. *Logistics Information Management*, 13(6), 353-361.

Chau, Y. K., & Jim, C.F. (2002). Adoption of electronic data interchange in small and medium enterprises. *Journal of Global Information Management*, 10(4), 61-85.

Chatterjee, D., Grewal, R., & Sambamurthy, V. (2002). Shaping up for e-commerce: Institutional enablers of the organizational assimilation of web technologies. *MIS Quarterly*, 26(2), 65-89.

Chiemeke, S.C., Evwiekpaefe, O., & Chete ,F. (2006). The Adoption of Internet Banking in Nigeria: An Empirical Investigation, *Journal of Internet Banking and Commerce*, 11(3), [Online] Available: http://www.arraydev.com/commerce/jibc/.

Chin, W. (1998). Issues and opinion on structural equation modeling. *MIS Quarterly*, 22(1), vii-xvi.

Chircu, A.M., & Kauffman, R.J. (2000). Limits to value in electronic commerce-related IT investments. Journal of Management Information Systems, 17(2), 59–80.

Cloete, E., Courtney, S. & Fintz, J. (2002). Small business acceptance and adoption of e-commerce in the Western-Cape province of South-Africa, Electronic Journal of Information Systems in Developing Countries 10(4), 1–13.

CIA WorldFact (2011). Nigeria reports. Retrieved April 3, 2011, from https://www.cia.gov/library/publications/the-world-factbook/geos/ni.html.

Davis, F.D. (1989). Perceived usefulness, perceived ease of use, and user acceptance of information technology. *MIS Quarterly, 13(3),* 318-339.

Doolin, D., Mcleod, L., McQueen, B., & Watton, M. (2003). Internet strategies for establishing retailers: four New Zealand case studies. *Journal of Information Technology Cases and Applications,* 5(4), 3–19.

Dongen, J., Maitland, C., & Sadowski, B. (2002). Strategic use of the Internet by small- and medium-sized companies: An exploratory study. *Information Economics and Policy,* 14(1), 75-93.

Economist Intelligence Unit. (2007). Government E-Payments Adoption Ranking: A briefing paper from the Economist Intelligence Unit. Retrieved December 16, 2008 from http://corporate.visa.com/md/dl/documents/downloads/GEAR_Paper.pdf

Emordi, C.N.O., (2007). Recent development in Nigeria's Payment System, *CBN Briefs,* Series No. 2006-2007/03, pp. 23-30.

EIU (Economic Intelligence Unit) (2011). Global intelligence and analysis. Retrieved March 27, 2011, from http://www.eiu.com/public/.

Eze, U.C. (2008). E-business deployment in Nigerian financial firms: An empirical analysis of key factors. *International Journal of E-Business Research, 4(2),* 29-47.

Ezeoha A. E. (2005). Regulating internet banking in Nigeria: problems and challenges - Part 1." Retrieved October 13, 2010 from http://www.arraydev.com/commerce/jibc/.

Farhoomand, A.F., Tuunainen, V.K., & Yee, L.W. (2000). Barriers to global electronic commerce: A cross-country study of Hong Kong and Finland, Journal of Organizational Computing and Electronic Commerce, 10(1), 23-48.

Fornell, C., & Larcker, D.F. (1981). Evaluating structural equations models with unobservable variables and measurement error. *Journal of Marketing Research,* 8(1), 39-50.

Gholami R., Ogun A., Koh E., & Lim J. (2010). Factors affecting e-payment adoption in Nigeria. *Journal of Electronic Commerce in Organizations, 8(4),* 51-67.

Grau. J. (2008). *Canada B2C e-Commerce: A work in progress.* Availabel at < http://www.emarketer.com/Reports/All/Emarketer_2000547.aspx >. Accessed 20 July 2010.

Hair, J.F. Jr., Anderson, R.E., Thatham, R.L., & Black, W.C. (1998). *Multivariate data analysis.* Upper Saddle River, NJ: Prentice-Hall International, Inc.

Iacobucci, D., & Churchill, G.A. (2009). *Marketing research: Methodological foundations (with Qualtrics Card)* (10th. ed). Cincinnati, OH: South-Western College Publishing.

Iacovou, C.L., Benbasat, I., & Dexter, A.S. (1995). Electronic data interchange and small organizations: adoption and impact of technology. *MIS Quarterly,* 19(4), 465–485.

Ifinedo, P. (2005a). Measuring Africa's e-readiness in the global networked economy: a nine-country data analysis. *The International Journal of Education and Development using Information and Communication Technology, 1(1),* 53-71.

Ifinedo, P. (2005b). E-government initiative in a developing country: strategies and implementation in Nigeria, *In Proceedings of 6th. World Congress on Electronic Business,* Hamilton, Ontario, Canada, pp. 1-11.

Ifinedo, P. (2008). Internet commerce and SMEs in Sub-Saharan Africa: Perspectives from Nigeria, *Conference on Information Technology and Economic Development (CITED2008),* Calabar, Nigeria, July 25 - 27, 2008, pp. 1- 8.

Ifinedo, P. (2011a). An empirical analysis of factors influencing Internet/e-business technologies adoption by SMEs in Canada, International Journal of Information Technology & Decision Making, 10(4), 731–766.

Ifinedo, P. (2011b). Internet/e-business technologies acceptance in Canada's SMEs: An exploratory investigation, Internet Research, 21(3), 255-281.

Igbaria, M., Zinatelli, N., Cragg, P., & Cavaye, A.L.M., 1997. Personal computing acceptance factors in small firms: A structural equation model. MIS Quarterly, 21(3), 279-305.

Internetworldstats (2011). Country reports. Retrieved April 3, 2011, from http://www.internetworldstats.com/

ITU International Telecommunication Union (2011). Weekly Update. Retrieved April 13, 2011, from http://www.itu.int/en/pages/default.aspx.

Laukkanen, T. & Pasanen, M. (2008). Mobile banking innovators and early adopters: How they differ from other online users? Journal of Financial Services Marketing, 13(2), 86-94.

Lee, M. (2009). Factors influencing the adoption of internet banking: An integration of TAM and TPB with perceived risk and perceived benefit. Electronic Commerce Research and Applications, 8(3), 130-141.

Legris, P. Ingham, J., & Collerette, P. (2003). Why do people use information technology?: A critical review of the technology acceptance model. *Information and Management,* 40(3), 191-204, 2003

Leadpile (2010) 2006, United States E-commerce Sales to Top 120 Billion, says Leadpile. Available at < http://www.leadpile.com/press/2006-10-24_press1.html >. Access 27 July, 2010.

Love, P.E.D., & Irani, Z. (2004). An exploratory study of information technology evaluation and benefits management practices of SMEs in the construction industry. *Information & Management,* 42, 227–242.

Mbarika, V.W., Okoli, C., Byrd, T.A., & Datta, P. (2005). The neglected continent of IS research: a research agenda for Sub-Saharan Africa. *Journal of the Association for Information Systems, 6(5),* 130-170.

Mehrtens, J., Cragg, P.B., & Mills, A.M. (2001). A Model of Internet adoption by SMEs. *Information and Management,* 39(3), 165-176.

Molla, A., & Licker, P.S. (2005). ecommerce adoption in developing countries: a model and instrument. *Information &* Management, 42, 877–899.

Nunnaly, J.C. (1978). *Psychometric theory.* New York, NY: McGraw-Hill.

Ramayah, T., Ling, C-Y, Suki, N. M., and Ibrahim, A. (2005).Determinants of intention to use an online bill payment system among MBA Students, E-Business, 9, 80-91.

Reid, M. & Levy, Y. 2008. Integrating trust and computer self-efficacy with TAM: An empirical assessment of customers' acceptance of banking information systems (BIS) in Jamaica, Journal of Internet Banking and Commerce, 12 (3), 1-8.

Ozkan S. (2010). Facilitating the adoption of e-payment systems: theoretical constructs and empirical analysis, Journal of enterprise information management, 23(3), 305-325.Pearson, M. & Grandon, E. (2004). E-commerce adoption: perceptions of managers/owners of small and medium sized firms in Chile. *Communications of the Association for Information Systems*, 13, 81-102.

Podsakoff, P.M., MacKenzie, S.B., Lee, J.Y., & Podsakoff, N.P. (2003). Common method biases in behavioral research: A critical review of the literature and recommended remedies. Journal of Applied Psychology, 88(5), 879-903.

Premkumar, G., & Roberts, M. (1999). Adoption of new information technologies in rural small businesses. Omega: International Journal of Management Science, 27(4), 467–484.

Ringle, C.M., Wende, S., & Will, A. (2005). SmartPLS 2.0 (M3) beta, Hamburg: http://www.smartpls.de.

Saffu, K., J.H. Walker, & Hinson R. (2007). An empirical study of perceived strategic value and adoption constructs: the Ghanaian case, Management Decision, 45(7), 1083 - 1101.

Scupola, A. (2003). The adoption of Internet commerce by SMEs in the South of Italy: An environmental, technological and organizational perspective. Journal of Global Information Technology Management, 6(1), 52-71.

Simpson, M., & Doherty, A. J. (2004). E-commerce adoption support and advice for UK SMEs. Journal of Small Business and Enterprise Development, 11(3), 315-328

Tan, J., Tyler, K., & Manica, A. (2007). Business-to-business adoption of ecommerce in China. *Information and Management, 44,* 332-351.

Tan, Z., & Wu, Q. (2003). Globalization and e-commerce I: Factors affecting e-commerce diffusion in China. *Communications of the Association for Information Systems*, 10(2), 25-35.

Teo, H.H., Tan, B.C.Y., & Wei, K.K. (1997). Organizational transformation using electronic data interchange: the case of TradeNet in Singapore. *Journal of Management Information Systems, 13(4),* 139-166.

Thong, J.Y.L., Yap, C.S., & Raman, K.S. (1996). Top management support, external expertise and information systems implementation in small business. Information Systems Research, 7(2), 248-267.

Tornatzky, L.G., & Fleischer, M. (1990). *The processes of technological innovation*. Lexington, MA: Lexington Books.

Turban, E., King, D., & Lang, J. (2010). *Introduction to electronic commerce.* New York, NY: Prentice Hall, NY.

Tuunainen, V.K. (1998). Opportunities of effective integration of EDI for small businesses in the automotive industry. *Information & Management*, 34, 361-375.

Vassiliou, C. (2004). Electronic payment systems and marketing: A literature review. Available at: http://mis.uoa.gr/Portals/57ad7180-c5e7-49f5-b282-c6475cdb7ee7/Temp/e-Payment%20Systems_Full%20Review.pdf

WEF (World Economic Forum) (2011). Global competitiveness 2009-2010. Retrieved April 2, 2011 from http://www.weforum.org/reports.

Zhu, K., Kraemer, K., & Xu, S. (2003). Electronic business adoption by European firms: A cross-country assessment of the facilitators and inhibitors. European Journal of Information Systems, 12(4), 251-268.

3

Further Development of a Secured Unified E-Payment System in Nigeria: A Critical Viewpoint

Charles K. Ayo[1] and Wilfred Isioma Ukpere[2]
[1]Dept of Computer and Information Sciences, Covenant University, Ota, Ogun State
[2]Department of Industrial Psychology and People Management, Faculty of Management, University of Johannesburg
[1]Nigeria
[2]South Africa

1. Introduction

e-Payment systems refer to the automated processes of exchanging monetary value among parties in business transactions and transmitting this value over the ICT networks. The common e-Payment channels include the payment cards (debit or credit), Online Web Portals, Point of Sales (POS) terminals, Automated Teller Machines (ATM), Mobile Phones, Automated Clearing House (ACH), direct debit/deposit and Real Time Gross Settlement (RTGS) system (Nnaka, 2009).

The wider patronage of e-Commerce is dependent on the availability of a secured and trusted e-Payment System (Baddeley, 2004). The various categories of e-Commerce include Business-to-Business (B2B): business transactions between organizations that involve companies buying and selling to each other; Business-to-Consumer (B2C): business transactions between organizations and consumers where goods and services are sold directly to the consumer; Consumer-to-Business (C2B): business transactions between consumers and organizations, where consumers can fix prices for both goods and services offered; and Consumer-to-Consumer (C2C): business transaction between consumers among others (Ayo, 2009). Therefore, appropriate considerations must be given to these categories so that the most suitable e-Payment system can be adopted.

According to Anderson (cited in Sumanjeet, 2009), e-Payment system was classified into:

- Online Credit Card Payment System
- Electronic Cheque System
- Electronic Cash System, and
- Smart Card-based Electronic Payment System.

Regardless of the adopted system, the problems militating against e-Payment as listed by Sumanjeet (2009), generally revolve around:

- Integrity: to ascertain that transmitted financial information is unchanged in transit.

- Non-repudiation: to ascertain that all parties have non-deniable proof of receipt.
- Confidentiality: to ascertain that transactions are protected from possible eavesdroppers.
- Reliability: to ascertain that there is reduced possibility of failure.
- Authentication: to ascertain that there are reliable proofs of identities of all parties involved.
- Authorization: to ascertain that individuals are recognized and granted the desired rights and privileges.

Therefore, any reliable e-Payment System should guarantee privacy, integrity, compatibility, efficiency, acceptability, convenience, mobility, anonymity and low financial risk. The smart card-based e-Payment system is essentially a credit card sized plastic card with memory chips and probably an embedded microprocessor that offers greater storage capacity than the ordinary credit card. While the credit card stores a single charge account number in the magnetic stripe, the smart card can hold hundreds of such data, and can serve multiple identification purposes such as personal identification, bank account identification and transactions, health insurance identification among others (Sumanjeet, 2009). Therefore, the objectives of this paper is to design a unified (single) smart card-based e-Payment system that can be used for banking transactions in all the banks in Nigeria as well as serving other forms of identification.

Zulu (2006) identified the challenges of e-Payment in Africa as inadequate telecommunication infrastructure which include: connectivity failure in telephone lines; low Internet bandwidth; high Internet cost, unavailability of dedicated data service networks; and close financial networks as well as frequent power interruption. Similarly, he identified lack of proper legal and regulatory framework and low level of credit access as the other challenges. The threats notwithstanding, there are standard security features already developed to handle them. Some of the available solutions include public-key cryptography, digital signature and certificate, secure socket layer (SSL), and secure electronic transaction (SET) as well as the introduction of biometrics authentication among others (Pesonen, 1998; Zulu, 2006 and Ayo, 2009).

One of the greatest threats to e-Banking is the increasing trends of identity theft, which is a major challenge to the Internet age (Helmbrecht, 2008). Therefore, there is need for a technology that is safe, convenient and not too demanding on the part of the user because of the level of literacy in the developing nations of the world, particularly Nigeria.

The other part of the paper is arranged as follows: section 2 presents the state of e-Payment in Nigeria; section 3 presents the research design; section 4 presents the system design; while section 5 presented the economic consideration of the design and; the conclusion of the work is presented in section 6.

2. The state of e-payment in Nigeria

Nigeria is predominantly a cash-based economy with a lot of cash in circulation. Analysts opined that the cash-based nature of payments in the country is responsible for the abysmally low level of participation in e-Commerce where the acceptable medium of settling transactions is e-Payment (Ojo, 2004; Ayo, 2007; & Ovia, 2002).

The Governor of the Central Bank of Nigeria embarked on bank recapitalization exercise as a strategic move to save the Nigerian banking sector from incessant failure and collapse (Nwachuku, 2005 and Gbolahan, 2005). The result of the exercise brought about a reduction of the 89 banks to 25 solid and strong banks through mergers, acquisition and recapitalization of asset base. As reported by Ayo et al. (2007), virtually all the 25 banks in Nigeria that survived the recapitalization exercise engaged the use of ICT for efficient service delivery. All the banks have one form of e-Payment system or the other.

Alao (2009) reported the colossal amount of money lost in Nigeria to ATM fraud through ATM card cloning, PIN theft among others and government had resorted to removing ATM from public places as well as installing security cameras at the ATM locations to track the activities of fraudsters. However, the level of ICT usage notwithstanding, the level of adoption of e-Banking by the citizen is still very low. Table 1 shows the distribution of the amount of currency in circulation from 2004 to 2008 in Nigeria.

Year	**Amount (₦billion)**
2004	545.7
2005	642.4
2006	770.1
2007	960.5
2008	1,155.1
2009	1,184.3

Source: CBN Annual Reports: 2006, 2007, 2008, 2009

Table 1. Distribution of the amount of Currency in Circulation.

The table raised a lot of issues about the influence of ICT on e-Banking and the banking habit of Nigerians, particularly the volume of cash in circulation. The amount of currency in circulation has continued to increase in view of the various efforts of government. Tables 3 and 4 will help to shed more light on the inhibiting factors which probably revolve around lack of safety, trust and security.

It is evident from table 2 that the most prominent form of e-Payment system in Nigeria is the ATM card. It remained dominant over the years both in volume and value. The other media such as the Internet payment, POS and Mobile payments are still at their infancies. The level of involvement of these instruments of payment presents a clearer picture of the low level of involvement of Nigerians in e-Commerce, knowing fully well that ATM cards are not suitable for international settlement of transactions.

Payment Instruments	Volume %			Value %		
	2006	2007	2008	2006	2007	2008
ATM	93.16	88.7	91.0	73.35	88.5	90.5
Web (Internet)	1.71	5.1	2.4	3.51	7.1	5.7
POS	4.83	2.4	1.8	23.04	4.3	3.7
Mobile	0.31	3.8	4.8	0.11	0.1	0.2

Source: CBN Annual Reports: 2006, 2007, 2008

Table 2. Level of adoption of e-Payment system.

Payment Instruments	Value (₦' Billion) ($1 = ₦155)		
	2007	2008	2009
ATM	131.5	399.7	548.6
Web (Internet)	10.6	25.05	84.5
POS	6.4	16.12	11.04
Mobile	0.09	0.07	1.26

Source: CBN Annual Reports: 2007, 2008 and 2009

Table 2. Level of adoption of e-Payment system.

3. Research design

The research design is two-fold. On one hand, a set of questionnaire was designed and administered randomly to 300 respondents out which 239 were returned representing about 80%. Cronbach's reliability value of 0.782 was obtained, which attests to the reliability of the instrument. Pertinent questions about the demographic profile of respondents as well as the state and operations of ATM Card were asked and the data collected was analysed based on descriptive statistics using the SPSS and the results were presented in tables 3, 4 and 5. On the other hand, a design of the proposed unified Smart Card-based ATM was presented as well as its activity diagram.

Gender of Respondents		
	Frequency	Percent
Male	140	58.6
Female	99	41.4
Total	239	100%
Age of Respondents		
	Frequency	Percent
<20	25	10.4
21 - 30	77	32.2
31 - 40	95	39.7
41 - 50	28	11.7
51+	14	5.9
Total	239	100%
Educational Level of Respondents		
	Frequency	Percent
Valid NONE	26	10.9
Primary School	4	1.7
High School	11	4.6
OND/NCE	24	10
BSc/HND degree	58	24.3
Post Graduate	102	42.7
Others	14	5.9
Total	239	100%
Sector where Respondents Work		
	Frequency	Percent
Valid Others	36	15.1
Finance	47	19.7
Manufacturing	33	13.8
Oil & Gas	13	5.4
Aviation	4	1.7
Education	21	8.8
IT & Telecom	85	35.6
Total	239	100%

Table 3. Demographic profile of Respondents.

3.1 Discussion

Out of the 239 respondents, about 59% of them are male while about 41% of them are female. From the age distribution, over 90% of the respondents are at least 20 years old. Keeping in mind that persons below the age of 18 years are not permitted to operate a bank accounts in Nigeria because that is seen as the age of apprenticeship. Furthermore, about 90% of the respondents have at least the first school leaving certificate (primary school), while only 10% of them (26 out of 239) did not indicate to have had any formal education at any level. Majority of the respondents (35.6%) work in the IT and Telecoms sector, followed by the finance sector (19.7%), the manufacturing sector (13.8%), the education sector (8.8%) and those outside the finance, manufacturing, oil and gas, aviation, education and IT and Telecoms account for 15.1% of the respondents.

Have Bank Accounts		
	Frequency	**Percent**
Valid None	2	8
No	3	1.3
Yes	234	97.9
Total	239	100
Number of ATM Cards Possessed		
	Frequency	**Percent**
Valid None	4	1.7
One	24	10
Two or More	211	88.3
Total	239	100

Table 4. Distribution of the respondents and banking transactions.

It is interesting to note that majority (about 98%) of the respondents operate a bank account. Also, about 88% of the respondents have two ATM cards or more. This gives validity to the proposed unified e-Payment system.

Most of the respondents attested to the convenience of the ATM services (59%) as well as its simplicity (69%). However, its reliability (25%), safety (16.3%) and privacy (31.8%) are in doubt. Therefore, a greater percentage of the respondents disagreed with its reliability, safety and privacy features. However, most of the respondents favour the desirability of having a unified (single) ATM card for all banking transactions (36.8%) as well as the inclusion of a fingerprint reader on the teller machine (66.9%).

	Agree	Disagree	Neutral	Do not Know	Total
Reliability of ATM Services	60 (25.1%)	97 (40.6%)	64 (26.8%)	18 (7.5%)	239 (100.0%)
Covenience of ATM Services	141 (59.0%)	56 (23.4%)	27 (11.3%)	15 (6.3%)	239 (100.0%)
Simplicity of ATM Services	165 (69.0%)	26 (10.9%)	31 (13.0%)	17 (7.1%)	239 (100.0%)
Safety of ATM Services	39 (16.3%)	123 (51.5%)	59 (24.7%)	18 (7.5%)	239 (100.0%)
Privacy of ATM Services	76 (31.8%)	90 (37.7%)	50 (20.9%)	23 (9.6%)	239 (100.0%)
Desirability of One ATM Card	88 (36.8%)	76 (31.8%)	36 (15.1%)	39 (16.3%)	239 (100.0%)
Include Fingerprint on ATM Machines	160 (66.9%)	19 (7.9%)	23 (9.6%)	37 (15.5%)	239 (100.0%)

Table 5. Distribution of the respondents experience with ATM cards.

4. System design

A typical ATM has a keypad that is composed of:

1. Numeric Keys (0-9)
2. Character Keys (A - Z)
3. Operational buttons (Accept, Correction, Cancel)

The screen has eight (8) buttons arranged at the two sides (4 at each side). The features of the ATM are presented in table 6 and a typical picture shown in figure 1.

Bank	Features		
	Numeric Keys • (0-9)	**Character Keys** • (A-Z, *, #, -, +)	**Operation buttons** • OK/Enter/Accept • Cancel • Correction/Change/Clear/Blank
UBA	Yes	Yes	OK, Change, Cancel and Blank
Oceanic	Yes	Yes	Accept, Correction, Cancel and Blank
InterContinental	Yes	Yes	Accept, Correction, Cancel and Blank
CMFB	Yes	No	Enter, Clear, Cancel and Blank

Table 6. Features of ATM Cards.

Table 6 shows the features of the ATM of four banks (UBA, Oceanic, Intercontinental and CMFB) in Nigeria. It is obvious that no special design is required. A common choice for the design is one that has numeric keys (0-9), character keys (A-Z, *, #, -, +), and operation buttons (OK, Change, Cancel), while the blank button can be replaced with the biometric fingerprint reader.

The structure in figure 2 represents the unified Smart Card-based ATM Card that has the possibility of being used for multiple identifications. Four (4) different ATM Cards for the four banks were considered and their features incorporated to arrive at this design. Furthermore, considering the spate of identity fraud, the law enforcement agencies should be able to check at random the various ATM locations to verify the identity of the carrier, though less frequently, hence the inclusion of the holder's passport, gender and or signature. Similarly, in case of accident the blood group is included. All other details are contained on the National Bank's Databank which is a repository of the identities of all banks' customers in Nigeria.

Fig. 1. A typical ATM.

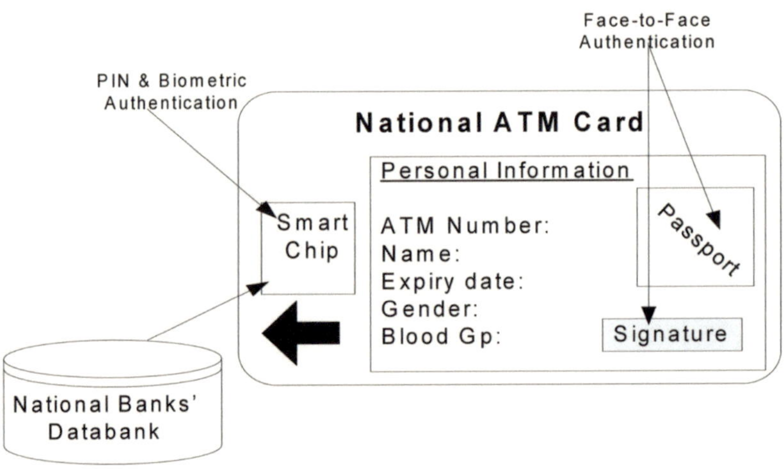

Fig. 2. Smart Card-based ATM Card.

The activity diagram is shown in figure 3. It shows an additional layer of information, which is the selection of bank to transact business with since a single card is being used for several banks, after which the usual (old) display follows: User identification (PIN) but now with fingerprint capture; Selection of Operation (Enquiry, Withdrawal etc); Selection of amount of money; Request for receipts and Exit.

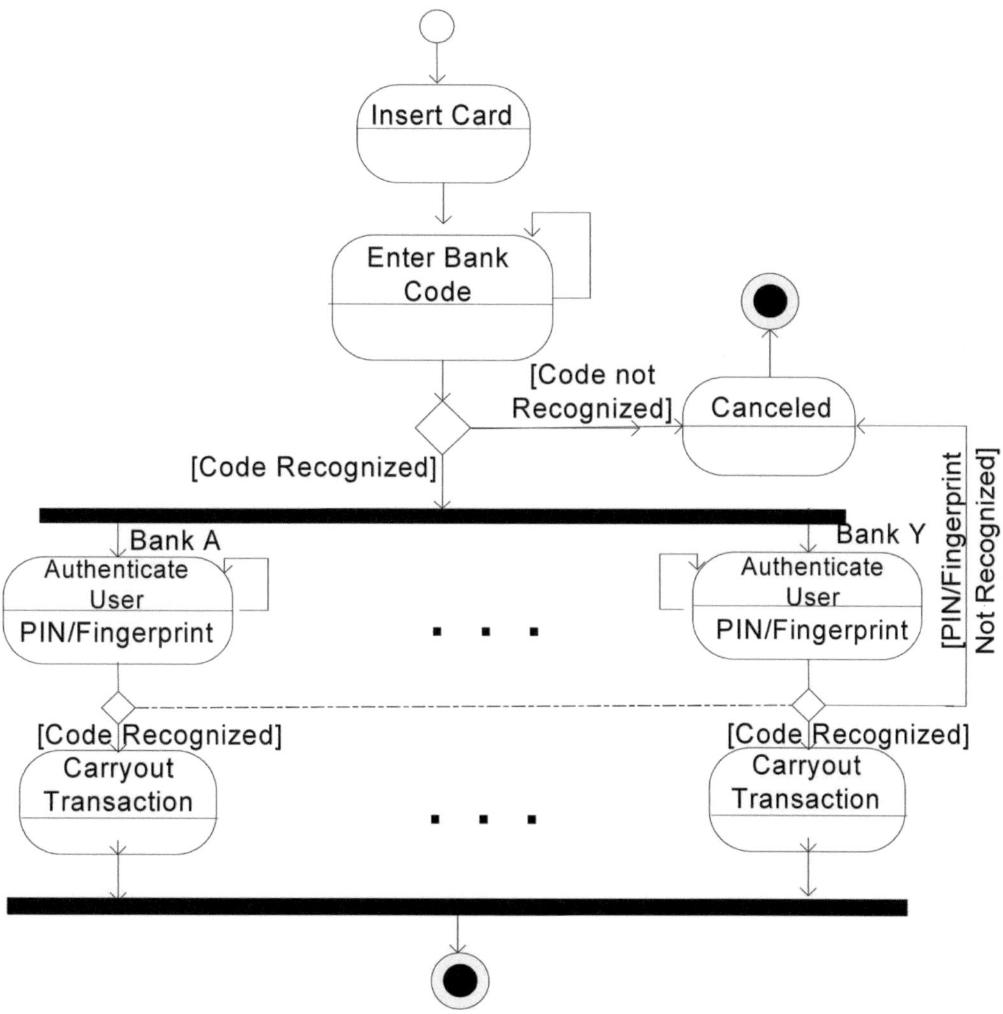

Fig. 3. Activity diagram of the proposed system.

Furthermore, all other changes are software based. The ATM monitor has 8 operational buttons distributed at both sides of the screen. There are 25 banks in Nigeria, modeled banks A to Y, therefore 7 banks can be listed per screen while the 8th key reads "More" for the next screen of 7 banks and the "More" Key, more and more until all the banks are displayed.

5. Cost implication of the design

The cost implication of this design is very minimal on the part of the operators (banks). All the Keypads have a blank button which can be replaced with fingerprint reader through the USB Connection to the CPU. Similarly, the cost of card redesign is not considered a major challenge since each card has expiry date. Therefore, the cost of a new card is borne by the card holder. Similarly, all other changes are software based: the selection of banks and fingerprint authentication which can be taken for regular software update and the cost borne by the operator. However, the major task is the integration of the various banks accounts into the National Banks' Databank. This design approach will most likely be a cheaper alternative than installing security cameras at each location in addition to the cost of relocating the machines to more secure premises.

6. Limitations of the study

From available statistics, 80% of the Nigerian populace are unbanked and 70% of the populace are illiterate (Ayo, 2009 and Okoegwale, 2011). Therefore, the limitations of the system include: high illiteracy level and lack of banking culture arising from lack of confidence and trust in the banking system.

7. Scope for future research

Future research should investigate the Usability of the system as it is likely to impart positively on the banking habit if it is user friendly, reliable and efficient. Furthermore, since the Voting and Banking age is 18years, with increased percentage of the banking populace the card could be further developed for use as the voter's card with a reliable databank formed from the combined databases of the switching companies. Also, the incorporation of voice processing can help persons with disability, particularly the visually impaired to transact banking businesses.

8. Conclusion

The level of adoption of ICT in the banking sector in Nigeria is on the increase, yet the amount of cash in circulation is equally increasing, a situation which is attributable to lack of safety, security, privacy and reliability in the e-Payment instruments. Therefore, the introduction of a smart card-based ATM with biometric authentication will ameliorate these challenges. More than that, the design of a unified smart card-based ATM with biometric authentication is cost-effective and secured. No special design is required as the current system can accommodate the proposed features at minimal cost.

The fingerprint scanner can be accommodated on the keypad while a slight software redesign is required to accommodate a layer of service that will enable the user select a bank of choice. Most importantly, the number of ATM required is drastically reduced, which reduces the cost of production and renewal, and there is enhanced safety, security, and privacy. Furthermore, the fingerprint authentication will be a cheaper alternative than to relocate all ATMs in Nigeria (several thousands of them), to safer premises and the inclusion of security camera at each location.

9. References

Alao Salimon (2009): Need to guard against ATM frauds, *Financial Standard*, Vol. 9, No. 479, pp17-18.

Ayo C. K. (2009): "Information Systems and Technologies". McKay Educational Series, 649p.

Ayo Charles K., Uyinomen O. Ekong, Fatudimu Ibukun Tolulope, and Adebiyi Ayodele A, (2007): M-Commerce Implementation in Nigeria: Trends and Issues, *Journal of Internet Banking and Commerce*, August 2007, Vol. 12, No.2, Available at: http://www.arraydev.com/commerce/JIBC/2007-08/Ayo_final_PDF%20Ready.pdf

Ayo Charles. K and Babajide Daniel O (2006): Designing a Reliable E-payment System: Nigeria a Case Study, *Journal of Internet Banking and Commerce*, August 2006, Vol. 11, No.2, Available at: http://www.arraydev.com/commerce/JIBC/2006-08/AYO.asp

Baddeley M. (2004): Using e-Cash in the new Economy: An Economic Analysis of Micropayment Systems, *Journal of Electronic Research*, Vol. 5, No. 7, pp239-253

CBN Report (2006): "CBN Annual Report for the Year 2006", Access date: June 2009, Available at: http://www.cenbank.org/documents/annualreports.asp

CBN Report (2007): "CBN Annual Report for the Year 2007", Access date: June 2009, Available at: http://www.cenbank.org/documents/annualreports.asp

CBN Report (2008): "CBN Annual Report for the Year 2008", Access date: June 2009, Available at: http://www.cenbank.org/documents/annualreports.asp

CBN Report (2009): "CBN Annual Report for the Year 2009", Access date: June 2009, Available at: http://www.cenbank.org/documents/annualreports.asp

Okoegwale Emmanuel (2011): "Nigeria Mobile Payment & Agency Banking Risk", accessed date: May, 2011, available at: http://mobilemoneyafrica.com/?p=3422

Gbolahan Dada (2005): Banking Sector Consolidation - Integration of IT applications is key, *Finacial Standard*, Vol. 6, No. 11, pg 24.

Helmbrecht U. (2008): The electronic identity card - A safe tool for unambiguous identification on the Internet, Acess date: Sept. 2009, Available at: https://www.bsi.bund.de/cae/servlet/contentblob/486520/publicationFile/31152/231008ANTS_VOE_pdf.pdf

Pesonen Lauri (1998): Electronic money, electronic identity impact on telecommunications Smart Card based solutions, Access date: June 2009, Available at: http://www.netlab.tkk.fi/opetus/s38001/s98/Session7_1.pdf

Nnaka Priscilia (2009): The Nigeria e-Payment System, *Nigeria Monthly*, Vol. 4, No. 8. pp25-27

Nwachukwo Chris (2005): Recapitalization: Bank Workers endorse categorization, access date: 2005, Available at: http://allafrica.com/stories/200504010318.htm

Ojo A. T. (2004): "Enhancing the efficiency of the payment system: Conceptual Framework", A paper presented at the 9th CBN Monetary Policy Forum, Abuja, May 2004.

Ovia Jim (2002): "Payment System and Financial Innovations", A paper presented at the Annual Policy Conference, Nov. 2002.

Sumanjeet S. (2009): Emergence of Payment Systems in the age of Electronic Commerce: The State of Art, *Global Journal of Business Research*, vol. 2, no. 2, pp17-36.

Zulu Brenda (2006): E- payment a challenge for Africa, Access date: Sept. 2009, Available at: http://brendait.blogspot.com/2006/03/e-payment-challenge-for-africa.html

4

Knowledge Management with Multi-Agent System in BI Systems Integration

Dejan Lavbič
University of Ljubljana, Faculty of Computer and Information Science
Slovenia

1. Introduction

There is a growing recognition in the business community about the importance of knowledge as a critical resource for enterprises. The purpose of knowledge management is to help enterprises create, derive, share and use knowledge more effectively to achieve better decisions, increase of competitiveness and fewer errors. In order to run business effectively an enterprise needs more and more information about competitors, partners, customers, and also employees as well as information about market conditions, future trends, government policies and much more. There are several products and technologies available on the market that support advanced Business Process Management (BPM) and advanced decision support. Enterprises expect these applications to support wide range of functionalities - analyses of customer profiles, building and analysing business strategies, developing customer-specific products, carrying out targeted marketing and predicting sales trends. Amount of documents in the Web, enterprise data repositories, and public document management systems with documents they persist are all growing. This huge amount of data is managed in some extent, but knowledge workers, managers, and executives still have to spend much of their working time reading dozens of various types of electronic documents spread over several sources in process of making decisions. There is just too much information to digest in a daily life. The tremendous amount of documents that is still growing has far exceeded the human ability for comprehension without intelligent tools. Different applications within information systems (IS) that support wide range of functionalities need to be integrated in order to provide the appropriate level of information support. One of the prominent approaches for IS integration is the use of ontologies and Multi-Agent Systems (Fuentes, Carbo et al. 2006; Soo, Lin et al. 2006).

The approach presented in this chapter is targeted towards using ontologies for several tasks, where emphasis is on using business rules (BR) approach for interoperability between business user and IS. By introduction of BR approach business users do not have to be fully familiar with the technology to manipulate the common understanding of a problem domain in a form of ontology and therefore enabling agents to execute defined analyses models. The use of ontologies in MAS environment enables agents to share a common set of concepts about contexts, user profiles, products and other domain elements while interacting with each other. Agents can exploit the existing reasoning mechanisms to infer high-level unknown contexts from known contexts, to make decisions and to adapt to the environment, current status, and personal setting of the user. The purpose of this chapter is to present integration of several information resources for Decision Support in Enterprises using agent-oriented approach based on ontologies. The goal of our research is to minimize the gap between business users and agents as special type of application systems that perform tasks in their behalf. The intention was to apply BR approach for ontology manipulation in MAS. Ontology used in our Multi-Agent System for Decision Support in Enterprises (DSS-MAS) was divided into task and domain ontologies while business users were enabled to manipulate them directly in a user friendly environment without requirement of detailed technical knowledge.

The remainder of this chapter is structured as follows. First we present some background in the following section 2 with emphasis on agents, ontologies and related work with clear definition of the problem and proposal for solution. Next, in section 3, we introduce our case study of integrated Multi-Agent environment from the domain of mobile communications with emphasis on architecture and the roles of agents and ontologies. The case study is focused in one of the mobile operators and furthermore oriented to supply and demand of mobile phones. After presentation of system architecture and decomposition of ontology of every agent from DSS-MAS will be presented in detail. Details of case study implementation will be given in section 4. Finally the last section 5 presents conclusions.

2. Multi-agent systems and ontologies

Multi-Agent Systems (MAS) offer a new dimension for cooperation and coordination in an enterprise. The MAS paradigm provides a suitable architecture for a design and implementation of integrated IS. With agent-based technology a support for complex IS development is introduced by natural decomposition, abstraction and flexibility of management for organisational structure changes (Kishore, Zhang et al. 2006). The MAS consists of a collection of autonomous agents that can define their own goals and actions and can interact and collaborate through communication means. In a MAS environment, agents work collectively to solve specific enterprises' problems. MAS provide an effective platform for coordination and cooperation among multiple functional units in an enterprise. The research on agents and MAS has been on the rise over the last two decades. The stream of research on IS and enterprise integration (Lei, Motta et al. 2002; Kang & Han 2003; Tewari, Youll et al. 2003) makes the MAS paradigm appropriate platform for integrative decision support within IS. Similarities between the agent in the MAS paradigm and the human actor in business organisations in terms of their characteristics and coordination lead us to a conceptualisation where agents in MAS are used to represent actors in human organizations.

Today, semantic technologies based on **ontologies** and inference are considered as a promising means towards the development of the Semantic Web (Davies, Studer et al. 2006). In the field of Computer Science and Information Technology (IT) in general ontology has become popular as a paradigm for knowledge representation in Artificial Intelligence (AI), by providing a methodology for easier development of interoperable and reusable knowledge bases (KB). The most popular definition, from an AI perspective, is given in

(Gruber 1993) as follows: "An ontology is an explicit specification of a conceptualization", where a conceptualization is an abstract, simplified view of the world that we wish to represent for some purpose. Ontologies can be considered as conceptual schemata, intended to represent knowledge in the most formal and reusable way possible. Formal ontologies are represented in logical formalisms, such as OWL, which allow automatic inferencing over them. An important role of ontologies is to serve as schemata or intelligent views over information resources. Thus they can be used for indexing, querying, and reference purposes over non-ontological datasets and systems, such as databases, document and catalogue management systems. Because ontological languages have a formal semantics, ontologies allow a wider interpretation of data that is inference of facts which are not explicitly stated. In this way, they can improve the interoperability of the conceptualization behind them, their coverage of arbitrary datasets. Ontology can formally be defined as specific sort of knowledge base and can be characterized as comprising a 4-tuple (Davies, Studer et al. 2006):

$$O = \langle C, R, I, A \rangle \quad (1)$$

Where C is set of classes representing *concepts* we wish to reason about in the given domain (Offer, Finding, Phone, Customer etc.). R is set of *relations* holding between those classes (Message hasRecipient Actor). I is a set of *instances*, where each instance can be an instance of one or more classes and can be linked to other instances by relations (Nokia isA PhoneBrand; Finding309 hasValue 11,23). A is a set of *axioms* (If a new customer buys Nokia E71, promotional discount of 10% should be offered). It is widely recommended that knowledge bases, containing concrete data (instance data or ABox) are always encoded with respect to ontologies, which encapsulate a general conceptual model of some domain knowledge, thus allowing easier sharing and reuse of KBs.

3. Related work

Decision support systems (DSS) have evolved significantly and there have been many influences from technological and organizational developments (Shim, Warkentin et al. 2002). DSS once utilized more limited database, modelling, and user interface functionality, but technological innovations enabled more powerful DSS functionality. DSS once supported individual decision makers, but later DSS technologies are applied to workgroups or teams, especially virtual teams. The advent of the Web has enabled inter-organizational DSS and has given rise to numerous new applications of existing technology as well as many new decision support technologies themselves. Internet facilitates access to data, information and knowledge sources, but at the same time, it threatens to cognitively overload the decision makers. Authors in (Vahidov & Kersten 2004) claim that internet technologies require a new type of decision support that provides tighter integration and higher degree of direct interaction with the problem domain. Based on that they propose a generic architecture where dynamic and highly complex electronic environments DSS's should be situated in the problem domain. Chen et al. conducted an interesting research about integrated interactive environment for knowledge discovery from heterogeneous data resources (Chen, Zhu et al. 2001). Their work is grounded on acquiring, collecting, and extracting relevant information from multiple data sources, and then forming meaningful knowledge patterns. The proposed system employs common DW[1] and OLAP[2] techniques to form integrated data repository and generate database queries over large data collections from various distinct data resources.

Regarding the domain of DW and OLAP analyses research has dealt with Document Warehousing (Tseng & Chou 2006) where extensive semantic information about the documents is available but still not fully employed as in traditional DW. The use of ontologies was found useful as a common interpretation basis for data and metadata. Furthermore research has extended to Web DW (Marotta, Motz et al. 2002) with the emphasis on managing the volatile and dynamic nature of Web sources. Utilization of ontologies is also addressed in Information Retrieval (IR) where it has been used for fuzzy tagging of data from the Web (Buche, Dibie-Barthelemy et al. 2006; Macias & Castells 2007), query construction tool in semi-automatic ontology mapping (Suomela & Kekalainen 2006) and semantic based retrieval of information from the World Wide Web (Shan, Jun et al. 2003; Garces, Olivas et al. 2006). Use of ontologies in DM has also been considered in (Bernaras, Laresgoiti et al. 1996; Zhou, Booker et al. 2002; Singh, Vajirkar et al. 2003; Cao, Chao et al. 2004) where ontology was used for representation of context awareness and handling semantics inconsistencies.

Several approaches (Tewari, Youll et al. 2003; Rivest, Bedard et al. 2005; Kishore, Zhang et al. 2006; Soo, Lin et al. 2006) deal with agent support for integration and decision support. Research in (Kishore, Zhang et al. 2006) showed that MAS paradigm provides an excellent approach for modelling and implementing integrated business IS. Authors within that research proposed a conceptual framework for MAS based integrative business IS. Results from other research in (Tewari, Youll et al. 2003; Rivest, Bedard et al. 2005) also deal with merging of data within DW, but they put more emphasis on geospatial component and location-sensitive information. Some promising results were also found in (Soo, Lin et al. 2006), where authors propose a cooperative MAS platform to support the invention process based on the patent document analysis. The platform allows the invention process to be carried out through the cooperation and coordination among software agents delegated by the various domain experts in the complex industrial R&D environment.

In context of domain knowledge representation ontology has been widely used for data, application and information integration (Qiu 2006). Jovanović in (Jovanović & Gašević 2005) concludes that the need for knowledge sharing and interoperable KBs exists and the key element for achieving interoperability are domain ontologies. In that approach XSLT[3] transformation is used to enable knowledge interoperability. Furthermore some attempts have also been made towards ontology programming in dedicated languages such as Go! (Clark & McCabe 2006) that is distinguished from OWL-like languages where stress is on logic and object oriented programming. Authors in (Vasilecas & Bugaite 2006; Lavbič, Lajovic et al. 2010) use ontologies for ontology based IS development. Another work presented in (Fuentes, Carbo et al. 2006) uses heterogeneous domain ontology for location based IS in a MAS framework with the emphasis on context-aware MAS. They propose a

[1] Data Warehouse (DW)
[2] OnLine Analytical Processing (OLAP)
[3] XSLT (XSL Transformations) is a declarative, XML-based language used for the transformation of XML documents into other XML documents.

global ontology to let agents work with heterogeneous domains using a wireless network and the intention is to provide customization about different environment services based on user location and profile. An important aspect is also continuous evaluation of developed ontologies that authors deal with in (Lavbič & Krisper 2010).

4. Problem and proposal for solution

The review of related work presented in previous section pointed out that modern DSS's changed quite substantially especially with the advent of the Web and availability of extensive information in online repositories. For managing complexity and integration issues with decision support many approaches relied on MAS paradigm and used ontologies as knowledge representation mechanism. The existing approaches mainly focused on either supporting existing business processes or improving decision support at some level of detail or integration of several structured resources to achieve better decision support. To our knowledge none of the approaches addressed the problem of enriching data from internal data sources with unstructured data found on internet. The interactivity of reviewed solutions is also limited; meaning that business users are usually limited to small set of parameters they can define to alter default behaviour of the system. These user requirements are usually entered directly into the system and no abstraction layers are provided as in business rules managements systems (BRMS) to enable users without technical skills to manipulate the content.

This chapter introduces a novel approach in integration of unstructured information found in the Web with information available in several internal data sources (e.g. database, DW, ERP[4] etc.). For implementation purposes MAS paradigm with agents was used, mainly because related work pointed out that is a very appropriate solution for integration of business IS. One of the reasons to choose agents is also modelling notion where business users and agents are modelled in a very similar manner. Problem of interaction between human actors and computer programs is also addressed by introduction of ontologies as knowledge representation mechanism. The approach presented in this chapter is targeted towards using ontologies for several tasks, where emphasis is on using BR approach to ensure interoperability between business user and IS. Not only that ontology is used by every agent to represent the interpretation of a problem domain but also for communication between agents and business users. The use of ontologies in MAS enables agents to share a common set of facts used in user profiles, products and other domain elements, while interacting with each other. With exploiting reasoning mechanisms new knowledge can be derived from known facts and improve the KB. To simplify this communication template system based on BR was introduced to enable users with less technical skills manipulation of knowledge within the system and control behaviour of individual agent. The approach will be further explained in the following section 3. The case study presented in this chapter is from the domain of mobile telecommunications and in section 4 is presented in detail with the impact it has on improving decision support within enterprise. In the domain of mobile communications that was used for case study we had to define several tasks in DSS-MAS, needed for decision support - OLAP analyses, DM, IR, context and profile definition, notification etc.

[4] Enterprise Resource Planning (ERP)

5. DSS-MAS

5.1 DSS-MAS architecture

DSS-MAS that we propose in this chapter is introduced in Fig. 1. The case study presented in this chapter is from the domain of mobile telecommunications and is based on business environment and information resources from one of the mobile operators. DSS-MAS is situated in the environment of several existing systems, like Data Mining Decision Support System (DMDSS), or DW and various resources available outside of an enterprise on the World Wide Web.

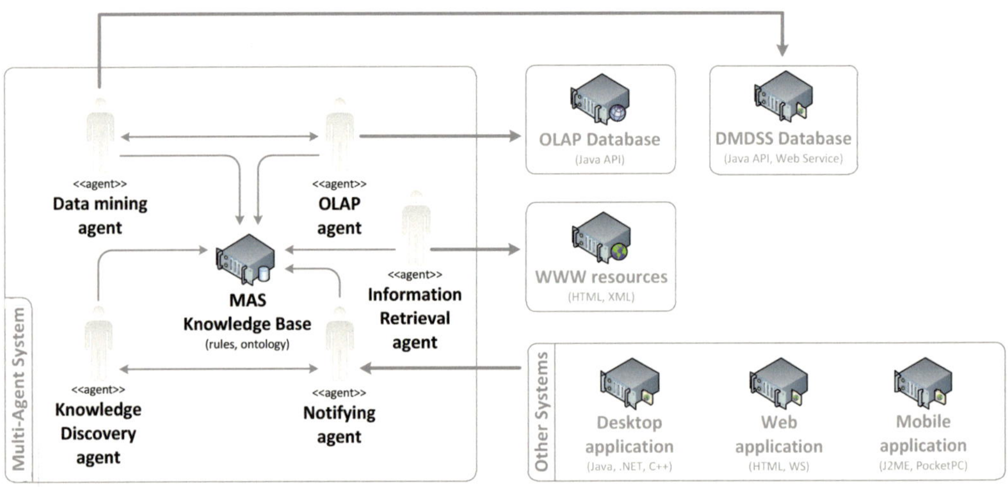

Fig. 1. Architecture of MAS used for Decision Support in Enterprises.

Global goal that agents in DSS-MAS should achieve is to support decision making process while using existing systems for business analysis and employing information from environment where enterprise resides. To support this goal DSS-MAS includes several agent roles that are as following: **Data Mining Agent (DMA)**, **OLAP Agent (OLAPA)**, **Information Retrieval Agent (IRA)**, **Knowledge Discovery Agent (KDA)**, **Notifying Agent (NA)** and **Mobile Agent (MA)**. Ontologies are used as a main interconnection object for domain knowledge representation, agent-to-agent communication and most important for agent-to-business user communication. An important element of an environment is the World Wide Web, where agents play information retrieval role for the purpose of decision making. The information retrieved is saved in a KB and available for further employment for Data Mining (DM) and DW analyses. After all information from internal and external sources is gathered it is then furthermore considered by KDA, where inference over several task ontologies used by individual agents (DMA, OLAPA, IRA etc.) is performed. Moreover the sub goal of DSS-MAS is delivering of the right information at the right time and to the right users. The system needs to be context aware and consider the relevant features of the business, i.e. context information such as time, location, and user preferences (Liao, Xu et al. 2005). Business users in DSS-MAS are able to employ agents to perform tasks on their behalf. For example, managers in enterprises have to request reports from their systems - OLAP or from transactional databases, and managers have to review reports every appointed period of time (day, week, month etc.). This task of information acquisition is predecessor for decision making and is more or less straightforward - business user sends a request for analyses and reviews the content according to some Key Performance Indicators (KPI). KPI is simply a measure of performance and is commonly used in enterprises to evaluate how successful they. In DSS-MAS tasks like this are automated and user participation is reduced as much as possible. An initial analysis model (e.g. OLAP or DM) has to be captured in the ontology by business users, while execution and optimisation is left for agents. Business users first define initial parameters for analyses to be performed, while agents perform these analyses and recommend improvements. When some action is required from business user, he is notified and has the ability to act or change rules of agent's execution.

To enable these functionalities we introduce ontologies as a mediation mechanism for knowledge exchange between actors (agents and business users) that cooperate in DSS-MAS. The following section will present the structure and organization of ontologies we have used for the case study.

5.2 The role of ontology

According to (Guarino 1998) ontology can be structured into different sub-ontologies - upper ontology, domain ontology, task ontology and the application ontology. Following similar guidelines we have defined upper ontology named **Common ontology** and combined domain and task ontologies in **Notifying ontology**, **Information retrieval ontology**, **Data Mining and Warehousing ontology** (see Fig. 2). The proposed clustering of ontologies is based on the common understanding of the problem domain being defined in Common ontology. Every agent has its own interpretation of a KB, which is a specialization of a Common ontology with detail definition of knowledge required by individual agent. Common ontology is limited to abstract concepts and it covers reusable dimensions, which are primarily used by KDA. Task ontologies specify concepts of notification, IR, DM and DW. Mobile communications in our case is the domain of all task ontologies and the emphasis is on supply and demand of mobile phones. As already mentioned we used in our research the knowledge management approach where every agent has knowledge about its own problem domain. In this case whenever new facts about the common knowledge are discovered, which might be of interest for other agents, they are updated to the common ontology.

The role of ontology in our approach is therefore twofold: (a) knowledge representation mechanism used by agents and (b) common understanding of problem domain used for communication between business users and agents by utilizing business rules manipulation with introduced templates (see section 4.2).

Fig. 2 shows an excerpt from intersection of several ontologies used in our case study. This part of ontology clearly defines the common elements being used for communication between agents and business users (domain specific elements such as phones, new phones and customers, all described with domain specific characteristics). A part of OLAP elements needed for conducting OLAP analyses is also presented. Ontology also presents notification with taxonomy of various warning levels and business users classification by organizational unit and decision making level.

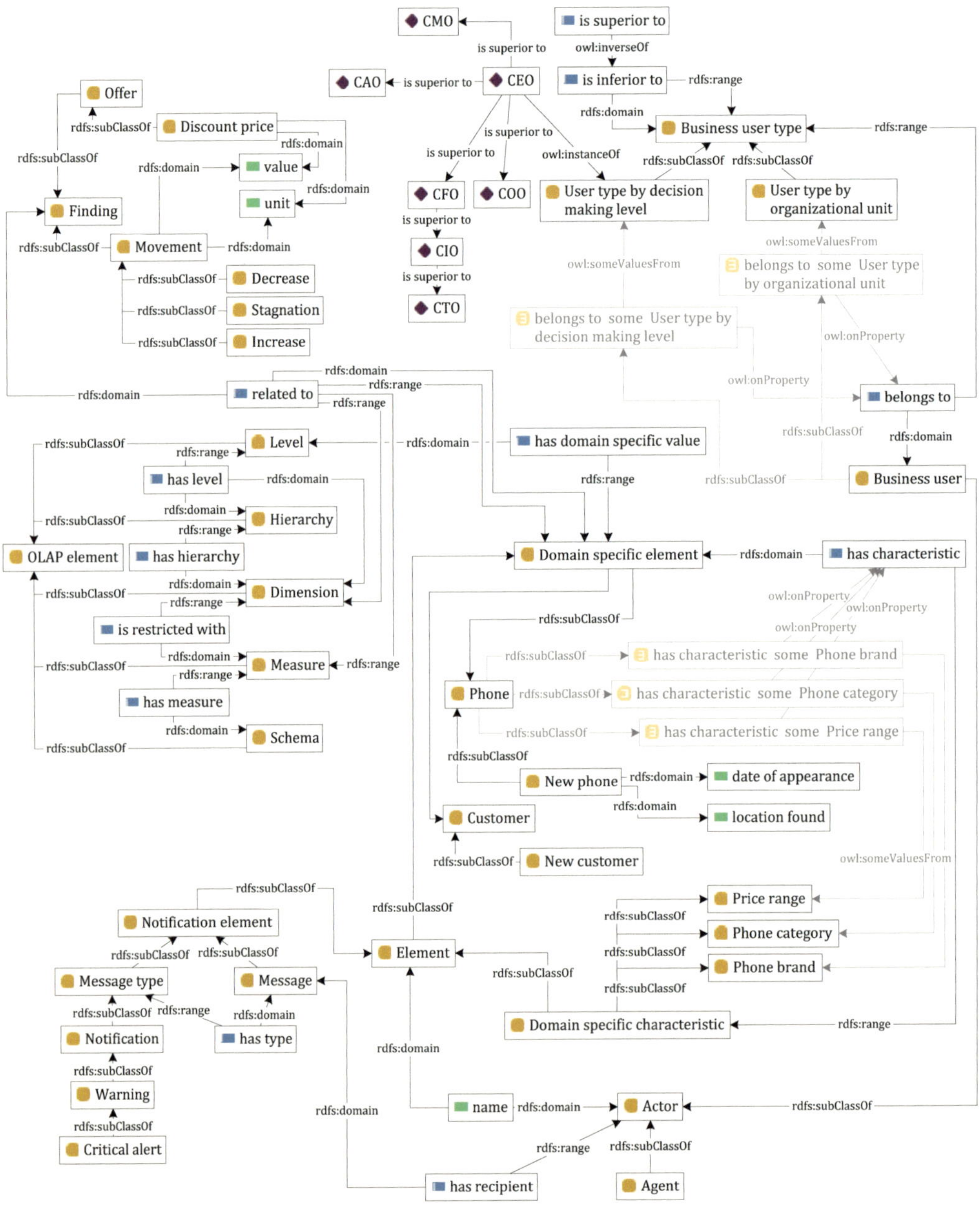

Fig. 2. Excerpt from intersection of several ontologies used in our case study.

5.3 The role of agents

Our case study uses domain of mobile telecommunications as a platform where we focus on the sales of mobile phones and their accessories. Manipulation with internal data storage is handled by two types of agents - OLAPA and DMA. They both have distinct tasks but still share common goal - periodically or on demand autonomously execute analyses models. Business users at first define these models and describe them with all required parameters (e.g. search for anomalies in sales of Nokia phones in last month period). The information about the execution is stored in the ontology (based on business user preferences) or is requested by another agent of the system. Business user preferences in this context define the execution parameters about the analysis, for example the period at which the analysis is performed (e.g. perform analysis every other day at 13:00). OLAPA has on first hand straightforward task of performing OLAP analyses on behalf of an agent or a business user and reporting its findings back to the requesting entity and all other entities that should be informed, according to the business policy. Nevertheless OLAPA does much more - after each execution it prepares the report for business user based on findings - movements and KPIs. If certain finding is substantially different from finding obtained in previous case further analysis is performed to discover the reason of change by drilling down (more detailed) or up (less detailed) the hierarchies and levels.

By acquiring the knowledge in ontology we enable business users to change the behaviour of agents with changing the ontology using graphical user interface. This interface incorporates all logical restrictions defined in ontology and does not allow users to enter unacceptable values and the most important is that it does not require technical knowledge from users. Previous experiences we obtained have shown that business users have great difficulties especially with setting the parameters required to run DM and DW analyses models, and so user interface really has to be friendly and intuitive. In our approach this issue was solved by introducing the architecture depicted in the next chapter at Fig. 3 and using templates as further discussed in section 4.

Nowadays Web-based information retrieval systems are widely distributed and deeply analysed from different points of view. The main objective of all of such systems is to help users to retrieve information they really need (obviously as quickly as it is possible) (Garces, Olivas et al. 2006). While the techniques regarding DW, multi-dimensional models, OLAP, or even ad-hoc reports have served enterprises well, they do not completely address the full scope of existing problems. It is believed that, for the business intelligence (BI) of an enterprise, only about 20% of information can be extracted from formatted data stored in relational databases (Tseng & Chou 2006). The remaining 80% of information is hidden in unstructured or semi-structured documents. This is because the most prevalent medium for expressing information and knowledge is text. For instance, market survey reports, project status reports, meeting records, customer complaints, e-mails, patent application sheets, and advertisements of competitors now are all recorded in documents. For that reason in DSS-MAS we introduced IRA for retrieval of data mainly from the World Wide Web. The tasks that IRA performs in presented case study can be grouped into three categories:

- identification of new online shops,
- analysis of mobile phones presented online and
- extending Data Warehouse with information found online.

First two tasks are concerned about the supply of mobile phones at various online shops worldwide. Identification of new online shops is conducted with web crawling and the use of several existing services on the Internet, such as Google, Froogle and Bing. Not only these internet resources are managed through ontology, but also rules for text extraction are defined as rules which make all domain knowledge available in IR ontology and not encoded in agent itself. More details about implementation of DSS-MAS case study can be found in section 4. Furthermore every shop found online is analysed to identify unique patterns for searching phones. Using these search patterns IRA is searching through online shops and determines phones with their market prices and stores this information into IR ontology to be available for further knowledge inference by KDA. Information of found phones is used to determine new market trends, enable price comparison between competitors, facilitate possible inclusion in enterprise's sales program etc. One of the tasks that IRA also performs is extending DW with information found online. While business users performs OLAP analyses, they deal with only internal information about the business, but in process of decision making other resources also have to be examined, e.g. news about the suppliers and competitors, opinions about certain products and organisations etc. IRA therefore scans the DW dimension data (through hierarchies and levels) from DW dimensional schema and uses this information for searching several internet resources (news archives, forums, stock changes, Google trends etc.). When users review OLAP reports these data from the Internet is also displayed according to their restrictions in dimensions. For example, when business user are making decision whether to increase support to Nokia or Sony Ericsson phones it only has reports about sales of selected brand names from their market program. Using our approach the user is provided with additional data that is found online and what will make decision better founded.

KDA is important element of DSS-MAS since it consolidates all findings from IR, DM and DW and furthermore delivers derived findings to NA. To employ inference capabilities over several ontologies the enterprises' BR are essential. While business concepts are captured in ontology, these concepts further have to be restricted to define specific meaning. Generally BR are prepared by business users and also some parts of BR in enterprises tend to change frequently; therefore we introduced architecture (see Fig. 3) for BR management (further discussion in section 4). Findings of KDA are presented as instances of **Domain-specific-element** and **Findings** classes (see ontology in Fig. 2).

As it can be seen from Fig. 1 NA represents an interface to DSS-MAS for all external applications and business users. The main role of NA is the information dissemination by simply delivering the right information at the right time to the right users. While in vast majority of today's applications users have to request the information using so called "pull model" in our approach we implemented the "push model", where information is proactively delivered by agents to the user without a specific request. This is achieved by making system context aware and considering the relevant features of the business, i.e. context information such as time, location, position in the organisational hierarchy etc.

All knowledge about notification is defined in Notifying ontology, where every user has his own context defined and the position within organisation across two dimensions - organisational unit (e.g. Marketing, Sales, Human resources etc.) and decision making level (e.g. Chief Executive Officer (CEO), Chief Information Officer (CIO), Chief Financial Officer

(CFO), Chief Marketing Officer (CMO), Chief Analytics Officer (CAO) etc.). According to that position rules for delivery of several message types are defined. These message types range from Notification to Warning and Critical alert. Each message also addresses the domain of specific organisational unit, e.g. when a new mobile phone is found online at competitor's website, CMO and CAO have to be notified. Organisational structure, as part of Notifying ontology, also defines that both CMO and CAO are inferior to CEO therefore he is also notified, but only in a case of a Critical alert. According to the business user profile, notification can be sent using several technologies from Windows Alert, e-mail, Really Simple Syndication (RSS), Short Message Service (SMS) etc. These notification types are also ordered by priority for each business user and according to this type the content is also adapted.

Mobile agent is an example of an application that can reside on a mobile device (e.g. Personal Digital Assistant (PDA), mobile phone etc.) and uses resources of DSS-MAS through NA. The typical use case includes sending mobile agent across network to DSS-MAS, where all needed information according to owner context is collected and then the mobile agent is returned back to originating location on a mobile device and presents the collected data to business user. When the process of acquiring data is in progress, business user does not have to be connected to the network, he can just wait offline until mobile agent is ready to return with the findings.

In the following section details about the case study implementation will be presented with technologies used, templates for business rules acquisition and presentation of one specific scenario from case study.

6. Case study implementation and discussion

6.1 Technology

The selected language for ontology presentation is OWL DL (Russomanno & Kothari 2004), since it offers the highest level of semantic expressiveness for selected case study and is one of the most widely used and standardised ontology language nowadays that has extensive support in different ontology manipulation tools. Besides OWL logical restrictions, Semantic Web Rule Language (SWRL) rules were also used due to its human readable syntax and support for business rules oriented approach to knowledge management (Horrocks, Patel-Schneider et al. 2005). SWRL rules are stored as OWL individuals and are described by OWL classes contained in the SWRL ontology. The use of SWRL enables storing schema, individuals and rules in a single component, which makes management much easier. SWRL rule form in a combination with templates that is introduced in the following subsection 4.2 is very suitable for knowledge formalization by business users that do not have extensive technical knowledge.

The user interface for ontology manipulation for business users is based on Protégé editor (Stanford Medical Informatics 2006) and SWRL Tab (Stanford Medical Informatics 2006) for Protégé. It enables entering OWL individuals and SWRL rules where a step further is made towards using templates for entering information (see Fig. 3). At the execution level KAON2 inference engine is used to enable inference capabilities. Due to limitation of *SHIQ(D)* subset of OWL-DL and *DL-safe* subset of SWRL language, before inference is conducted, semantic validation takes place to ensure that all preconditions are met. We selected FIPA[5] compliant MAS platform JADE[6] in DSS-MAS because it offers broad range of functionalities and is most widely used platform. This is due very good support and availability of agent framework, where a lot of common agents' tasks are already implemented (i.e. agent communication at the syntax level, agent management, migration of agents etc.). For Mobile Agent implementation an add-on JADE-LEAP[7] was used to support the mobility of agents.

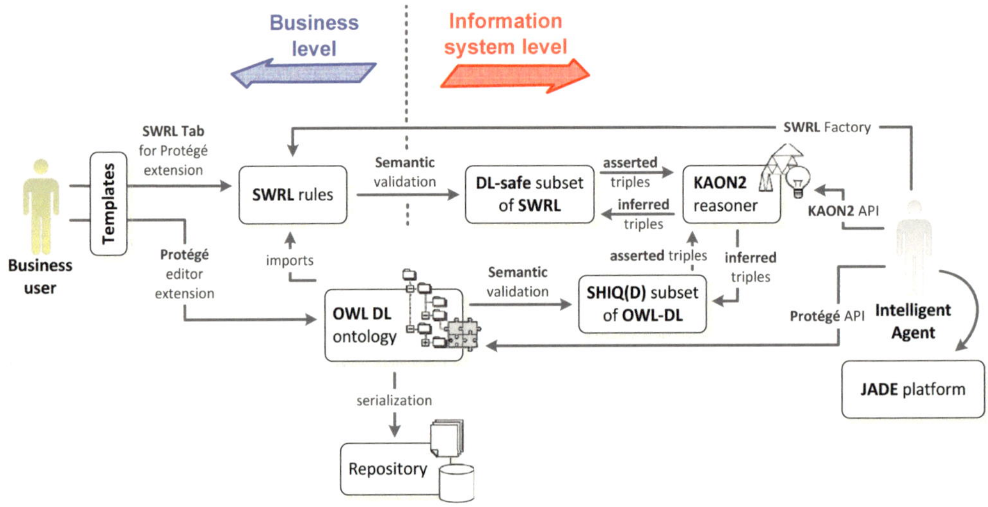

Fig. 3. Prototype of selected case study.

6.2 Mediation with BR templates

Using templates with ontology, business logic is excluded from the actual software code whereas the majority of data for templates is acquired from ontology axioms and natural language descriptions in ontology, while other templates are prepared by users with technical knowledge. The main goal of using mediation with BR templates is to enable acquiring knowledge from actual knowledge holders i.e. business users and enable transformation of this high-level knowledge into information system level, where this data together with concepts from business vocabulary can be directly used for inference purposes and bring added value without any further programming by technically educated users.

When acquiring new knowledge into the system from business users, the process always starts with focusing on concepts of business vocabulary that are persisted in a form of ontology. Users can freely traverse through this information space, select concepts and further manipulate all related information within the selected context. Altering and adding new information is all time limited to formal definition of concepts that is defined in ontology. For easier manipulation business user is aided with template and business vocabulary, so BR building process is simplified as it will presented in detail in the following section.

[5] Foundation for Intelligent Physical Agents (FIPA)
[6] Java Agent DEvelopment Framework (JADE)
[7] Java Agent Development Environment-Lightweight Extensible Agent Platform (JADE-LEAP)

IF
Condition := { $\exists x : x \in$ **Domain specific element** $\cup$ **Finding** } $\wedge$ | Condition | ≥ 1
THEN
Result := { $\exists y : y \in$ **Finding** } $\wedge$ | Result | ≥ 1

Fig. 4. BR template for general finding definition.

Fig. 4 presents an example of BR template that is used for definition of aggregation of findings or domain specific elements. The user interface that is available is directly linked to ontology, where constraints on classes, properties and individuals are considered in real-time. This approach allows to minimize the risk of entering wrong constraints. The DSS-MAS system supports entering of new statements in several forms from simple IF-THEN form to decision table or decision tree.

IF
First finding is **Increase (Finding)** which {
is **related to** first amount sold which is **Measure (OLAP element)** AND
is **related to** first date which is **Dimension (OLAP element)** AND
is **related to** first phone which is **Phone (Domain specific element)** which {
has **characteristic** brand which is **Phone brand (Domain specific characteristic)**
}
} AND
Second finding is **Increase (Finding)** which {
is **related to** second amount sold which is **Measure (OLAP element)** AND
is **related to** second date which is **Dimension (OLAP element)** which {
is *greater than* first date
} AND
is **related to** second phone which is **Phone (Domain specific element)** which {
has **characteristic** brand which is **Phone brand (Domain specific characteristic)**
}
} AND
Found phone is **New phone (Domain specific element)** which {
has **characteristic** brand which is **Phone brand (Domain specific element)** AND
has **date of appearance** found date which is **Dimension (OLAP element)** which {
is *greater than now – 14 days*
}
} AND
New customer is **New customer (Domain specific element)**
THEN
Promotion discount is **Discount price (Finding)** which {
is **related to** new customer AND
is **related to** found phone AND
has **value** "10" AND
has **unit** "%"
}

Fig. 5. Example of a rule, developed by using template.

The following example in Fig. 5 represents a BR that states: *If there exist two consequent increases of sold phones of the same phone brand and a new phone of this phone brand was found online within last 2 weeks, then offer a promotion discount of 10% on this new phone to all new customers.*

When constraint presented at Fig. 5 is transformed to execution form at information system level, standardized SWRL and OWL languages are used to enable reusability (see Fig. 6). By this transformation a rule is produced that can be directly used in the inference engine to produce results in a form of inferred triples that are presented to the user.

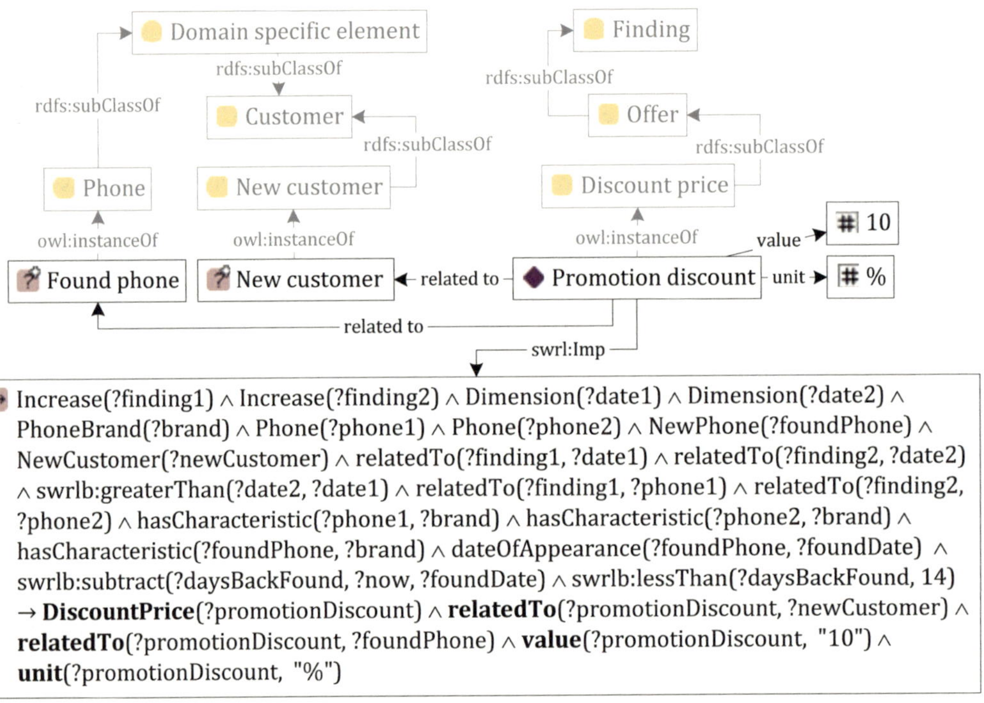

Fig. 6. Constraint presented in ontology in SWRL and OWL syntax.

6.3 Case study

One of the most common cases of using DSS-MAS system is combing information found online with BI reports (DW, DM, IR etc.) developed on internal data in enterprise DW. Fig. 7 presents one of this scenario.

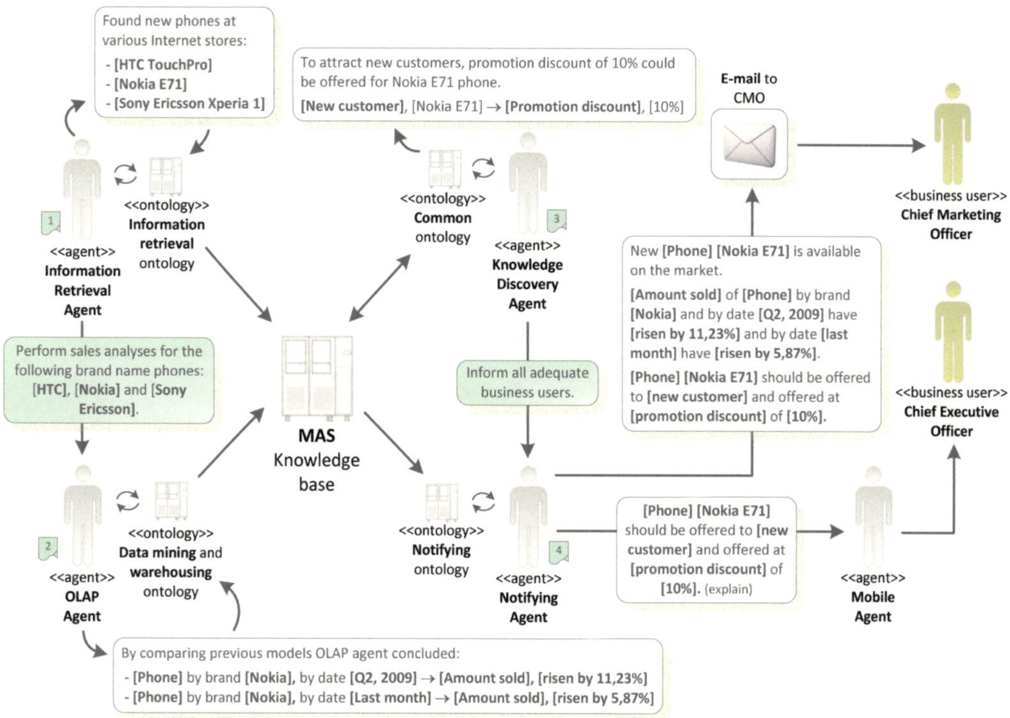

Fig. 7. Case study of using DSS-MAS in mobile phone domain.

Scenario presented at Fig. 7 is triggered by results of IRA activity, when three new mobile phones: HTC TouchPro, Nokia E71 and Sony Ericsson Xperia 1 are found by IRA at online mobile shops. According to the execution policy from Common ontology, OLAPA is notified with a request to rebuild all DW reports where brands of identified phones can be found in dimension elements. After running OLAP on Sales schema with constrains of Nokia brand in Phone dimension and last year in Date dimension OLAPA creates a report as depicted in Fig. 8.

[Phone] by brand **[Nokia]**, by date **[Q2, 2009]** → **[Amount sold], [risen by 11,23%]**
[Phone] by brand **[Nokia]**, by date **[Last month]** → **[Amount sold], [risen by 5,87%]**

Fig. 8. Business Intelligence findings.

At the information system level the first finding is represented as an excerpt from ontology and is depicted in Fig. 9.

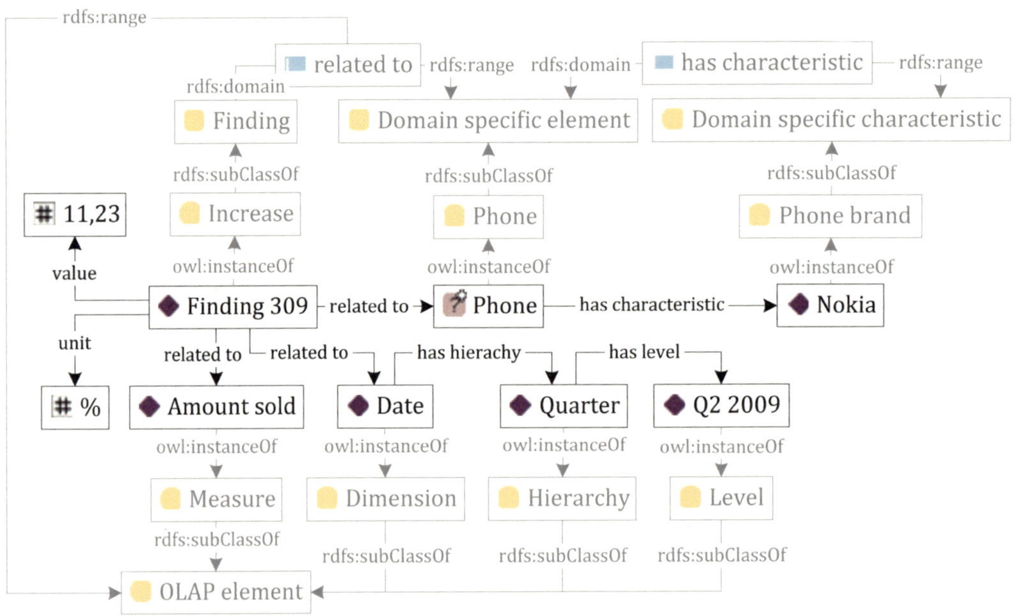

Fig. 9. Example of representing the finding in ontology.

The fields that appear in the report are all instances of **Domain specific element, OLAP element** and **Finding** from ontology (see Fig. 2). After these findings have been asserted, KDA will be executed to derive new knowledge. Based on these new facts represented at Fig. 8 and enterprise business rules (see example in Fig. 5), the KDA produced results represented in Fig. 10, by using inference engine knowledge is asserted in ontology.

[New customer], [Nokia E71] → **[Promotion discount]**, [10%]

Fig. 10. Derived finding.

After consolidation of all new findings KDA sends message to NA with request to forward notifications to appropriate users. The result of triggered activity of NA is the list of business users that have to be notified about this event. The list shows that in this case CMO and CEO have to be notified whereas their context has to be considered. According to CMO's preferences an e-mail is sent with the following content presented in Fig. 11.

FACTS New **[Phone] [Nokia E71]** is available on the market. **[Amount sold]** of **[Phone]** by brand **[Nokia]** and by date **[Q2, 2009]** have **[risen by 11,23%]** and by date **[last month]** have **[risen by 5,87%]**.
CONCLUSION **[Phone] [Nokia E71]** should be offered to **[new customer]** and offered at **[promotion discount]** of **[10%]**.

Fig. 11. Report of findings with explanation.

The CEO uses a Mobile Agent on his mobile device and is also notified by a truncated message with new finding, while explanation is available upon request.

7. Conclusion

In this chapter we discussed DSS-MAS where internal and external data is integrated using agent-oriented approach and ontologies as a common understanding of a problem domain and for communication between business users and agents. Agents were used due to their mentalistic notions for modelling, similarities between the agent in the MAS paradigm and the human actor in business organisations, and also possibilities for the use of ontologies as means of agents' internal knowledge base representation. The external information from the Web was integrated by IRA agent with the data in organisation's DW and after applying BR new knowledge was derived by employing agents' inference capabilities. Tasks like information retrieval from competitors, creating and reviewing OLAP reports are autonomously performed by agents, while business users have control over their execution through manipulation of knowledge base. The research also emphasized agent-to-business user communication and trying to minimize that gap. This was accomplished by introducing different views on ontologies for business user and agent. While agents dealt with formal description of business concepts, logical constraints and rules, business user had simplified view of formal description of knowledge. User is able to manipulate with ontology through templates, where little technical knowledge is required. The role of the mediation mechanism is then to transform these business level concepts into formal specification at the level of information system.

Presented approach was verified and implemented using a case study from the domain of mobile telecommunications, where the aim was to provide the knowledge worker an intelligent analysis platform that enhances decision making process. The application domain was reduced to its sub domain dedicated for supply and analysis of demand of mobile phones in one of the mobile operators. DW system is constructed from several heterogeneous data sources where majority of those sources are internal to the enterprise. Our approach added information found on the Web (i.e. competitors' offers, stock rates etc.) to these internal data sources and improved the decision support process within the enterprise. The proposed approach also addressed business users and their communication with the system which was simplified by using templates to define some business requirements that were transformed into analyses models (OLAP, DW etc.), automatically performed by agents which reported results back to users in charge. The case study presented in the chapter was implemented in Java and using mainly open source technologies.

8. Future work

It should be noted that some limitations related to our approach do exist. One of the concerns is associated with performance issues. When amount of data used for reasoning grows the overall performance of the system declines and additional mechanism are required to achieve expected results. There are several on-going research activities about reasoning on the Semantic Web that deal with formal models and their applicability. The results of that research would be greatly beneficial to our approach.

The mechanism of BR templates used in our approach is aimed to bridging the gap between business users and information systems. Templates are used to enable business users without extensive technical knowledge to formalize their expert knowledge about selected problem domain and therefore enable agent to act autonomously on their behalf. This separation of business and information system level proved useful but further research is needed in finding more innovative ways for expressing BR templates and defining more templates. The use of NLP[8] can provide additional aid to business users in semi-automatic acquisition of business rules from documentation.

The role of IRA is to extend DW with information online and by doing that it employs general purpose search engines, custom defined online stores etc. Future work will focus on extending the variety of sources included in our system, especially by integration with DBpedia[9] and Freebase[10]. One of the coming tasks is also integration of selected subsets of data with Linked Data and contributing in connecting distributed data across the Web.

Our approach was verified on a case study from the domain of mobile telecommunications, but the results can be easily applied to various problem domains as the architecture of DSS-MAS is modular with clear separation of layers. This enables us to syntactically and semantically integrate internal structured data with external data that is mainly in unstructured form.

9. References

Bernaras, A., I. Laresgoiti, et al. (1996). Building and resusing ontologies for electrical network applications. European Conference on Artificial Intelligence (ECAI '96).

Buche, P., J. Dibie-Barthelemy, et al. (2006). Fuzzy semantic tagging and flexible querying of XML documents extracted from the Web, *Journal of Intelligent Information Systems* Vol. 26, No. 1, pp. 25-40.

Cao, L. B., L. Chao, et al. (2004). Ontology services-based information integration in mining telecom business intelligence, *Pricai 2004: Trends in Artificial Intelligence, Proceedings* Vol. 3157, No., pp. 85-94.

Chen, M., Q. M. Zhu, et al. (2001). An integrated interactive environment for knowledge discovery from heterogeneous data resources, *Information and Software Technology* Vol. 43, No. 8, pp. 487-496.

Clark, K. L. & F. G. McCabe (2006). Ontology oriented programming in Go!, *Applied Intelligence* Vol. 24, No. 3, pp. 189-204.

Davies, J., R. Studer, et al. (2006). *Semantic Web technologies - trends and research in ontology-based systems,* John Wiley & Sons, Chichester, England.

Fuentes, V., J. Carbo, et al. (2006). Heterogeneous domain ontology for location based information system in a multi-agent framework, *Intelligent Data Engineering and Automated Learning - Ideal 2006, Proceedings* Vol. 4224, No., pp. 1199-1206.

Garces, P. J., J. A. Olivas, et al. (2006). Concept-matching IR systems versus word-matching information retrieval systems: Considering fuzzy interrelations for indexing Web

[8] Natural Language Processing (NLP)

[9] DBpedia (http://dbpedia.org) extracts structured information from Wikipedia.

[10] Freebase (http://www.freebase.com) is an open, Creative Commons licensed repository of structured data.

pages, *Journal of the American Society for Information Science and Technology* Vol. 57, No. 4, pp. 564-576.

Gruber, T. R. (1993). A Translation Approach to Portable Ontology Specifications, *Knowledge Acquisition* Vol. 5, No. 2, pp. 199-220.

Guarino, N. (1998). Formal Ontology and Information Systems. FOIS'98, Trento, Italy, IOS Press.

Horrocks, I., P. F. Patel-Schneider, et al. (2005). OWL rules: A proposal and prototype implementation, *Journal of Web Semantics* Vol. 3, No. 1, pp. 23-40.

Jovanović, J. & D. Gašević (2005). Achieving knowledge interoperability: An XML/XSLT approach, *Expert Systems with Applications* Vol. 29, No. 3, pp. 535-553.

Kang, N. & S. Han (2003). Agent-based e-marketplace system for more fair and efficient transaction, *Decision Support Systems* Vol. 34, No. 2, pp. 157-165.

Kishore, R., H. Zhang, et al. (2006). Enterprise integration using the agent paradigm: foundations of multi-agent-based integrative business information systems, *Decision Support Systems* Vol. 42, No. 1, pp. 48-78.

Lavbič, D. & M. Krisper (2010). Facilitating Ontology development with continuous evaluation, *Informatica* Vol. 21, No. 4, pp. 533-552.

Lavbič, D., I. Lajovic, et al. (2010). Facilitating information system development with Panoramic view on data, *Computer Science and Information Systems* Vol. 7, No. 4, pp. 737-768.

Lei, Y., E. Motta, et al. (2002). IIPS: An Intelligent information presentation system. 7th International Conference on Intelligent User Interfaces, San Francisco, USA.

Liao, L. J., K. Q. Xu, et al. (2005). Constructing intelligent and open mobile commerce using a semantic web approach, *Journal of Information Science* Vol. 31, No. 5, pp. 407-419.

Macias, J. A. & P. Castells (2007). Providing end-user facilities to simplify ontology-driven web application authoring, *Interacting with Computers* Vol. 19, No. 4, pp. 563-585.

Marotta, A., R. Motz, et al. (2002). Managing source schema evolution in Web Warehouses, *journal of the Brazilian Computer Society* Vol. 8, No. 2, pp. 20-31.

Qiu, R. G. (2006). Towards ontology-driven knowledge synthesis for heterogeneous information systems, *Journal of Intelligent Manufacturing* Vol. 17, No. 1, pp. 99-109.

Rivest, S., Y. Bedard, et al. (2005). SOLAP technology: Merging business intelligence with geospatial technology for interactive spatio-temporal exploration and analysis of data, *ISPRS Journal of Photogrammetry and Remote Sensing* Vol. 60, No. 1, pp. 17-33.

Russomanno, D. J. & C. R. Kothari (2004). Expressing inter-link constraints in OWL knowledge bases, *Expert Systems* Vol. 21, No. 4, pp. 217-228.

Shan, F., M. Jun, et al. (2003). A programmable agent for knowledge discovery on the web, *Expert Systems* Vol. 20, No. 2, pp. 79-85.

Shim, J. P., M. Warkentin, et al. (2002). Past, present, and future of decision support technology, *Decision Support Systems* Vol. 33, No. 2, pp. 111-126.

Singh, S., P. Vajirkar, et al. (2003). Context-based data mining using ontologies, *Conceptual Modeling - Er 2003, Proceedings* Vol. 2813, No., pp. 405-418.

Soo, V. W., S. Y. Lin, et al. (2006). A cooperative multi-agent platform for invention based on patent document analysis and ontology, *Expert Systems with Applications* Vol. 31, No. 4, pp. 766-775.

Stanford Medical Informatics. (2006). Protégé. Available from http://protege.stanford.edu.

Stanford Medical Informatics. (2006). SWRLTab. Available from http://protege.cim3.net/cgi-bin/wiki.pl?SWRLTab.

Suomela, S. & J. Kekalainen (2006). User evaluation of ontology as query construction tool, *Information Retrieval* Vol. 9, No. 4, pp. 455-475.

Tewari, G., J. Youll, et al. (2003). Personalized location-based brokering using an agent-based intermediary architecture, *Decision Support Systems* Vol. 34, No. 2, pp. 127-137.

Tseng, F. S. C. & A. Y. H. Chou (2006). The concept of document warehousing for multi-dimensional modeling of textual-based business intelligence, *Decision Support Systems* Vol. 42, No. 2, pp. 727-744.

Vahidov, R. & G. E. Kersten (2004). Decision station: situating decision support systems, *Decision Support Systems* Vol. 38, No. 2, pp. 283-303.

Vasilecas, O. & D. Bugaite (2006). Ontology-based information systems development: The problem of automation of information processing rules. Advances in Information Systems, Proceedings. 4243: 187-196.

Zhou, L., Q. E. Booker, et al. (2002). ROD - Toward Rapid Ontology Development for Underdeveloped Domains. 35th Hawaii International Conference on System Sciences.

5

Web Services-Enhanced Agile Modeling and Integrating Business Processes

Fatima-Zahra Belouadha, Hajar Omrana and Ounsa Roudiès
Siweb (Information System and Web), SIR Laboratory,
Ecole Mohammadia d'Ingénieurs, Mohammed V-Agdal University,
Morocco

1. Introduction

In a global business context with continuous changes, the enterprises have to improve their productivity and their brand image according to a given strategy. They are expected to face big challenges in order to overcome hard competition and meet the growing demands of clients. Indeed, they should capitalize on the potential of new information and communication technologies to enhance their operational efficiency, to react more quickly and to ensure the flexibility of their business processes. Therefore, they should use e-business methods, mechanisms and techniques. In simple terms, e-business refers to the use of Intranet to network, to enhance and to empower intra-enterprise business processes, and of Internet to serve customers and to collaborate with business partners reusing external processes. Nevertheless, e-business aims cannot be resumed to a simple design of Intranet applications or Web sites to share business data or publish products and business services. It is necessary to note that e-business engages managing business processes. It intends particularly to model, to integrate and to make business processes able to exchange data. Indeed, Business Process Management (BPM) must be done in the most appropriate way to ensure interoperability between both intra and inter enterprises information systems, and to guarantee business process agility and dynamic integration.

The ability to exchange data between heterogeneous systems has been for a long time a prime concern of researchers in this field. Nevertheless, e-business is not limited to a simple exchange of data. Exchanged data are just the product of a set of collaborative business processes identified according to the enterprise business strategy. These processes are implemented by both internal and external systems. Thus, it is necessary to manage both internal and external business processes, implemented on either compatible or heterogeneous systems, while ensuring the data exchange between them. In other terms, it is necessary to ensure the systems' interoperability but it is also important to be able to manage the processes they execute.

BPM aims to discover, design, deploy, execute as well as interact with, operate, analyze and optimize business processes, and essentially to do this at the design level (Smith et al., 2002). Therefore, before deploying end executing a business process, it is necessary to model it as finely as possible at the design-time. Well describing processes is a prerequisite for their strategic alignment. In addition to an expanded specification of business processes, it is also necessary to integrate them in order to achieve a given business goal. However, in an evolving collaborative context, this integration should be dynamic and easy to make the enterprise's information system agile. To achieve this goal in the global economic context, we think that the e-business mechanisms have to provide the means to quickly and easily discover the appropriate business processes through Internet.

In this chapter, we propose a model-driven approach, based on Web services standards, for modeling and integrating agile business processes using Web services. The choice of focusing on Web services technology was not arbitrary. The large and broad adoption of this technology by enterprises will lead most business processes to be performed using Web services. Besides, the added value of Web services and their great interest to business process management are beyond doubt. Web services produce, on the one hand, loosely coupled applicative components. On the other hand, they are the most widely used implementation technology of SOA (Service-Oriented Architecture), which is based on the large experiences of software and distributed component technologies. Being founded on the XML (eXtensible Markup Language) language, the SOAP (Simple Object Access Protocol) protocol and the UDDI (Universal Description Discovery and Integration) repository, this technology can be considered as an appropriate mean to ensure interoperability, data exchange and the publication and discovery of business processes when they can be implemented as Web services. Furthermore, Web services standards developed by the W3C (World Wide Web Consortium) consortium fit well with required standards in e-business context (Belouadha & Roudiès, 2008), and therefore they can be used in case of business processes.

Our approach aims to benefit from Web services characteristics for managing business processes. The purpose is to enable the production of agile business processes through an enhanced modeling and dynamic integration. Therefore, we propose to describe them from a business point of view. We consider that a process is a set of activities that can be mapped to Web services. Thereby, a business process can be implemented by composing a set of published Web services. Besides, agility can be achieved by the ability of updating a given process through reuse of Web services dynamically discovered from Internet. A rich Web services' repository available in the Web as well as the high interoperability of Web services facilitate integration. This chapter is structured in seven sections. Section 2 introduces the concept of business process. Sections 3 and 4 are respectively devoted to the description of modeling languages and integration solutions used to design and integrate business processes. Section 5 presents the proposed approach and illustrates it by a sample scenario. Section 6 explores future research opportunities to build on this work. Finally, Section 7 discusses our contribution by comparing it with related works, and specifies its impact, advantages and also limitations.

2. Business process

The term "process" (in Latin "procedere") is defined (in Oxford dictionaries[1]) as a series of actions or steps taken in order to achieve a particular end. Specific and several meanings may be assigned to this concept according to the domain of use: juridical, biological, scientific or technical domain. In the technical domain we are interested in this chapter, a process is often denoted using the term "business process".

[1] http://oxforddictionaries.com/definition/process

A business process denotes a set of activities to be performed by given actors through specific tools and methods according to a defined procedure. Many definitions have been conferred on this term. For example, Hammer et al. define an operational process as a sequence of activities which, from one or several inputs, produces a result (output) that represents an added value for a client (Hammer et al., 1993). Lorino considers a process as a set of activities connected together, using information flows and combined to provide an important and well-defined material or immaterial product (Lorino, 1995). For Tarondeau, a business process is a set of activities which are organized into network, in a sequential or parallel manner, and which combine and implement multiple resources, capabilities and competences to produce a result or output of value for an external client (Tarondeau, 1998). Brandenburg and Wojtyna consider it as a chain of activities or activity sets, which is supplied by inputs, has resources and adds value relative to the goal in order to create outputs (Brandenburg and Wojtyna, 2003). Besides, Morley et al. use five notions: goal, activity, role, resource and event to define a business process (Morley et al., 2011). They identify it as a set of activities undertaken in a determinate objective, assigned in total to an actor or in part to several actors corresponding to different roles, performed using resources, and may be conditioned by events of internal or external origin. They also introduce the notion of process structure that corresponds to the arrangement of process activities. Finally, the ISO 9000 standard defines a business process as a set of correlated or interacting activities which transforms inputs into outputs. All of these definitions commonly agree on the fact that a process is a set of activities which, from a set of inputs, produces a set of outputs that allow achieving a given goal. Moreover, we note that activities are performed by human actors or machines and can require resources. They are sometimes conditioned by events. Moreover, they can also interact and they run in a determinate order according to expected events. To specify business processes, it is therefore necessary to use concepts such as activity, input, output, goal, role, resource and event.

In the literature, an activity refers to tasks. Lorino identifies it as a set of elementary tasks, homogeneous from the point of view of their cost and performance behaviors, which produce an output from a set of inputs (Lorino, 1991). An input is an object on what the activity must operate to produce an output. The output is simply a result produced by the activity. The goal of a given process is what this process aims to achieve or to accomplish in order to meet the enterprise strategy. The role refers to a prescribed or expected behavior associated with a particular status in the enterprise. It corresponds to a responsibility assigned to an internal or external actor which can be a person, an organizational entity (which includes a group of persons) or a system. We can consider that a role corresponds to one or more activities that are performed by the same actor. However, an actor may play several roles. It is therefore appropriate to specify a business process by eliciting the roles rather than the actors. Besides, the concept of resource refers to a mean required to perform an activity. It can be for example a database, a software or a hardware tool. Last but not least, the event constitutes a fact that occurs and which can trigger an activity. It can, for example, correspond to a time deadline or an occurring result (output).

Finally, we note that the activity is the core of a business process. We can therefore apprehend this one as a decomposable macro-activity and consider the task as the smallest unit of decomposition. The process approach is, in fact, a systemic approach that distinguishes several levels of analysis. These ones can be, in general, summarized into four levels (Brandenburg & Wojtyna, 2003): the macro-processes, the elementary processes, the sub-processes that we choose to call micro-processes in this chapter trying to avoid any confusion with the term sub-processes used in the BPMN (Business Process Management Notation) standard (Object Management Group [OMG], 2011), and finally the activities. A macro-process provides added value and meets a strategic goal of the company. A multi-activity enterprise can use several macro-processes. Each macro-process is, in fact, decomposed into elementary processes, and each elementary process is simply decomposable into activities or even micro-processes when its activities are performed by different entities. In this last case, each group of activities constitutes a micro-process. We can say that a micro-process is simply a part of a business process composed of activities, performed by a same entity and hence corresponding to a same role. After this analyze of the process concept, let's consider in the following section its representation in the literature.

3. Languages and formalisms for modeling business processes

Modeling business processes has, for long time, been attracting much research interest. Many languages, formalisms or even frameworks have been developed over time to meet that goal. We cite, as examples, Petri nets, the CIMOSA (Computer Integrated Manufacturing Open System Architecture) framework, the RAD (Role Activity Diagrams) notation, the EPC (Event Driven Process Chain) notation, the IDEF (Integration Definition Language) methods, the OSSAD (Office Support Systems Analysis and Design) method, the Merise method, the UML (Unified Modeling Language) language and the BPMN notation. In this section, we study these formalisms in order to show their fundamentals as well as their limitations. However, we cannot describe all of them here. We focus on three standard languages: IDEF, UML and BPMN. We have chosen these three languages because we think that they trace the evolution in modeling business processes over the years. IDEF has been the first brick proposed in this area. UML has accompanied the object-oriented paradigm and has been widely adopted by designers. Finally, the BPMN notation is a recent standard that is known to be the most adapted standard to model business processes.

3.1 IDEF

In 1970's, U.S. Air force has launched a project for integrated computer-aided manufacturing. This project has led to the IDEF family of methods. Today, this family includes fifteen methods recommended to describe and specify business processes. The first two methods, IDEF0 and IDEF1, known as SADT (Structured Analysis and Design Technical) (Lissandre, 1990), have been developed to respectively represent the functions and information. IDEF1 focuses on describing company data models, whereas IDEF0 has been devoted to the description of the processes.

IDEF0 had great success and became an IEEE standard in 1998. It considers that a complex system is iteratively decomposable into simpler subsystems that interact to achieve a goal. This decomposition consists in splitting the system into a set of functions, starting from a global function to dissect into sets of sub-functions, until reaching elementary functions. IDEF0 provides a structured system representation with hierarchical levels. It adopts a graphical notation and a simple syntax in order to describe and organize the system in a tree. This method represents in fact, a business process as a tree whose nodes constitute functions described using diagrams. Each diagram includes one or more functions which constitute nodes of the business process tree and belong to a given level of decomposition.

To describe a function, IDEF0 considers it as an activity or a sub-process that transforms ingoing objects into outgoing ones, through mechanisms that correspond to material, software or human means (resources, tools, actors, etc.). It also assumes that its behavior can be influenced or triggered by a set of conditions that form its control directives. Indeed, IDEF0 describes each function as a box, expresses its goal simply using a text and represents its interface using arrows indicating its inputs, outputs, mechanisms and controls. A business process model would thereby be modeled as shown in Figure 1. A node number can be mentioned under a box in the IDEF0 diagram to indicate that the corresponding function is a composite activity which is decomposed and described in another diagram denoted by the same node number. In Figure 2, *Node 0* is described by a graph with two activities and a sub-process (*Node 2*).

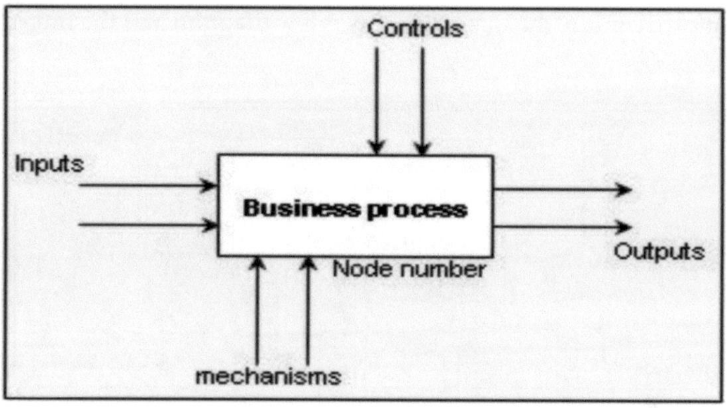

Fig. 1. IDEF0 Business process model.

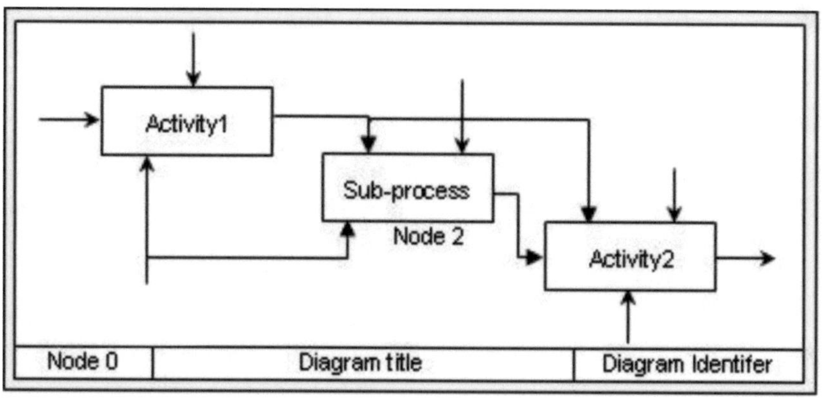

Fig. 2. Sample model of a diagram decomposing a node in IDEF0.

Although the IDEF method had remarkable success in industrial and military domains, it has some limitations. On the one hand, IDEF0 does not provide a flexible way to describe the process activities and requires describing each box (activity) by at least an output and a control. It also leads to an ambiguous description of concepts: since the actors, roles and resources are all represented by ingoing or outgoing arrows, it is not always easy to distinguish, for example, an actor from a role, or even an actor from a resource. On the other hand, IDEF3 does not allow building a well-developped representation of the process behavior, and informally describes any additional information concerning a process by simple comments. Several years later, UML has focused on non ambiguous description of systems.

3.2 UML

UML is an object-oriented modeling language (J. Gabay & D. Gabay, 2008; Charroux et al., 2010). It was created by merging the methods OMT (Object Modeling Technique), OOD (Object Oriented Design) and OOSE (Object Oriented Software Engineering), and became an OMG (Object Management Group[2]) standard in 1997. UML Version 2 proposes thirteen diagrams to describe a system. To formalize a process, it is useful to use, among them, the use case diagram, the transition-state diagram, the activity diagram, the sequence diagram, the communication diagram, the interaction overview diagram and the time diagram shown in Figure 3.

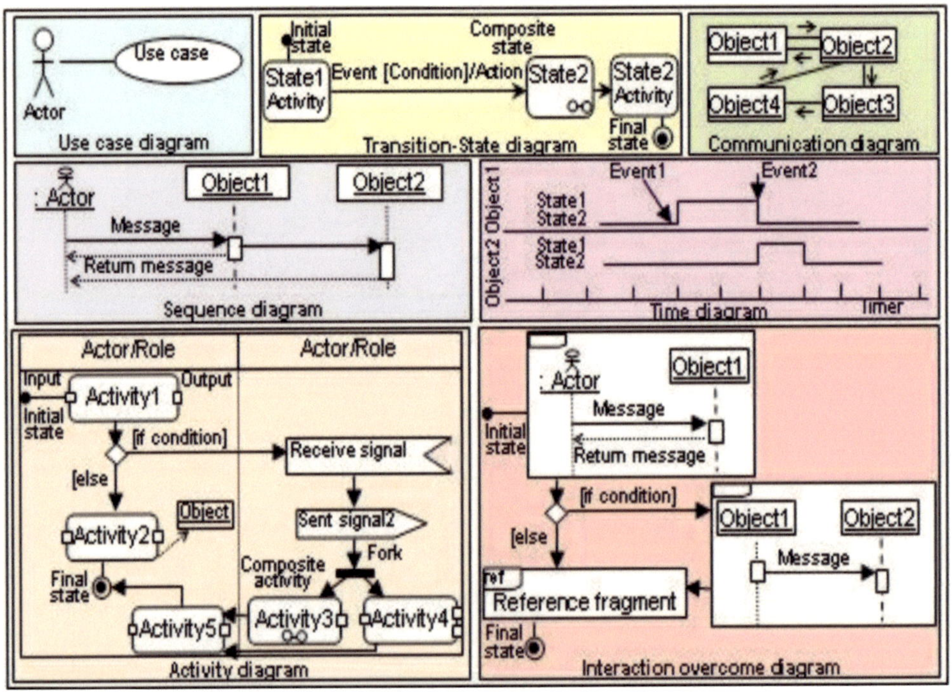

Fig. 3. View of UML behavioural diagrams used to describe business processes.

The use case diagram describes a system from the point of view of the user. The state-transition diagram represents the lifecycle of an object and its main states. Just as the transition-state diagram, the UML 2 activity diagram also illustrates the behavior of the system by introducing new elements to provide a rich description of activities and their sequence. It specifies the activities using input/output pins, describes data flows (objects), and uses specific nodes to describe control flows such as decision, fork and synchronization. It also introduces specific communication actions to represent events such as a signal or a

[2] www.omg.org

time flow. In addition, it can be organized into partitions, each one including a group of activities that often correspond to organizational units or actors. Finally, the activity diagram is the core of process description, in which micro-processes can be elicited using partitions. Besides, the sequence diagram is a temporal description of a collaboration scenario between objects. The communication diagram, as for it, only indicates interactions between objects. The interaction overview diagram merges the activity and sequence diagrams to provide more detail. Finally, the time diagram allows to better visualize the state changes and the interactions between objects in respect of time constraints.

All of the diagrams mentioned above can be used to model macro-processes in UML. The use case diagram serves to show the use of elementary processes by different actors. These elementary processes can be further specialized in micro-processes to provide more details. As for the activity diagram, it is used to formalize the activities and tasks of each elementary process. The aim is to describe the control flow between all of the micro-processes constituting an elementary process, since their activities are interdependent. This description could be performed considering as many partitions as there are actors, or even micro-processes. Besides, the communication diagram can be used to describe interactions (exchanges) between micro-processes, and the sequence diagram would be useful to precisely describe their chronology. In addition, the interaction overview diagram improves the visibility of each elementary process conduct by merging the activity and sequence diagrams. The object state transitions, as for it, can be described using the state-transition diagram, but also the time diagram when these states change over time depending on their interactions with other objects.

Finally, we note that modeling a business process is spread over seven UML diagrams, each one provides an accurate modeling focusing on a given aspect. Therefore, the activity diagram, which is fundamental for specifying the process behavior, does not cover all of the elements describing a process such as the events or resources. It denotes a resource as a simple comment, and does not show the events triggering activities, except for communication actions which can be considered as signal type events. The events are, rather, described at the level of the state-transition diagrams in which the activities are encapsulated in objects states. Thus, the activity diagram cannot be directly mapped to an executable process. In addition, details on the processes' inputs and outputs can only be given through an eighth diagram: class diagram. However, this one only provides information about the data types of these parameters. After these two generic process notations, let's consider in the following sub-section BPMN standard which is devoted to business processes design.

3.3 BPMN

BPMN is a flowchart representation of business processes. It aims to provide, on the one hand, a fully graphical notation, easy to use and usable at both business and technical levels, and on the other hand, a mechanism to generate executable processes directly without using another language. It was developed at the initiative of the BPMI (Business Process Management Initiative) organization in 2004 and adopted as OMG standard in 2006. Version 2 of the BPMN standard (OMG, 2011) uses five main concepts for this purpose: the swimlanes, the flow objects, the connectors (connecting objects), the data and the artifacts. As illustrated in Figure 4, all of these concepts are used together into a specific diagram to describe in particular the dynamic behavior of a business process.

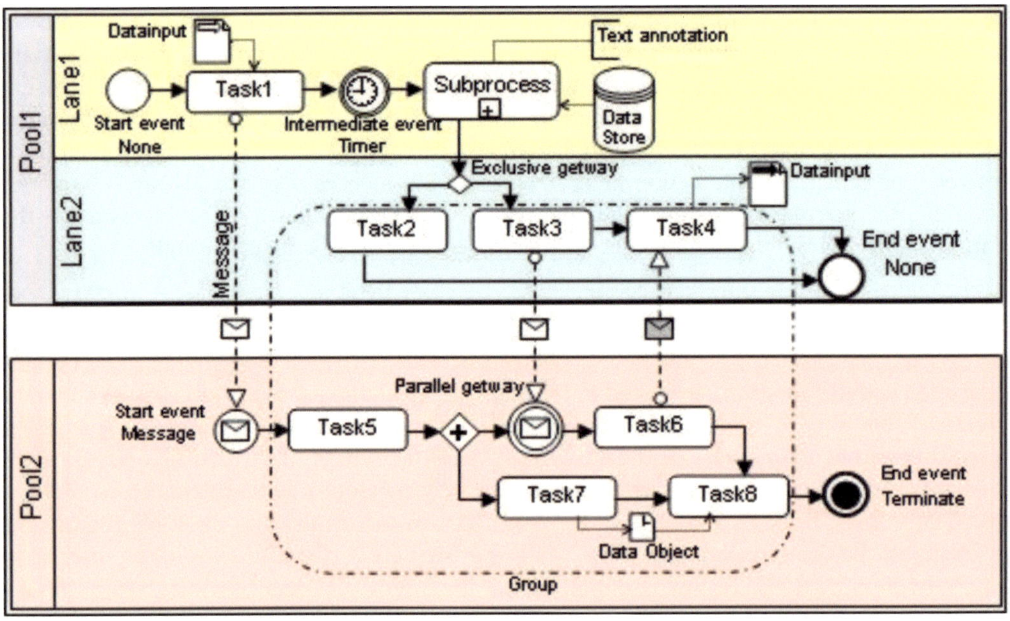

Fig. 4. Sample model of BPMN diagram used to describe business processes.

The swimlanes (pools and lanes) are used to create activity partitions in order to organize processes. Each pool includes activities performed by a participant in an interactive process. The pools are activities' containers, whereas the lanes are a way to organize these activities within the pool. Besides, the flow objects constitute graph nodes that represent the activities (tasks or sub-processes), events and gateways. The tasks are atomic activities and the sub-processes are composite activities. The events are something that happens and affects the process execution. They often have a cause and a result, and can start, interrupt or terminate a flow. The gateways are elements representing the control of activities flows. They are divided into exclusive, inclusive, parallel, event-based, and complex gateways, to represent different conditional branching such as "Fork", "Join" and "Merge." The connectors are information flows that represent sequence flows, message flows, associations or data associations. The sequence flows link the activities within a lane to explicit the order in which they will be executed. They connect together activities, events and gateways, and can be conditional flows. The message flows represent the messages exchanged between the pools. The data associations are used to model the data flow between data objects and activities or events. They can, for example, associate inputs or outputs with an activity. The associations express relationships between information or artifacts and flow objects. For example, an annotation (user-defined text) can be associated with a graphical element. The artifacts (groups or text annotations) provide additional information about the process. The groups are used to highlight sets of activities that may belong to different lanes and/or pools. The text annotations are associated with the BPMN diagram elements to describe them. Besides, the data refer to data objects, data inputs, data outputs, data stores or messages. The data inputs and data outputs are respectively input to/output of the entire process as whole. They can be associated with its activities using data associations. As for the data objects, they represent either objects used by the activities, or objects that the activities produce (business documents, emails, etc.). The data stores are places where the activities can retrieve or update stored information, e.g. databases. Finally, the messages describe the contents of a communication between peers of participants.

3.4 Conclusion

BPMN is a standard inspired from a myriad of methodologies and notations such as UML, IDEF, ebXML BPSS (Electronic Business using eXtensible Markup Language Business Process Specification Schema), RosettaNet, and EPC. Nowadays, it is considered as the most adapted notation to business process specification. This standard proposes a set of concepts that can be described in a concise, clear, but also compact (not fragmented) manner. The resulting descriptions are understandable by all business users, and produce interoperable process management systems. The main advantage of BPMN is that it provides processes representations that we can directly implement and execute without having to perform translations.

In this section, we analyzed how to represent business processes and we conclude with the leading position of BPMN. In the next section, we will consider the ways to integrate business processes.

4. Business process integration solutions

The integration consists in adopting a technique to ensure the coherence of an information system constituted of different components, create collaboration pathways, reuse functions, share data, and ensure the agility of the enterprise information system. Various solutions have been experimented to achieve the integration of applications. They can be divided into seven classes, each one uses a specific technique: the conversion, standardization, middleware, EAI (Enterprise Application Integration), ERP (Enterprise Resource Planning systems), Workflow and BPEL (Business Process Execution Language) based solutions.

4.1 Conversion

The conversion consists in using peer to peer converters in order to convert the models and data exchange formats between applications. This type of integration is chronologically the first integration technique that was specifically used for data exchange. Using a converter allows converting the sender's data format into the receiver format. However, it requires using as many converters as there are used formats. Thus, exchanging data with an application which uses a new format requires conceiving a new converter. In addition, the updating of the data format adopted by a given company application involves the updating of all converters concerning this application. This technique leads to a complex interfacing. Furthermore, it assumes that partners are known in advance, and thereby it is adapted to A2A (Application to Application) integration and not B2B (Business to Business) one.

4.2 Standardization

The data integration solutions based on standardization have been developed to avoid the problems of the conveters-based integration. They specifically consist in unifying representation and data exchange models. This class includes, as examples, the EDI (Electronic Data Interchange) standards, and recently the XML-based standards, RosettaNet and ebXML.

The EDI standards like X12 (American intersectoral standard) and EDIFACT (Electronic Data Interchange For Administration, Commerce and Transport) have opted for standardization as an efficient mechanism for intersectoral and international electronic data exchange. These standards have attempted to standardize, according to the domain context, the way, the means and the format used to exchange data. Their aim was to enable partners, belonging to the same sector, to communicate. However, they were designed to support business transactions between a limited set of known trading partners (Albrecht et al., 2003). They also do not provide a standardized representation of information supporting different areas and do not allow indexing for discovery purposes (Truman, 1998).

The standards proposed in 1998 by the RosettaNet consortium, help trading partners collaborate through commercial transactions based on a formalized data exchange. They are developed to be used in a layered infrastructure that partners must necessarily adopt to be able to collaborate. These standards are used to define business process templates, partner interface processes, architecture of exchange and transaction dictionaries. However, they are adapted to e-commerce transactions and require adapting used systems according to the proposed infrastructure.

The ebXML standard was proposed in 1999 by the UN/CEFACT (United Nations Centre for Trade Facilitation and Electronic Business) and OASIS (Organization for the Advancement of Structured Information Standards). As recommended by ISO 15000, it uses five layers of data specification (Chauvet, 2002). These layers are used to describe business process interfaces, define collaboration protocol profiles and agreement, specify reusable data structures, define message transport and routing, and indicate mechanisms required to use repositories and registers. The ebXML BPSS specification uses activity diagram concepts to formalize a business process. It describes it as a set of choreographed business transaction activities which exchange XML business documents to perform, in particular, binary collaborations. The ebXML standard is adapted to business interchanges between commercial partners. It is also a non flexible solution which assumes that multi-party collaborations are very restricted. Furthermore, it is intended for exchanging documents which match with predefined data patterns, and imposes agreed interchanges using only predefined interaction patterns.

4.3 Middlewares

The middlewares are used as intermediate software components that make applications communicate and abstract the heterogeneity of their platforms. They mainly ensure messages transport and routing, but also other services such as data transformation and transaction management. Middlewares, such as JDBC (Java DataBase Connectivity) and ODBC (Open DataBase Connectivity), ensure data access regardless of the databases used. Those such as API RMI (Java Remote Method Invocation) and MOM (Message-Oriented Middleware) are based on the RPC (Remote Procedure Call) techniques or message exchange to make communicate remote systems. Besides, the component-based middlewares are among the most important ones. They constitute a solution to integrate heterogeneous and distributed applications. Being based on remote methods or procedures invocation, they make communicate, according to specific communication models, components distributed across network. Examples of this type of middlewares are CORBA (Common Object Request Broker Architecture) of OMG, COM/DCOM (Component Object

Model/Distributed Component Object Model) of Microsoft, J2EE (Java 2 Enterprise Edition) of Sun and DotNet of Microsoft.

Finally, the component-based middlewares have, in general, the advantage of ensuring portability, security, scalability, load balancing, and reusability. However, they have limitations that can be summarized in the complexity of implementation, the cost of platforms used, the tight software coupling that makes the produced applications non flexible, the dependence on the development environment due to the use of specific communication buses, and therefore the complex integration of heterogeneous systems. Furthermore, some of these middlewares are proprietary and non standardized softwares.

4.4 EAI

EAI provides formatting, technical gateways and process management services (Octo Technology, 1999). They allow, in general, conveying messages, accessing applications through interfaces provided by connectors, transforming and conveying data in a format adopted by the target application using a pivot format, ensuring messages routing and also orchestrating applications in the case of some EAI. BEA Weblogic Integration, Microsoft Biztalk and IBM Websphere Business Integration are among the EAI technologies used in the market. These technologies have the advantage of integrating heterogeneous applications using connectors, and reducing the connections between these applications by centralizing them at the EAI level. However, the connectors are proprietary and difficult to maintain. In addition, implementing EAI is a complex operation, and the interoperability they provide depends on the EAI which constitutes a central intermediate.

Besides, the ESB (Enterprise Service Bus) technology, proposed by the Gartner Group in 2003, constitutes a new generation of EAI. It uses diverse standards such as XML, JMS (Java Message Service), JCA (Java Connector Architecture), JMX (Java Management Extensions) and also Web services standards. An ESB provides a set of services (Mullenders, 2009): dynamic services discovery, their automatic orchestration, strong distribution services on the network or Internet, messages communication, XML data transformations, content-based intelligent routing, and in some case, business Activity Monitoring, and business process management. Several ESB exist in the market. They are proprietary as well as open source, such as: IBM WebSphere ESB, Microsoft BizTalk Server, Oracle Enterprise Service Bus (BEA Logic), Apache ServiceMix and Open ESB. The ESBs are based on bus architecture, exploit Web services and use an integration engine which is distributed in the service adapters. It follows that they provide highly distributed integration and lead to loosely coupled applications. However, the administration of these tools may be complex depending upon the integrated systems. Besides, they are more costly, vendors depending, and require more work upfront. They also assume the use of unified messages models. Finally, the ESB may become a single point of failure since all application communications are performed across it. These indirect communications may lead in increased latency and decreased performance.

4.5 ERPs

ERPs are computer systems which use advanced communication and information technologies to process enterprise management information. They constitute, indeed, a solution that performs all of the crucial enterprise business processes such as the commercial management of the supply chain, from product production to its sale. They consist in a set of independent applicative modules and use a workflow engine to propagate real-time data between these modules. SAP, Oracle/Peoplesoft, SAGE ADONIX, and Microsoft are examples of proprietary ERPs. As for Compiere/Adempiere, Ofbiz, Openbravo and Open ERP (previously denominated Tiny ERP), they are among Open ERPs. All of these systems are considered as the most popular ERPs in the market.

Besides, ERPs have, in general, the advantage of overcoming the difficulty of information access due to the incompatibility of platforms, databases, data formats and semantics used by different business applications. They are among the solutions adapted to A2A process integration. However, they require major investments (high costs of license, maintenance, technical assistance, training and material infrastructure), a dependence of the supplier in case of technical problems and a complex implementation. Implementing an ERP project requires, in fact, to conduct an analysis and preliminary study in the long term to perform the ERP customization, update it if the version has been changed, create appropriate interfaces to integrate the ERP with existing applications, and make organizational changes and adaptations according to the business processes defined by the ERP.

4.6 Workflow

Workflow engines aim to automate business processes by automating the coordination of the tasks and the circuits routing documents as well as information between a set of actors. We cite, among them, Windows Workflow Foundation, WORKEY and Activiti . They allow executing one or more workflow definitions described using workflow languages. These languages are used to represent a process by an activity flow specifying the exchanged documents and information as well as the actions of each actor.

WPDL (Workflow Process Definition Language) is, for example, a workflow definition language that was defined by the Workflow Management Coalition (WfMC) in 1994. It is based on a meta-model (objects model) and allows describing the basic elements of a workflow management system with a focus on the interfaces to external systems. Its use can enable the exchange of models and documentation between heterogeneous worlflow systems of different vendors (Workflow Management Coalition [WfMC], 1998). For the purpose of using an internationally defined standard encoding language, WPDL uses today XML to exchange processes, and is denominated XPDL (XML Process Definition Language). However, this language is not a formal language and does not provide flow semantics, and thereby, its implementation and use impose problems. In addition, although the workflow languages enable to easily define a workflow between human actors, the integration of the workflow to an application or a system still remains a complex task.

4.7 BPEL

The BPEL language, originally called BPEL4WS (Business Process Execution Language for Web Services) is a recent language appeared in 2003. It was inspired from the WSFL (Web Services Flow Language) and XLANG (XML Business Process Language) standards. This language is intended to execute synchronous and asynchronous business processes. Besides, it is fundamentally based on the use of XML standard to describe an executable process with all the necessary technical specifications. It is also worth noting that this language allows the rapid and easy deployment of executable processes on a business process engine.

Version 2 of BPEL constitutes an OASIS standard appeared in 2007 (Organization for the Advancement of Structured Information Standards [OASIS], 2007). This standard allows interacting with Web services to exchange XML data, and managing exceptions and compensation in the case of rollback transactions. It describes the process activities using flow control structures (sequence, iteration, parallelism, etc.), defines the data manipulated in containers and organizes Web services, when used, as partners. In the BPEL context, each activity consists in a service invocation, a message reception or transmission, or an exception (error message) reception. As for the exception and compensation routines, they are respectively described using specific elements, namely, *faultHandlers* and *compensationHandler*.

4.8 Conclusion

One main feature of BPEL is that it constitutes, in fact, the standard language for Web services composition. Thereby, it is a recent and recommended standard for orchestrating transactional and distributed business processes. It is, moreover, adapted for the specification of executable as well as abstract business processes, in particular, those apprehended as Web services. That's why we adopt this language in combination with BPMN standard in order to model and integrate business processes. The main lines of our approach for business processes are introduced in the next section.

5. Our approach for modeling and integrating business processes

In this section, we propose a Web service and model-oriented approach for modeling and integrating business processes. The aim is to produce flexible and scalable systems. These systems would be able to use agile business processes that can be dynamically integrated and subsequently, become adaptable to changes. To achieve this goal and realize efficient information systems, we think that enterprise must adopt a development cycle fundamentally based on modeling and integrating business processes. It could begin with designing its abstract business processes according to its needs and regardless of its competences, then implement or simply discover Web services that can be used in order to perform those processes if it decides to collaborate with business partners. Finally, it is this discovery aspect in which we are interested, since it leads to a dynamic integration producing changeable business processes. However, dynamic services discovery, in this case, can only be performed if the business processes design covers their functional, non-functional and semantic aspects. Eliciting what a process exactly do, its non-functional properties (e.g., security and quality of service), and the semantics of its inputs/outputs as well as its functionality, is crucial to manage processes, and in particular to discover and integrate them. Thereby, three main phases define our global approach: business process modeling, dynamic Web services' discovery and deployment.

The initial modeling phase consists, first of all, in describing all abstract business activities making up the global process, using UML and BPMN diagrams and taking advantage of the concepts used in Web services standards. It must obviously cover the business process's functional, non-functional and semantic aspects. This phase delivers generated BPEL files corresponding to the abstract business processes. The second phase of dynamic Web services discovery consists in searching, among Web services published in repositories, those that are appropriate to automate the abstract business processes. As for the deployment phase it simply consists in automatically replacing each invocation of an abstract activity in BPEL files generated in advance, by a concrete invocation of the corresponding Web service. The objective is to make business processes executable by adding the relevant technical information (binding information in the Web services context) to their BPEL files. In the following section, we explain the details of our approach concerning the two main phases: business process modeling and Web services dynamic discovery. We first present the modeling principles that will be illustrated using a sample scenario. Then, we discuss the proposed discovery mechanisms.

5.1 Business processes modeling

The BPMN standard adopts an activity-oriented representation for specifying business processes. This type of representation is adapted for describing the behavior of processes. However, it does not describe their functional, non-functional and semantic aspects. In fact, even if the BPMN standard introduces elements such as the goal and inputs/outputs to specify a business process, it does not describe it in an expanded and disambiguated manner. In this subsection, we propose an approach that exploits the concepts used in the W3C standards recommended to describe Web services, in order to model business processes. This approach does not ignore the importance of the activity-oriented representation proposed by BPMN. It, indeed, adopts it to model the behavioral aspect of business processes, but enriches and completes it by functional, non-functional and semantic representations using UML diagrams. Our business processes metamodel is illustrated in Figure 5. The metaclasses shown in yellow, blue, and pink respectively refer to concepts used to achieve the behavioral, functional and non functional description while considering the semantic of business processes. By analyzing all of the definitions and concepts previously presented, a business process may, indeed, either represent a micro-process, an elementary process or a macro-process. A macro-process is an aggregation of elementary processes, each one can aggregate one or more micro-processes. Each micro-process is an aggregation of activities and the activity is specialized into a task or a subprocess. According to the BPMN standard, we denote a task as an atomic activity and a sub-process as a composite activity. We have, therefore, used the composite pattern to specify the metaclass *Activity*.

As we previously noted, we are considering to specify business processes as Web services. A main question remains: how to introduce this technology in the business processes specification practices? To answer this question, we think that this can be performed through the business processes' activities. We consider that each activity part of a business process refers to an atomic or composite Web service, and each task corresponds to an operation. This mapping is justified by the fact that an activity, just as a Web service, includes a set of operational tasks (operations) that cooperate together to provide a specific function and produce added value. Thereby, the atomic activity can be performed by simply invoking an operation of an atomic Web service. Whereas, the sub-process is a composite activity that can be performed by an atomic or composite Web service, and thus requires orchestration of a set of operations of the same Web service or coordination of several Web services.

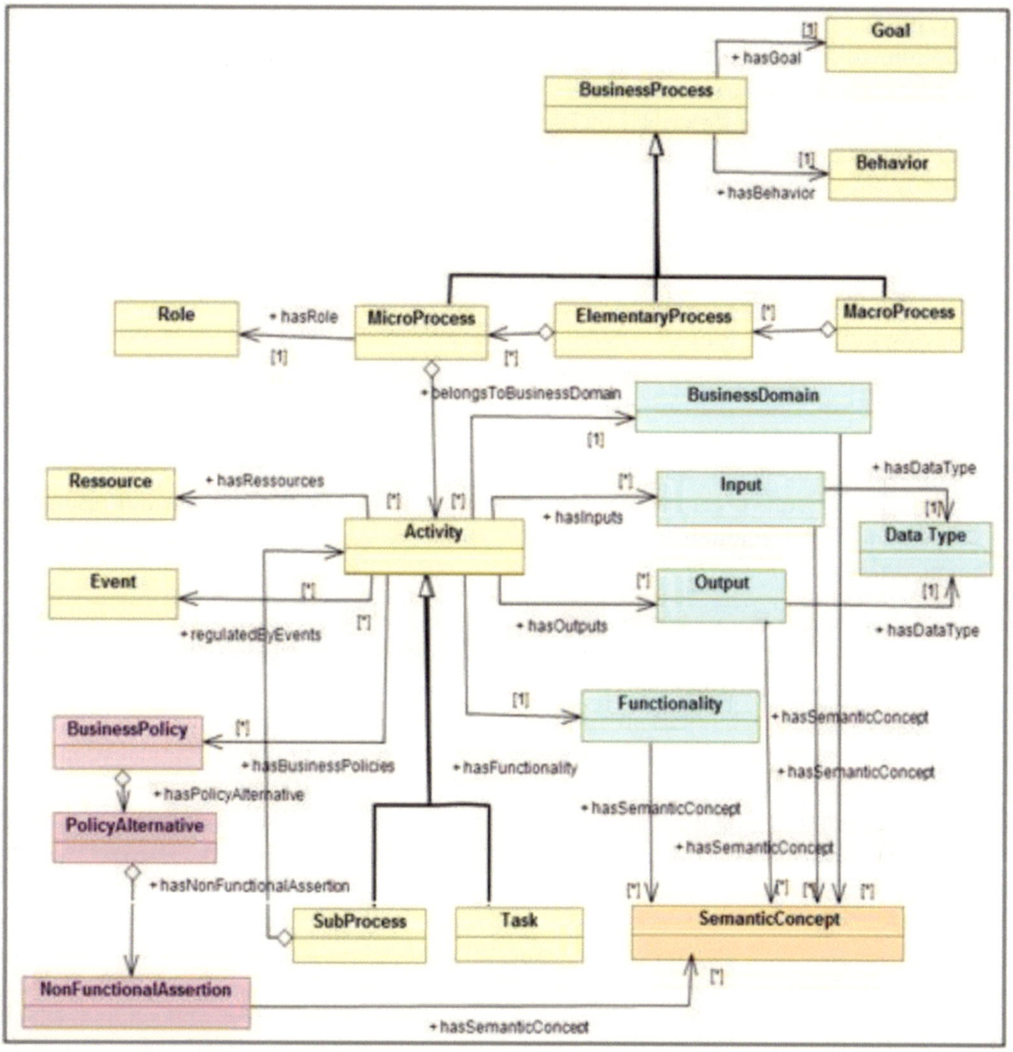

Fig. 5. Business process metamodel.

Besides, we recall that a business process can be described by a goal, activities, roles, resources, inputs/outputs and eventually a set of events. However, a global process is represented by its goal and eventually its decomposition into processes (Morley et al., 2011). The macro-processes and elementary processes are elements of great granularity from the point of view of analysis. They are, in reality, global processes that do not need to be described in detail. The details of their specification may in particular be given at the level of their fine-grained components. Thereby, it would be convenient to associate the metaclasses *goal* and *behavior* with the metaclass *business process*, in order to describe indifferently a macro-process, an elementary process or a micro-process by their goals as well as their behavior. Besides, the metaclass *role* should rather be associated with the micro-process which by definition includes a set of activities assigned to the same role. The micro-process specification also requires identifying its inputs/outputs, resources and events to which it reacts in order to understand its running. However, for a detailed description, these elements, represented by the metaclasses *Input, Output, Resource* and *Event* must be specified at the activity level to describe their implementation. Each input or output should also be described by its data type and each activity should be described by its business domain and its functionality. All of these elements will serve to specify an abstract business process which is not yet associated with one or more concrete Web services to become executable.

The W3C standard WSDL (Chinnici et al., 2007) specifies a Web service as an interface that belongs to a business category, and aggregates operations providing a given functionality and having input and output parameters. Our way to specify the business processes allows describing their functional aspect, while fitting harmoniously with this standard. It also introduces the concepts role, resource, event and behavior (orchestration in Web service context) to describe their dynamic aspect. This aspect may, indeed, be represented by a BPMN diagram. This one uses different workflow patterns to describe the arrangement of a business process, while organizing activities by role and highlighting events and resources. However, this is not enough to describe the semantics and non-functional properties of business processes.

To specify the business processes non-functional aspect, we reuse the concepts introduced in WS-Policy standard (Vedamuthu et al., 2007) recommended to describe Web services' policies. According to this standard, we complete the description of an activity by a business policy. We model this activity as an aggregation of alternative policies, each one constitutes an aggregation of assertions. A business policy refers, in fact, to non-functional properties that must be satisfied during the execution of an activity. It is expressed by mentioning sets of alternative non-functional properties. Each of these sets constitutes an alternative policy and each non-functional property is an assertion in the sense of WS-Policy. The Web service that will perform an activity must therefore have, as non-functional properties, all the assertions belonging to one of its alternative policies. Besides, to produce semantic business processes, we take our inspiration from the SAWSDL standard (Farrell et al., 2007). By analogy to the *ModelReference* element, we use the metaclass *SemanticConcept*. We associate this metaclass to the metaclasses *BusinessDomain, Functionality, Input* and *Output* which describe the business process functional aspect, and also with the metaclass *NonFunctionalAssertion* that specifies its non-functional aspect. The metaclass semanticConcept will allow describing all of these elements using ontological concepts that are semantically equivalent to them, and thereby will serve to dynamically discover Web services able to perform the concerned business processes.

5.2 Sample scenario

In this subsection, we present a scenario of selling silver by an enterprise supplier S to illustrate the use of our approach. We assume that when the enterprise S receives a new order from an enterprise client C, it conducts the preparation of the ordered quantity of the silver. Once the supplies are ready, it needs to identify the international current price of silver and convert it into euro before billing the order. Once the invoice is ready, the company C receives the invoice and supplies and must make the payment on delivery. Besides, we assume that the identification of the real-time price of silver and its conversion into euro according to the current exchange rate cannot be performed internally. Thereby, the enterprise needs to use external services provided by an eventual partner. It should indeed be able to discover Web services that provide these financial services and dynamically integrate them to its system.

As defined in this scenario, we can classify the business process activities performed by the company S into three categories: Internal, external and abstract activities. Internal activities are implemented by the information system of the company S, and consist of three activities: *ObtainSilverOrder*, *DeliverSilver* and *ReceivePayement*. External activities are performed outside the company S. They are implemented by the information system of the client C. These activities, denominated *Place SilverOrder*, *ReceiveSilver* and *Pay*, are statically integrated in the process of company S. Finally, abstract activities have to be dynamically integrated into the related business processes by discovering the appropriate Web services able to automate them. They consist of two financial services: *GetRealTimeSilverPrice* and *CurrenciesExchange*. To describe this scenario, we use the BPMN notation as shown in Figure 6.

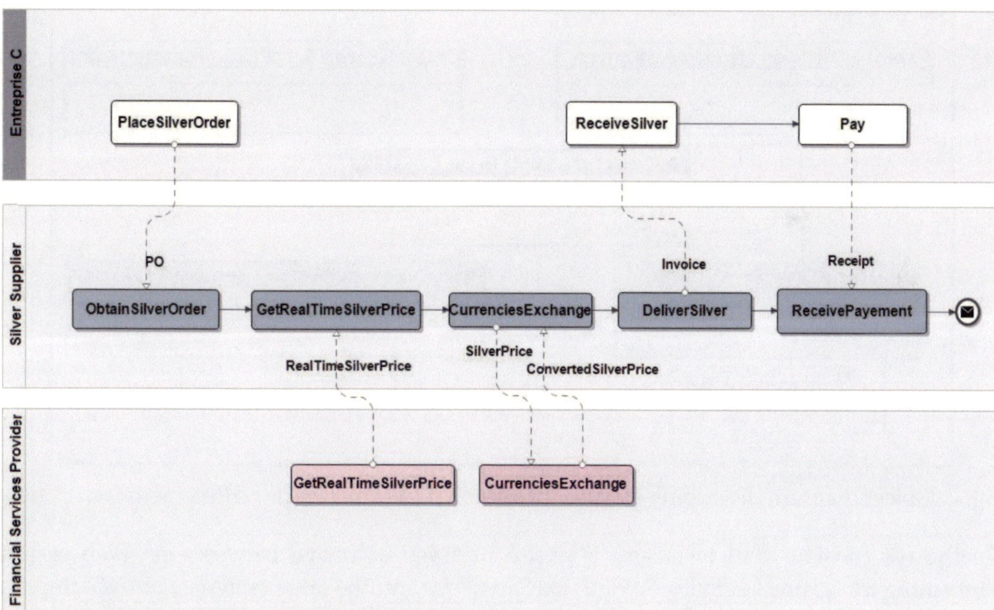

Fig. 6. Process of purchasing silver's metal.

The illustrated BPMN diagram (Fig. 6) is used to model the behavior of the business processes required by the enterprise S. It identifies three pools representing the concerned company, its customer and its external partner. The pool Silver Supplier represents the company S which constitutes the silver's supplier. The pool Enterprise C refers to the business customer of this one. Finally, the pool Financial Services Provider represents a partner that provides financial services and which has to be identified by the company S through discovery process. Each of these pools contains the activities performed by one of the three entities: the company S, the customer C and the abstract partner.

In order to dynamically discover Web services able to perform the abstract activities *GetRealTimeSilverPrice* and *CurrenciesExchange*, the company S must complete its BPMN diagram by two UML diagrams. These ones cover the description of the functional, non-functional and semantic aspects of the concerned abstract activities, in accordance with the metamodel previously exposed. In the remainder of this subsection, we present the case of the activity *GetRealTimeSilverPrice*. Modeling the second abstract activity *CurrenciesExchange* can be done similarly. Figure 7 illustrates an object diagram that specifies the functional properties of the *GetRealTimeSilverPrice* activity, and their corresponding semantics. The concerned activity is, indeed, described by its business domain, functionality, output and ontological concepts which constitute semantic annotations of these properties.

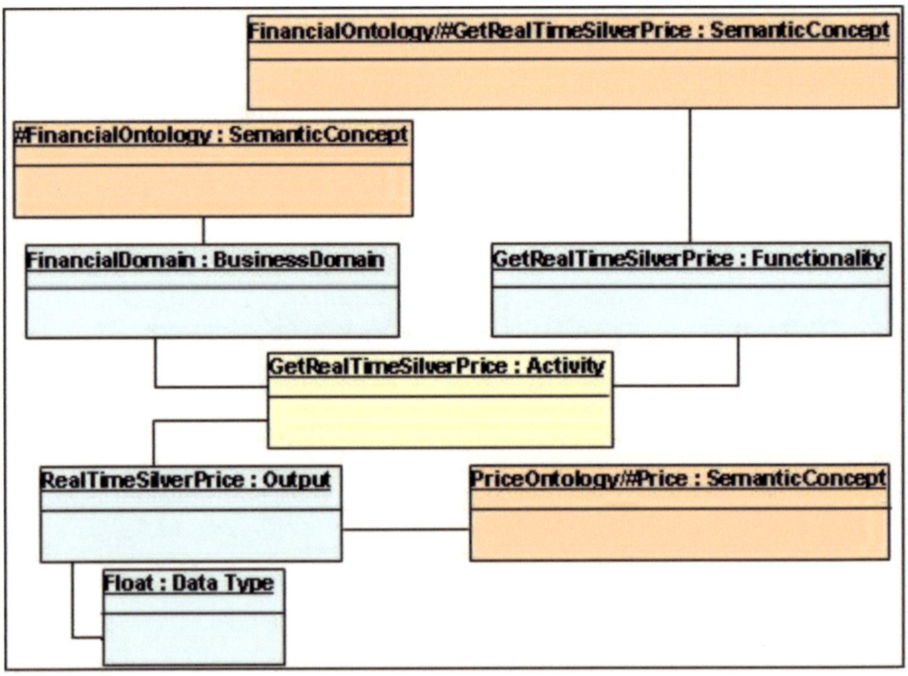

Fig. 7. Object diagram describing functional aspect of *GetRealTimeSilverPrice* activity.

Finally, we consider that to ensure a secure message exchange between the Web service performing the abstract activity *GetRealTimeSilverPrice* and the other activities of the company S, a security policy is required. This policy consists in using cryptography or digital signature to secure the exchange between all involved partners. Modeling this non-functional aspect is thereby essential to discover the appropriate Web service that meets this non-functional need. Figure 8 illustrates an object diagram that describes the involved non-functional constraints and their corresponding semantics. *GetRealTimeSilverPrice* activity is associated with a security policy that aggregates two alternatives policies: *Alternative 1* and *Alternative 2*. The first alternative policy requires the adoption of cryptography mechanism to secure the exchange using the assertion *EncryptedParts*. As for the second alternative policy, it requires the adoption of digital signature mechanism using the assertion *SignedParts*. Both *EncryptedParts* and *SignedParts* assertions are predefined in the WS-Security standard. In our example, they are annotated by ontological concepts to link them to their semantics.

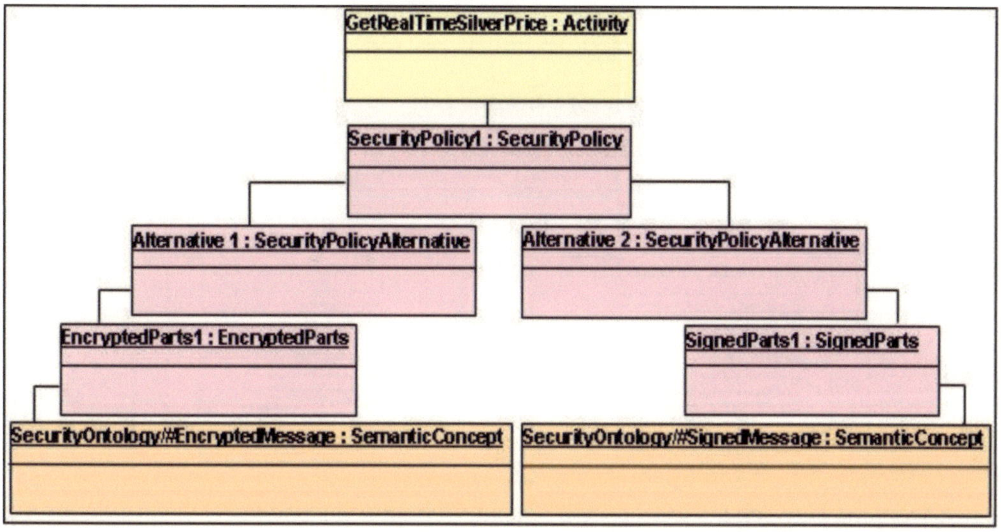

Fig. 8. Object diagram describing non-functional aspect of *GetRealTimeSilverPrice* activity.

In this section, we considered a sample scenario in order to illustrate how our approach designs business processes. In the next one, we address the Web services discovery issue.

5.3 Web services dynamic discovery

The second phase of the development cycle we propose consists in Web services dynamic discovery. This phase involves three basic steps: extraction, matching and selection. It consists, first, in extracting, from published WSDL files, the functional, non-functional and semantic properties of the corresponding Web services. To determine the set of Web services whose functionalities fit with those required, it is necessary to then perform a semantic matching of the published services functional properties with those required and specified in the description of the abstract business process activities. Finally, to identify the most appropriate Web services which satisfy the enterprise constraints and preferences, this phase uses the non-functional properties specified in the modeling phase as criteria used to select services. Two algorithms for matching and selection are thereby necessary to perform Web services' dynamic discovery.

The matching algorithm aims to determine, for each activity of the required abstract process, a list of Web services providing the desired functionality. To optimize this operation, we propose to proceed in a hierarchical manner. The idea is to semantically compare each element specified in the functional model of the abstract activity with its correspondent extracted from the SAWSDL file, following a determined order to avoid inutile comparisons. This hierarchical order is shown in Figure 9 which illustrates the mapping of the elements described in the abstract activity's functional model with those of Web service, as well as the order in which the matching should be performed. The semantic concepts, corresponding to the business domain, functionality, inputs and outputs of the required abstract activity, should respectively be compared in this order with the SAWSDL file contents tagged *modelReference*, and corresponding to the interface, operation, inputs and outputs elements.

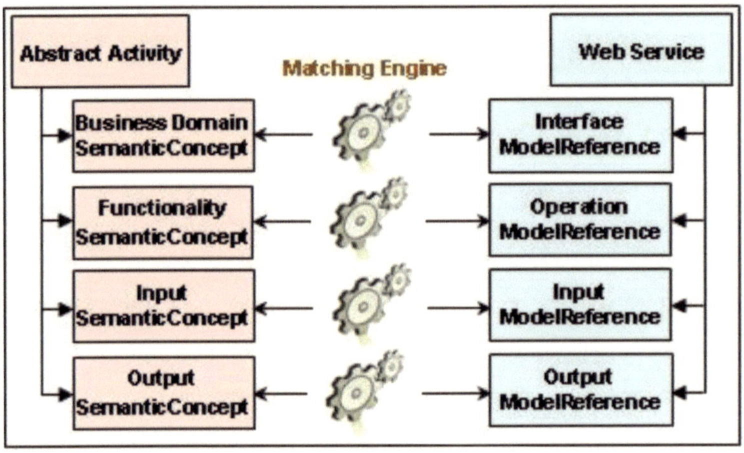

Fig. 9. Mapping between an abstract activity and Web service elements.

Besides, the semantic concepts do not usually perfectly match. There is often no exact matching between the matched concepts. To broaden the scope of the possible results by also covering the approximately similar concepts, we propose to enhance the matching algorithm by semantic relaxation mechanisms. This algorithm could, indeed, use the Edge-Counting Distance method (Hatzi et al., 2009) to calculate the semantic distance between two ontological concepts. This method calculates the distance between two concepts by counting the number of arcs of the shortest path connecting them in a given ontology. Calculating this metric allows determining the degree of similarity between two semantic concepts that can be either absolute or approximate.

Furthermore, data structures constituting the inputs/outputs types must be matched to determine the mapping between the data types used by an abstract process and those adopted by an invoked Web service. Calculating the semantic similarity, between the different concepts mentioned above, allows identifying Web services that match with the abstract business processes. However, the data types of their inputs and outputs can be heterogeneous. This can imply difficulties when integrating the various Web services that must interact to perform the different required business processes. To overcome this problem, it would also be necessary to make a matching of the inputs and outputs' data structures represented as XML schemas. We consider that a data type of a parameter used in an abstract business process and that corresponding to a parameter used by a published Web service are similar if they are equivalent or if the parameter's data type of the Web service covers that of the abstract process. When the matched data structures are heterogeneous, the matching algorithm should integrate data mediation mechanisms that make their mapping more flexible. This mapping would be useful for managing conflicts due to the heterogeneity of data exchanged during the Web services' invocation operation.

Finally, the selection algorithm adds a significant value to the discovery phase by specifying, among the list of discovered candidate services, those which suit the best to automate the enterprise's business processes. To perform the selection step, we propose to exploit the WS-Policy framework's abilities. This framework allows evaluating policies, and thereby, the non-functional properties of the discovered Web services, by comparing them with those related to the abstract business processes. The selection algorithm would, indeed, be important for ranking discovered Web services that are similar from the functional point of view. This ranking, based on the degree of their matching to the specific constraints and preferences of the enterprise, allows therefore refining the results of matching process.

6. Future research

The issue of modeling and integrating business processes using Web services is not limited to this work. There are several opportunities for future research that stem from the application of our approach. For instance, future works could build on the posited metamodel using Model Driven Architecture (MDA) to develop UML profiles for describing business processes. To explain the impact of this proposal, we recall that services' discovery is based on the matching of business processes properties with published Web services' elements. This imposes an issue due to the fact that these properties are encapsulated in UML diagrams that cannot be directly matched. To face this, we think that MDA techniques can be used in order to generate business processes' description files whose the syntactic structure is fully compatible, and thereby easily matched with that of Web services. In fact, similarly to our previous works in the Web services area (Belouadha et al., 2010a, 2010b; Omrana et al., 2010), we are actually considering to elaborate UML profiles in line with our metamodel and transformation rules in order to enable generating SAWSDL processes' files. This presents two advantages: on the one hand, the exploration of these files during the matching process would be easy, and on the other hand, its use for generating the BPMN diagram will enable generating a BPEL file which is patterned on Web services.

Second, future research can also be undertaken into the business ontologies to enable the semantic matching of business processes, and subsequently their dynamic discovery and integration. In fact, our approach uses SAWSDL principles in order to describe the business processes semantics. However, these principles are limited to semantic annotations. Indeed, the proposed metamodel only annotates the description elements used to design business processes and do not describe their semantics. For example, an ontology URL (Uniform Resource Locator) can be used to semantically annotate a given element describing a business process. Proposing sectorial ontologies or updating the existing ones in order to give semantic details concerning the diverse concepts related to business processes, particularly those considered in our metamodel, is important for supporting semantic processing such as the matching process. The required ontologies must consider the own characteristics of a given sector and give semantic relationships of different concepts, especially, business goals and functionalities, as well as the inputs and outputs of the related business processes. It can be built on the findings of the two main business schemas: North American Industry Classification System (NAICS) and Universal Standard Products and Services Classification (UNSPSC).

Lastly, future research can also build on our approach findings by shifting the emphasis more to the context-aware mobile business processes. The aim is to enable processes running in mobile environments benefiting from the potential of mobile devices. For instance, commercial agents often need to receive customers' orders on their cellular phones in order to activate the supply process and thereby rapidly satisfy the clients' requests. Thus, the main question remains: could contextual information, related to mobile devices properties (e.g., screen size and processor capacity) and users' preferences (e.g., preferred image or file formats), be considered at the business processes' design-time? In fact, our metamodel is based on Web services' W3C standards which are extensible. Thereby, we think that it will be possible to extend the proposed UML metamodel, and subsequently to obtain processes' description files including necessary contextual information. This information is considered as criteria for selecting appropriate mobile services which meet users' preferences and can run on specific mobile devices.

7. Discussion and conclusion

The Weakness of classical approaches for modeling and integrating business processes and the incessant need to create dynamic collaborative environments have consequently oriented the researchers in this area to explore the Web services. The emergence and the strengths of this technology have made it a prominent technology suitable for business process management and enterprise application integration. The interest of Web services to e-business has been discussed and confirmed by many researchers (Leymann et al. 2002; Albrecht et al., 2005; Zhang, 2005). This is what we have also addressed in this chapter.

Today, most enterprises use Web services to perform a part of their business processes, but they do not worry about how to design these processes, so that they become performed by Web services, and how to dynamically integrate them. However, this aspect is crucial to achieving complex business goals in a changing and evolving environment, and also being able to analyze and manage the enterprise business processes. Thereby, the approach we have proposed focuses on the use of Web services for process management in e-business. A number of recent works have been interested to this research orientation using different languages and formalisms. Papazoglou and Yang present a design methodology, based on WSDL and WSFL, for Web services and business processes (Papazoglou & Yang, 2002). They show how business process should be described so that services can be identified. Martens proposes a Petri nets-based method for modeling and analyzing business processes (Martens, 2005). Decker et al. propose an extension of BPEL to enable defining business process choreographies which are based on Web services (Decker et al., 2007). Gorton et al. present a workflow-based approach for business process modeling. This approach, founded on SOA, uses a simple graphical notation and the policy language Appel (Adaptable and Programmable Policy Environment and Language) to describe business processes, and aims to assemble and orchestrate available services in the business process (Gorton et al., 2009).

One of the advantages of our approach is that it enables to describe all business process aspects: functional, behavioral, but also semantic and non-functional. It is also completely aligned with the standards. To model and integrate business processes, it opts for the OMG standards, UML and BPMN, and the OASIS standard BPEL. Furthermore, it adopts design principles founded on the use of W3C standards, namely, WSDL, SAWSDL and WS-Policy. This leads to a business processes description which well fits with the standardized description of Web services. This compatibility of description allows, on the one hand, avoiding problems related to the heterogeneity of the description of the matched elements.

On the other hand, it allows leading to reliable discovery results since it could be possible to match all the concerned elements with their exact corresponding. Moreover, given the fact that the BPMN standard is directly mapped to BPEL, the use of this standard for orchestrating the activities of a business process or integrating many business processes allows to have business process files which are directly executable. It is also worth noting that the W3C standards used in our approach are extensible. This allows extending the proposed business process models in order to take into consideration unforeseen or specific aspects of business processes. Finally, our approach is a Web services-based and model-driven approach. It combines models and mechanisms of Web services' dynamic discovery to model and integrate business processes. The aim is not to show how to integrate a given Web service to legacy applications, when it is necessary to invoke it, but to define a way to develop enterprise information systems which can evolve and adapt to change, using agile business processes. Nevertheless, although our approach has advantages, it also imposes some limitations. First, it is only applied when business processes can be performed using Web services. Second, it can lead to a high cost in terms of dynamic discovery time due to the huge and evolving number of published Web services in Internet. Lastly, it assumes that the explored Web services are published in repositories according to new standards, namely, SAWSDL and WS-Policy.

8. References

Albrecht, C.C.; Dean, D.L. & Hansen, J.V. (2003). Market Place and Technology Standards for B2B, Ecommerce: Progress and Challenges. *MISQ Special Issue Workshop, MISQ Special Issue Workshop: Standard Making: A Critical Research Frontier for Information Systems, International Conference in Information Systems*, pp. 188-209, Seattle, Washington, USA, December 12-14, 2003

Albrecht, C.C.; Dean, D.L. & Hansen, J.V. (2005). Marketplace and Technology Standards for B2B, E-commerce: Progress, Challenges, and the State of the Art, *Information & Management*, Vol. 42, No. 6, (September 2005), pp. 865–875, ISSN 0378-7206

Belouadha, F.-Z. & Roudiès, O. (2008). Towards a UDDI based Semantic Solution for the E-business. *Proceedings of the 3rd IEEE International Conference on Information and Communication Technologies: from Theory to Applications ICTTA'08*, ISBN 978-1-4244-1752-0. Damascus, Syria, April 7-11, 2008.

Belouadha, F.-Z.; Omrana, H. & Roudiès, O. (2010a). A Model-driven Approach for Composing SAWSDL Semantic Web. *International Journal of Computer Science Issues (IJCSI)*, Vol. 7, Issue 2, No. 1, (March 2010), pp. 7-15, ISSN (Online) 1694-07 84, ISSN (Print) 1694-08 14, Retrieved from http://www.ijcsi.org/papers/IJCSI-Vol-7-Issue-2-No-1.pdf.

Belouadha, F.-Z.; Omrana, H. & Roudiès, O. (2010b). A MDA Approach for Defining WS-Policy Semantic Non-functional Properties. *International Journal of Engineering Science and Technology (IJEST)*, Vol. 2, Issue 6, (June 2010), pp. 2164-2171, ISSN 0975-5462, Retrieved from http://www.ijest.info/docs/IJEST10-02-06-115.pdf.

Brandenburg, H. & Wojtyna, J.-P. (2003). *L'approche Processus, Mode d'Emploi*. (2nd edition), Editions d'Organisation, ISBN 2-7081-3482-5, Paris, France

Charroux, B.; Osmani, A. & Thierry-Mieg, Y. (2009). *UML 2, Pratique de la Modélisation*, (3rd edition), Pearson Education France, ISBN 978-2-7440-7466-0, Paris, France

Chauvet, J.-M. (2002). *Services Web avec SOAP, WSDL, UDDI, ebXML*, Eyrolles, ISBN 978-2-212-11047-0, Paris, France

Chinnici, R.J.; Moreau, J.; Ryman, A. & Weerawarana, S. (June 2007). Web Services Description Language (WSDL) Version 2.0 Part 1: Core Language. W3C recommendation, In: *W3C Website*, 13.09.2011, Available from http://www.w3.org/TR/wsdl20/

Decker, G.; Kopp, O.; Leymann F. & Weske M. (2007). BPEL4Chor: Extending BPEL for Modeling Choreographies, Proceedings of IEEE International Conference on Web Services (ICWS 2007), pp. 296-303, 2007. ISBN 0-7695-2924-0, Salt Lake City, Utah, USA, July 09-13, 2007

Farrell, J. & Lausen, H. (August 2007). Semantic Annotations for WSDL and XML Schema, W3C recommendation, In: *W3C Website*, 13.09.2011, Available from http://www.w3.org/TR/sawsdl/

Gabay, J. & Gabay, D. (2008), *UML 2 Analyse et Conception : Mise en Oeuvre Guidée avec Etudes de Cas*, Dunod, ISBN 978-2-10-051830-2, Paris, France

Gorton, S.; Montangero, C.; Reiff-Marganiec, S. & Semini, L. (2009). StPowla: SOA, Policies and Workflows, In: *Service-Oriented Computing – ICSOC 2007 International Workshops, Vienna, Austria, September 17, 2007, Revised Selected Papers, LNCS Vol. 4907*, E. Di Nitto & M. Ripeanu (Ed(s).), pp. 351-362, Springer-Verlag, ISBN 978-3-540-93850-7, Berlin, Heidelberg, Germany, Retrieved from http://www.springer.com

Hammer, M. & Champy, J. (1993). *Le Reengineering – Réinventer l'Entreprise pour une Amélioration Spectaculaire de ses Performances*, Dunod, ISBN 2-10-002027-7, Paris, France

Hatzi, O.; Meditskos, G.; Vrakas, D.; Bassiliades, N.; Anagnostopoulos, D. & Vlahavas, I. (2009). Semantic Web Service Composition using Planning and Ontology Concept Relevance, *Proceedings of the IEEE/WIC/ACM International Joint Conference on Web Intelligence and Intelligent Agent Technologies (WI-IAT 2009)*, pp. 418-421, ISBN 978-0-7695-3801-3, Milan, Italy, September 15-18, 2009

Leymann, F.; Roller D. & Schmidt, M.T. (2002). Web Services and Business Process Management, *IBM Systems Journal*, Vol. 41, No. 2, pp. 198-211, ISSN 0018-8670

Lissandre, M. (1990). *Maîtriser SADT*. Editions Armand Colin, ISBN 2-200-42022-6, Paris, France

Lorino, P. (1991). *Le Contrôle de Gestion Stratégique, la Gestion par les Activités*, Dunod, ISBN 978-2-10-003080-4, Paris, France

Lorino, P. (1995). Le Déploiement de la Valeur par les Processus, *Revue Française de Gestion*, No. 104, (June-August 1995), pp. 55-71, ISSN 0338-4551

Martens, A. (2005). Analyzing Web Service based Business Processes. In: *Fundamental Approaches to software Engineering, 8th International Conference, FASE 2005, Held as Part of the Joint European Conferences on Theory and Practice of Software, ETAPS 2005, Edinburgh, UK, April 4-8, 2005 Proceedings, LNCS, Vol. 3442*, M. Cerioli (Ed.), pp. 19-

33, Springer-Verlag, ISBN 978-3-540-25420-1, Berlin Heidelberg, Germany, Retrieved from http://www.springer.com

Morley, C. ; Bia-Figueiredo, M. & Gillette, Y. (2011). *Processus Métiers et Systèmes d'Information : Gouvernance, Management, Modélisation,* (3rd edition), Dunod, ISBN 978-2-10-055705-9, Paris, France

Mullenders, A. (2009). e-DRH: Outil de Gestion Innovant. la Théorie - les Progiciels - le Cadre Juridique. Groupe De Boeck s.a., ISBN 978-2-8041-5975-7, Bruxelles, Belgique

Octo Technlogy. (1999). Livre Blanc de l'EAI - Intégration des Applications d'Entreprise, In: *Scribd,* 13.09.2011, Available from http://www.scribd.com/doc/6964800/octocom-livre-blanc-eai

OASIS. (April 2007). Web Services Business Process Execution Language Version2.0, OASIS standard, In: *OASIS Website,* 13.09.2011, Available from http://docs.oasis-open.org/wsbpel/2.0/OS/wsbpel-v2.0-OS.html

OMG. (January 2011). Business Process Model and Notation (BPMN), Version 2.0, OMG Document, In: *OMG Website,* 13.09.2011, Available from http://www.omg.org/spec/BPMN/2.0/PDF

Omrana, H.; Belouadha, F.-Z. & Roudiès, O. (2010). A MDA Approach for Describing Web Services Policies. *Proceedings of the 3rd IEEE International Conference on Web and Information Technologies (ICWIT'10),* pp. 449-460, ISBN 978-9954-9083-0-3, Marrakech, Morocco, June 16-19, 2010.

Papazoglou, M. & Yang, J. (2002). Design Methodology for Web Services and Business Processes. In: *Technologies for E-Services, Third International Workshop, TES 2002, Hong Kong, China, August 23–24, 2002 Proceedings, LNCS, Vol. 2444,* G. Goos, J. Hartmanis & J. van Leeuwen (Ed(s).), pp. 54-64, Springer-Verlag, ISBN 3-540-44110-7, Berlin Heidelberg, Germany, Retrieved from http://www.springer.com

Smith, H.; Neal, D.; Ferrara, L. & Hayden, F. (2002). The Emergence of Business Process Management, Report by CSC's Research Services, Version 1.0, In: *Alarcos Website,* N. Morgan & A. Pappenheim (Ed(s)),13.09.2011, Available from http://alarcos.inf-cr.uclm.es/doc/psgc/doc/lec/parte4b/csc-emergenceBPM.pdf

Tarondeau, J.-C. (1998). De Nouvelles Formes d'Organisation pour l'Entreprise : la Gestion par les Processus, *Les Cahiers Français,* No. 287, (July/September 1998), pp. 39-46. ISSN 00080217

Truman, G.E. (1998). An Empirical Appraisal of EDI Implementation Strategies. *International Journal of Electronic Commerce,* Vol. 2, No. 4, (June 1998), pp. 43-70, ISSN 1086-4415

Vedamuthu, A.; Orchard, D.; Hirsch, F.; Hondo, M.; Yendluri, P.; Boubez, T. & Yalçinalp, Ü. (September 2007). Web Services Policy 1.5 – Framework, W3C recommendation, In: *W3C Website,* 13.09.2011, Available from http://www.w3.org/TR/ws-policy/

WFMC, Work Group 1. (July 1998). Workflow Management Coalition, Interface 1: Process Definition Interchange Organisational Model, Document Number WfMC TC-1016-O, In: *WFMC Website,* 13.09.2011, Available from http://www.wfmc.org/Download-document/WfMC-TC-1016-O-Interface-1-Process-Definition-Interchange-Organizational-Model.html

Zhang, D. (2005). Web Services Composition for Process Management in E-Business. *Journal of Computer Information Systems*. Vol. XLV, No. 2, (Winter 2005), pp. 83-91.

6

E-Business and Research Institutes: When Technologies, Platforms and Methods Converge to Meet Users' Needs

Serena Pastore
INAF – Astronomical Observatory of Padova
Italy

1. Introduction

Research and educational institutes as well as business entities make massive use of the Internet and the web as the ideal platform to make their work and to promote their products. The main mission of a generic research or educational environment is to look at specific topics with studies and research, but one of the goals is disseminating and promoting such research, projects and activities. Even if not for-profit, such organizations need funds for their activities obtained as state funds or European contributions, or any other financing methods. The amount of financing is in some way related to the quality of the work done, the results in terms of scientific knowledge and technological transfer, but also is strictly related to the capacity of the institute to disseminate and promote researches, projects and activities. Studies, research and projects are the products and services of such organizations that still have a target market and therefore require the actions and methods of a typical business environment. In this perspective, we could apply to organizations such as research or education institutes some of the models and techniques of the business world to obtain successful results especially in today's hyper-connected environment. In general, models are defined by a combination of policies, operations, technologies and ideology. And a business model (Chesbrough, 2007) describes how an organization creates, delivers and captures value through a process known as a business strategy. Core aspects of the model include purpose, offering, infrastructure, trading practices and operational processes. An e-business (Smith, 2001) refers to a dynamic interdisciplinary topic, utilizing models, techniques and concepts that combine business and technology especially based on the Internet and the web. Generally, an e-business has an online presence that is exploited in different forms (i.e., selling, publicizing, trading, transacting over the web, etc.), but strategies that lead to a successful e-business such as customer relation management (CRM) (Greenberg, 2009) and supply chain management (SCM) (Hugos, 2011) are the same used by a general enterprise even if it takes advantage of Information and Communication technology (ICT) (Dutta & Mia, 2009) to boost efficiency and responsiveness. In addition other organization types must take account of the needs of their target audience, create a marketing plan geared to such needs and re-think their architecture from the point of view of the manager as well as that of the customer. The social revolution in how we communicate point outs the technological aspect as an added value factor for all types of organizations. The web platform and service-based activities guide the transformation of the key business processes through Internet technologies, its main applications and its evolving platform. Focusing on the products/services of a research institute (i.e., the research activities, projects, etc.), we apply models and practices from the e-business world since they share in some ways a common goal, which is the success of the organization. The main aspect is related to customers' expectations, and thus, a CRM strategy must be built in order to promote and advertise scientific culture as a way to have a return investment. Communication is an important mission of every organization selling products or services. The creation, development and suggestion to users of whatever product, go through a business process. The lifecycle of a product requires several activities that in a global market take advantage of the web world and its tools.

The chapter will describe the goal of providing an innovative cultural/scientific e-product related to astrophysical knowledge from an e-business point of view in order to take advantage of this perspective to obtain a successful result. Our aim is to develop and test a model to propose research and products results in order to reach many stakeholders and generate leads for the organization through several channels. Our research project starts from the need to provide a prototype product of a research institute designed from a business perspective and followed by a business plan, offered and "sold" with marketing techniques and thus with a specific marketing and strategic plan and developed with innovative ICT technologies. Starting from the contact point between the two organization types by considering a specific use case in testing the model, we will discuss platforms (i.e., newer Internet distributed infrastructures) and web technologies (i.e., languages, standards, etc.) that should be adopted to realize a good product. From a strategic perspective, technology is heading towards mobility in terms of hardware, software and network and a strong emphasis on information and its architecture (Spencer, 2010), which will be conveyed through a diversified set of rich multimedia web applications or services adhering to standards to satisfy the common goals of usability, accessibility, internationalization and multilingualism, interoperability, etc. An e-product for communication purposes implies a specific user interface for applications and/or services, platforms to deploy and execute such products and languages used for the development are the same regardless off the organization's type.

The organization of the chapter is as follows: Section 1 presents the Institute use case (the Italian national institute for astrophysics), describing its products from an e-business perspective. Section 2 emphasizes the common points of the two organizations types, describing some practical evidences such as social network tools and so-called tagging or data collection technologies. Section 3 highlights technological solutions that are divided into two main technical topics: the platform where the e-business and its tools work (i.e., distributed infrastructures) and the applications/services needed (i.e., web applications).

1.1 Research/educational institute products: the INAF case

The National Institute for Astrophysics (INAF) is an Italian research institute whose mission is to execute, promote and conduct scientific and technological research in astronomy and astrophysics. Moreover, the institute has the duty to disseminate and popularize its results in the school and society and to promote and to encourage technological transfer toward industries. The INAF is composed of 19 institutes spread all over Italy, most hosted in historical buildings such as medieval castles later converted into astronomical observatories located in tourist cities (i.e., Padua, Rome, Florence, Naples, etc.). In particular, astronomical observatories have a great history and hold a great cultural heritage as historical and modern scientific instrumentations and libraries. Due to the different aspects of this kind of institute, we could consider several products and services as outcomes of these organizations. We focus on products since they help us to model the organization as a business and apply a strategy coming from a business environment especially in terms of marketing and fundraising. We think that a research institute should provide outcomes analyzed through indicators that define the success or failure of a study and project and have implications for the survival and competitiveness of an institution. Outreach and public activities increase public visibility and enhance fund raising opportunities. In our opinion, research and educational institutes even if not for profit may be considered businesses since specific processes for retrieving funds for their survival, a marketing plan to promote the entity to citizens and the different categories of stakeholders especially in an epoch of economic crisis can be applied. Research, projects and their results especially in scientific disciplines contribute to new knowledge, discoveries, but could also produce outcomes in everyday life in different contexts even in an interdisciplinary contest. Many intersections and synergy are driven by technologies and the exploration of the universe. Disseminating and promoting such work help to finance the research and thus could be viewed with a marketing approach. Moreover, specific customer relationships processes and supply chain management especially in projects related to scientific instrumentations are becoming an integral part of researchers' work. Astrophysics is in fact a discipline that embraces several topics that are theoretical and practical: studies about the universe and its components require complex instrumentations that involve technological aspects. We focus however on specific products related to the communication and dissemination goal even if the field of application of such a topic involves every aspect of researchers and projects in this science. These products are actually realized with software tools that in a global networked environment are web applications executed through distributed architectures (Schewick van, 2010) and with client and server software on several kinds of devices in an online or offline mode using various communication networks.

1.2 Dissemination of projects' results and knowledge

Our experience in the outreach and dissemination of Astronomy has grown in the last few years (Boccato et al., 2005) thanks to several projects with different targets (Pastore, 2005), developed in a variety of contexts and heterogeneous content. Moreover, all these projects conducted over several years have had the same characteristics: the use of emerging technology regarding information and communication technology. Many branches of communication as well as everyday life are shifting on the Internet infrastructure and on the web platform. Especially now, we are approaching a new way of work that requires an always-on network connection. The new frontiers are user mobility and ubiquity, and these are aspects on which new dissemination should be based. The technological aspect is shared among organizations since citizens and thus customers' lives go through the Internet. In astrophysics, for example, outreach could be enhanced only through future Internet technologies and the evolution of the web as a platform. The first tool for disseminating and marketing outcomes is a website, but this facility is not sufficient and should be integrated with other applications and methods taken from the so-called web 2.0 environment (Oreilly,

2007). Social network facilities and all digital communication forms (i.e., blogs, SMS, etc.) are examples of relative new methods of implementing Internet or web marketing (Cox, 2003). And in this optics, science communication remains the main aspect of every research activity and project and needs methodologies and a detailed plan in order to guarantee a successful result. Finally, science produces a knowledge-based economy based on discovery and innovations that cannot be achieved without increasing and enhancing all the aspects related to the diffusion of scientific culture. This could be reached by establishing interdisciplinary activities, and a good approach is to combine newer developments in the ICT and e-business area.

1.3 The INAF case

With the idea of dissemination and outreach of astrophysics, its projects, and its heritage, we propose a method to design and implement new methods for doing research and projects. Most of the experiences done in the past by our institute related to this field (Pastore et al., 2008), took advantage of new technologies to disseminate information, but in our opinion were lacking in terms of marketing and in a return on investment. Focusing on the threads related to an e-business approach, the new trend in ICT technologies for wireless or contactless communication protocols, mobile devices and mobile apps (Anthes, 2011), we propose a model for a typical scientific product to be used in a ubiquitous environment and seen from a sales perspective.

We consider our institute business-like with products and services to be provided in a target market with a certain degree of concurrency and thus with the need to customize and propose a brand. We approach scientific products as a way to gain visibility for our Institute, its activities and its heritage. From this point of view, a business and a research institute even if they have different aims or goals could converge on some common objectives, and using methodologies, tools or processes that traditionally belong to the e-business world in the research institute environment could contribute to enhancing the visibility of an institution and provide an opportunity for growth. The newer products that we are going to plan should take advantage of different tools, facilities and methods seen from a technological point of view but in the optics of a business perspective in order to promote this science, its outputs and its outcomes. We are starting from the assumption that our institute is an organization that needs to promote its image as means of the scientific culture and astrophysical science. In this optics, we apply a business plan approach to the activities related to promoting sciences followed by specific market analysis and with the added value of using the Internet and the web as a platform and as tools to make this work. Analyzing the trend, we focus on a product developed for communication purposes that should be the way by which we promote our Institute such as:

- It is executed in the different categories of mobile devices regarding hardware or software capabilities;
- It takes advantages of different wireless and contactless communication protocols that are added on to mobile devices;
- It uses a web marketing approach for advertising;
- It is subject to a business plan analysis in order to test the need for investment and the capacity to become a successful product.

The mobile environment is taken as the platform due to its spread and fast diffusion thanks to the advance of devices regarding compute and storage capabilities with the richness of software. However the web platform remains the main way to distribute and execute software due the advances in communication technologies and the availability of bandwidth. The following paragraphs give an idea of this approach, which is relatively new for our institute. An example is the realization of a framework, as shown in Fig. 1, to provide the vast amount of information related to astrophysics with the activities at the different institutes' sites in terms of software executed on mobile devices.

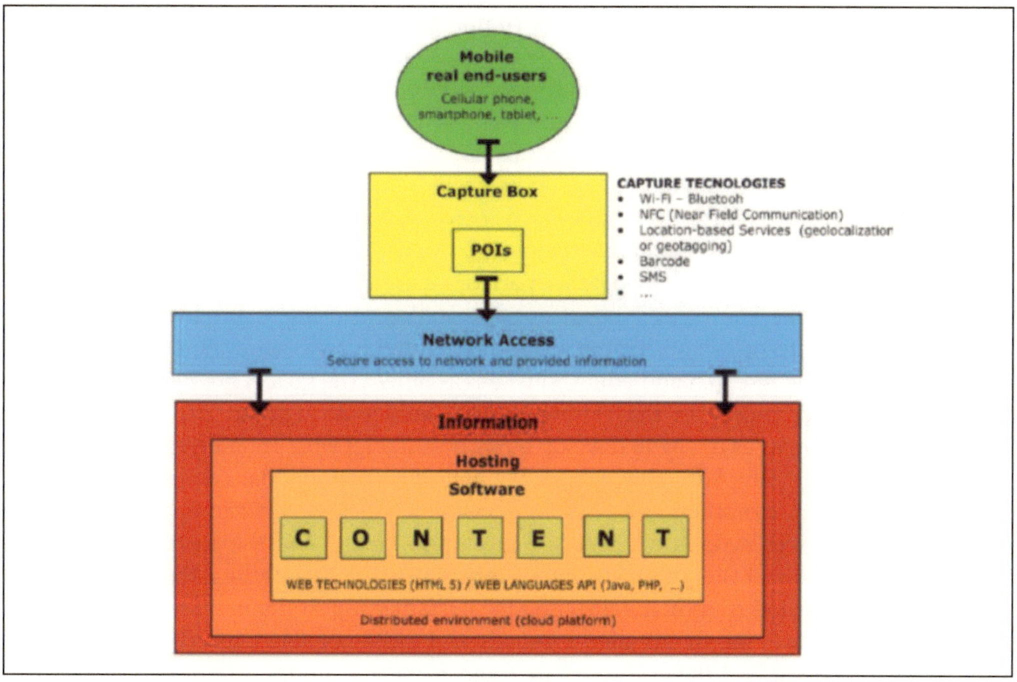

Fig. 1. Example of the e-product prototype framework.

Users with mobile devices are captured by using different communication technologies and could convey different kinds of information via a network application hosted on distributed platforms. Specifically, the information module will propose well-structured content (content module) in terms of web applications, tools or services using standard web technologies or languages (software module); these are hosted in a distributed environment (hosting module). This example could be applied even in a business context since platforms, applications and languages are the same regardless of the environment in which they are applied. The focus is on users and the satisfaction of their needs as a means for obtaining information regardless of the features of the users' devices. Among the techniques used to capture users, the use of a barcode is relatively new in such an environment. Extended two-dimensional barcodes, called 2D barcodes, act as tagging systems (Leder et al., 2010) and a marketing tool in a business environment. The 2D codes can store more complex information (alphanumeric characters, binary, URLs, SMS, e-mail, etc.) as an identification number to track a specific product. The approach, whose implementation is described later, could be easily implemented and allows many people to be reached. The main characteristic is the facility of realization and reading thanks to the standardization of the codes and the presence of free software able to produce and read such codes. This method successfully and in a relatively economic way disseminates content in order to promote an institution and to give visibility to its activities.

2. Where e-business and research/educational institutes converge

The business model describes how a company functions, how it provides a product or services and revenue and indicates how the business will create and adapt to markets and technologies. The business model has four components: the e-business concept, the value proposition, sources of revenue and business activities, resources and capabilities. A business model could describe how an organizations is funded on hierarchical principle and, interacts with other actors in a competitive market in order to produce an economic value. Adopting digital platforms allows a business to reduce costs (administrative and controls, internal management, etc.). It is the method of doing business by which a company can sustain itself, that is, generate revenue. Business models have been defined, categorized and implemented in many different ways (brokerage, advertising, community, etc.). Moreover, an organization may combine several different models as part of its overall Internet business strategy. A research institute, like any other e-business organization, exchanges products and services with other institutions or organizations, groups and individuals even if the mission diverges and in the case of the research and educational environment the goal is not making profit. An interesting reference model in the literature (Osterwalder & Pigneur, 2010) proposes the Business Model Canvas as a way to develop a business model with building blocks to be used as the model design template. This model distinguishes the four main areas of a business: infrastructure, offer, customers and financial viability. The infrastructure aspect helps to highlight key activities necessary to execute a business model and the resources needed to create value for customers and to define the pattern network. With offering, the area is defined as products and services and their value, and the customer aspect defines customer segments as the target audience, the distribution channels and customer relationships. Finally, in the finances definition we find the cost structure (outcomes) and the revenue streams (incomes). The applications of these nine basic building blocks to both organizations show the logic how a company and a research institute intends to have successful results. It should result in a strategy to be implemented through structures, processes and systems. However, all these areas have in some way interactions with the improvement of ICT and in specifically with newer Internet technologies to support activities' implementation. In this perspective, distributed platforms that need to support applications and services by guaranteeing some of the important features such as availability, fault tolerance, applications and services needed could be considered a further convergent point between the two organizations. Distributed architectures evolved from grid to cloud computing (Myerson, 2009) that makes on-demand resource provisioning a reality.

Moreover, when talking about applications, we refer to web applications for a decreased developing time and maintenance and for the usability and spread of the applications. Web applications are executed through a browser, a tool that is present in every device. Web apps are more successful than normal applications because the former are more user-friendly and thus are candidates to be successful products. With the newer specifications about web languages, the constraints related to always on connectivity are released due to

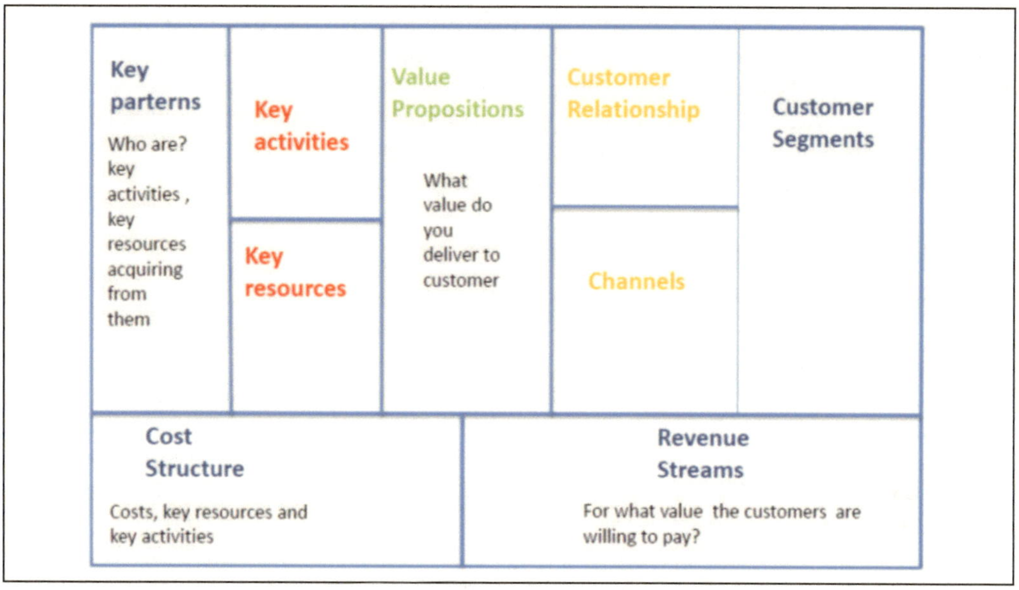

Fig. 2. Main building blocks of a business model according the business model canvas.

the capacity of offline web applications. Web languages (Cederholm, 2009) show new markup languages and different ways of using scripting languages to enhance user interaction and experience. Bringing a business to the web provides many benefits by offering personalized service, high-quality customer service and improved supply chain management. Moreover, operating on the web, requires specific technologies to build and run the service/product. Finally, the capabilities of web 2.0 such as collective intelligence, network effects, user generated content and self-improving systems that have a great impact on networking in terms of wireless communication protocols should be considered.

Focusing on a product as a core business that needs to be provided to heterogeneous stakeholders, there are platforms where single products made of applications or services are deployed to be hosted and/or distributed and languages used to develop the products. E-products are strictly related to hardware devices where the products are executed and/or provided and in this optics standards are the main requirement to provide important features for a successful product: usability, accessibility, interoperability and internationalization.

2.1 Points of convergence

We have highlighted two practical cases in the convergence of the methods and techniques of e-business and research organizations approaches. Both aim to gain results in terms of visibility or the successful of a product by using the Internet architecture and web platform. Many activities are made through web applications specifically developed for use in a collaboration mode and executed in specific frameworks according to the requirements of the distributed environment. We refer to the introduction of social media as a way to apply a web advertising model and the use of tagging technologies, even if with different aspects, to both organizations. Web advertising or web marketing is a method that offers content mixed with advertising messages different from banner ads. This tool takes advantage of technology to enhance the promotion of a specific product, service or the organization itself. There is a shift towards a new form known as contextual advertising/behavioural marketing and content-targeted advertising: the concept is to focus on the actual behaviour of potential customers that is going toward the use of mobile devices, mobile Internet and specific web applications to create a community model based on user loyalty.

2.2 Exploitations of social media platform

Social media technologies facilitate broad participation and enlarge the stakeholders of an organization. These technologies are seen as a means for economic revitalization through business innovation; however, they are not markets or hierarchies, but ecosystems: the reference business models are not limited to traditional economical exchanges, but require complex transactions. Their members are not only clients, but also stakeholders and thus have some interest in the organizations. The technologies could have different functions such as a reduction in design or production or marketing costs of products and services. Social networks from Facebook to Foursquare are not only seen as entertainment or free-time activities but have also become important tools in citizens everyday lives. This aspect of diffusion brings attention to the method of making money with these tools or at least taking advantage of the potential customers that the tools can reach. Each type of social network according to its spread, use or potentiality in different country could help to reach specific goals related to user attractions, needs and expectation. Specifically, each platform could give an added value in terms of helping customer communication, brand exposure, site traffic boost and search engine customization (SEO). As Table 1 shows, each platform could provide different marketing outcomes. Facebook is an excellent tool for customer communication by creating a central hub that companies can use to drive interactions even if the best tool remains Twitter.

Social media	SEO	Customer communication	Brand exposure	Boost site traffic
Facebook		X (excellent)	X	Little effect
Twitter		X (best)		
Flickr	X (great)			
Linkedin	X		X (very useful)	
YouTube				
Digg				X

Table 1. Social media and expected results.

Studies (O'Dell, 2011) have provided charts showing which social networks are best for organizations, CRM and marketing goals. Facebook and Twitter refer users to the content, and Flickr and YouTube allow to enhanced SEO.

2.3 Contactless and other technologies' communication protocol

With the widespread use of mobile devices, wireless-like communication technologies able to transfer few data are becoming more and more important as a business strategy.

Reaching customers through their own devices can guarantee direct and fast contact. Among the technologies, we distinguish the ancestor technology that is the barcode, evolved in 2D (bi-dimensional) code and short and medium wireless technologies ranging from Radio Frequency Identification (RFID) to Near Field Communication (NFC) and Wi-Fi. All these technologies contribute to providing ubiquitous and mobile information. RFID has been successfully used in the supply chain (Meyerson, 2006), 2D code technologies were developed in the marketing area since the ease of implementation and contactless technologies such as NFC are gaining importance as related to micro-payments made through mobile devices allowing evolution of the e-commerce topic (Reynolds, 2011). As an approach to test a marketing tool in a research environment, we implemented 2D barcodes as a way to disseminate information about our institute and its sites.

2.3.1 The INAF use case of 2D code

Two-dimensional codes, which show different standard implementations, are the square usually black-and-white images present in stores, magazines, and journals as a way to store an URL through which a business can promote itself or its products. However, the information coded in the matrix even if limited could be different and of various formats. 2D code technology helps to store information as squared images since the data are saved in both directions, forming a matrix rather then staked bars. Coded with software mostly available freely online (generators) and, normally printed in some support, a 2D code is read with specific client software by every device equipped with a camera. Born as ancillary technologies, now with the spread of mobile devices, 2D codes have begun to have an impact as the kind of functionality that commercial customers are starting to ask of mobile developers. Consumers owning a mobile device equipped with a camera and software reading such codes can scan the image and usually obtain information that could be easily remembered since the consumers could save it on their own devices.

Among the different standards developed, the QR (quick response) code specification allows up to about 4000 alphanumeric characters together with several other data types to be encoded in the matrix barcode (Denso Wave, 2009).

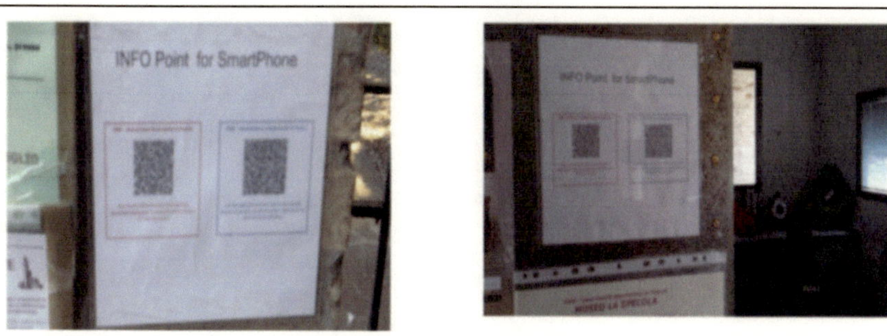

Fig. 3. QR codes experiment outside our institute buildings.

In our experiment, as Fig. 3 shows, we tested this technology by printing QR codes that we posted outside the main entrances of our institute buildings. QR codes have been easily implemented by using online software such as QR-code generators and are read by freely available client software, i-nigma for example. This is certainly a good method to exploit the potential of such technology and to contribute to creating curiosity about an organization, enhancing a visibility approach. Two-dimensional code give the first impact and information about an organization without the need to connect to the Internet and with the opportunity to store some information about the location directly on users' devices. Unfortunately, this technology does not have broader knowledge and needs to be promoted.

3. Software architecture and platforms: grid paradigms vs. Cloud paradigms

Regarding key resources needed for an e-business, software infrastructure plays a big role. Virtually all large computer-based systems are now distributed systems. Information processing, storing and publishing are distributed over several computers and systems rather than confined to single machines even if in a cluster structure. Distributed software engineering is therefore very important for an enterprise computing system. All systems share resources, openness, concurrency, scalability and fault-tolerance. The disadvantages are complexity, security, manageability and unpredictability. Distributed computing architectures and platforms have evolved recently from a cluster, to a grid and cloud system (Keahey et al., 2009) due to the increased requests made of computer resources in a broader meaning, not only in terms of computing and storage resources, but also any kind of service. Enhanced distributed platforms such as cloud and web standards play an important role since they are the main technologies that seem to provide a value-added and a medium-term life under guarantee. Moreover, they are necessary infrastructure needed by each organization. Table 2 reports a comparison of the three main architectures by considering the main features.

Category	Cluster	Grid	Cloud
Size	Small	Great	Small→great
Initial cost	Very high	High	Low
Resources type	Homogen ous	Heterogen eous	heterogeneou s
Typical ROI	Very High	Medium	High
Hardware	Very expensive	Expensive	VM use upon hardware
Network type	Private /Proprietar y	Private based on Ethernet	Public Internet on Ethernet
Security requirement	Low→ High	High	High
SUMMARY	Supercom puter	workstatio n	Groups of VM

Table 2. Differences in distributed paradigms.

Each platform has a specific action context that should be carefully analyzed in order to choose the best solution by making trade-off between costs and benefits.

3.1 The grid paradigm experience

The first experience of a distributed paradigm extending clustering computing in some way is the grid paradigm born with the idea of sharing distributed computing resources between trusted organizations called Virtual Organizations (VOs). The sharing is however regulated by a specific security model based on the Public Key Infrastructure (PKI), and thus, resources are released only to authenticated users in a trusted environment. The INAF, similar to most Italian research institutes, experimented on grid platforms (Pastore, 2004) thanks to European grid projects that were initially born as a platform for the Large Hydron Collider (LHC) project at CERN that has now become the European grid infrastructure (now known as EGI) grouping national grid projects and acting as underlying infrastructure for many scientific applications. However, different experiences in using this paradigm have demonstrated that an extension toward web applications and web services shared in a grid environment is complicated at least in the European infrastructure using gLite as the software framework (Pastore, 2008).

Moreover, the security infrastructure that guarantees the distribution of resources, could act as a limit in an environment such as the web. The main application seems to be in grouping computing and storage resources to be distributed among VO' users. Web applications that are executed through web servers seem to be better hosted in cluster environments, since they represent a closed structure, reliable and robust, but have some problems of scalability. In this optic, the application of the cloud paradigm, which declares the release of resources on demand, could be a solution that fits with services and applications with different traffic peaks. The main issues underlying such technologies are, for example, threshold policy, interoperability issues, hidden costs and unexpected behaviour that even if necessitating the adoption of such infrastructures have a great impact on cost structure in terms of the building blocks of the model. In the European grid, a difficult specific use case could be linked to the experimental characteristic of the European grid infrastructure that has shown the unexpected behavior of an application launched in the environment.

The vision that grid computing has and in part has realized in Europe, for example, with the EGEE infrastructure, even if started to solve the data management and the computing needs related to the LHC project that is devoted to a specific science project has been and actually is used for many applications in different science fields. Different researchers in different countries have been able to use shared resources and advantages from all the benefits that this infrastructure has brought. Choosing this platform compared to commercial grid solutions was inevitable in research institutes that in many cases embraces the open-source or the community philosophy. However, the EGI.eu objectives aim at providing a convergence between different paradigms and enhanced middleware software able to provide each type of resources' demanded.

3.2 The promises of the cloud paradigm

Some limitations and constraints of the grid paradigm have led to an extension of this vision in order to provide every kind of resource even if in a broader meaning (from computing resources to entire virtual machines). Cloud computing is the latest effort at delivering resources as a service. According the US National Institute of Standards and technologies (NIST), cloud computing is "a model for enabling convenient, on demand network access to a shared pool of configurable computing resources (e.g., networks, servers, storage, applications and services) that can be rapidly provisioned and released with minimal management effort on service provider interaction. "

Cloud represents a shift away from computing as a product that is owned to computing as a service that is delivered over the Internet from large-scale data centers or clouds. However, at present much ambiguity and uncertainty exist regarding the realization of these promised benefits, as there is currently much hype. Clouds (Linthicum, 2009) are categorized in term of type, distinguishing private, public, hybrid and community clouds and by the type of service offered. The first distinction is in terms of SaaS (Software as a Service) or AaaS (application as a service), PaaS (Platform as a Service) and IaaS (infrastructure as a Service). Next to the main three patterns, others, as Fig. 4 shows, are now considered a cloud category such as Storage as a Service (or disk space on demand that is related to the concept of grid computing), DaaS (database as a Service), or Information as a Service meaning the ability to consume any type of content available through a well-defined interface, and other models.

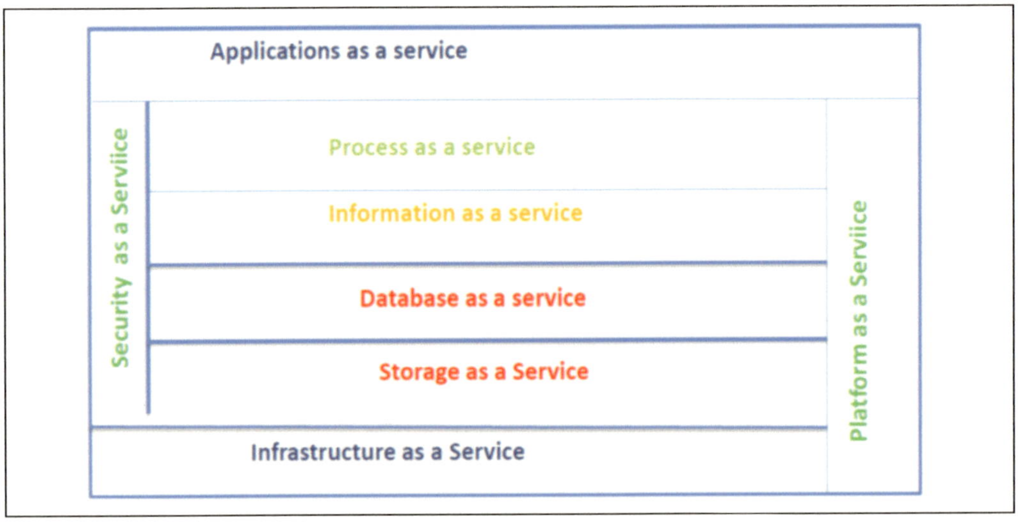

Fig. 4. Categories of cloud computing and environment representation.

Each implementation implies a complex software architecture essentially taking advantage of virtualization technologies based on the Service oriented Architecture (SOA). A SOA (Erl, 2008) is a technology framework that allows interconnected systems to expose and access services and information bound to those services. Such services could then be orchestrated to realize composite applications thanks to the addition of abstraction layers. This concept, which was referred to as inside an organization even if geographically distributed, is extended with a cloud, which means taking the SOA outside an enterprise. The diffusion of this technology in recent years has been an important factor in the evolution of the distributed paradigm allowing the sharing of a complex resource such an entire operating system and all the layered software that is executed over the system.

The cloud model comprises the following characteristics: on-demand provision of computing capabilities given as needed without requiring human interaction; ubiquitous network access by heterogeneous client platforms; location-independent and elastically resource pooling that is dynamically assigned and provisioned to scale up or scale down (Marshall, 2009).

The cost-based aspect, which is a pay-per-use view, allows the following consideration: capabilities are charged using billing models based, for example, on storage, bandwidth or computing resources consumed. Because adhering to open philosophy solutions should be taken by open source offerings, but academic and open source implementation is limited, and efforts related to its adoption should be carefully evaluated with the real cost of a commercial solution.

Both commercial and open source solutions follow cloud categorization. An example of a PaaS cloud is the Microsoft and Google solution that offer the entire platform (Microsoft Azure vs. Google Apps Engine) to develop and deploy web applications. IaaS solutions are those provided by a main commercial brand such as Amazon, VMware, Oracle and so on. The academic solutions Nimbus developed by researchers at the University of Chicago and Open Nebula designed by researchers at Madrid University aim at transforming a cluster in an IaaS and a data center in a cloud infrastructure that could adapt dynamically to the load request, respectively. These products seem to be oriented in sharing standard resources (storage and computer), but this concept should be inevitably expanded since applications are ported in a web environment. In this perspective development framework, different according the programming language used for the applications (i.e., PHP, Python, .NET framework, and so on) should be provided together with entire virtual machines hosting the software stack necessary for computer execution. Among the platforms providing this broader resource in the open-source field seem to emerge Eucalyptus and Xen Cloud Platform.

Eucalyptus is commercial, open-source software that implements a cloud framework based on different open-source virtualization techniques such as Xen and KVM. The open-source version allows private and public clouds to be created, and in this last field, a community cloud has been created in order to support the distributed cloud and spread the adoption of this framework. Moreover, this software is also used in the Ubuntu project as the cloud platform, and since this Linux distribution has been widely diffused, this software probably will be successfully adopted. On the other hand, Xen with VMware approssimally dividing the virtualization market has integrated its software with XCP, a complete infrastructure (Fig. 5) that realizes an IaaS.

Fig. 5. Details of the Xen Cloud Platform (provided by xen.org).

Due to the offers and the problem that surround cloud computing related to security and network demand, for example, there is some confusion about what different solutions offer regarding needs. Cloud is strictly related to a commercial brand that at this moment provides the effective implementations, and analysis of the costs-benefits should be done before choosing a solution. Specifically considering the availability of budget and workforce in many cases in a research environment, adopting the Google or Amazon platform seems to match the needs. From this point of view, the two organizations as regards in terms of choosing IT platforms seem to converge since e-business is going to the cloud to reduce the costs related to a hardware and software infrastructure management.

4. Web applications and services development: Standards and languages for making good products

The convergence present for software infrastructure remains in the category of applications used in both organizations. Due to the web platform, we are considering web applications (Desoza, 2011). A web application (or web app) is an application that runs on web platforms usually designed with web standards. Web standards describe the actual specifications of how a language or technology works on the web. They are specified by an industry standards body such as the World Wide Web Consortium (or W3C) that refers to techniques of applying the language or technology taken in most cases as best practices. Usually standards included in this definition refer to the model of application development that divides the content structure and semantics usually designed with the HTML markup language from its presentation realized through the style sheet languages (or CSS) and behavior implemented with a web programming language as Fig. 6 describes.

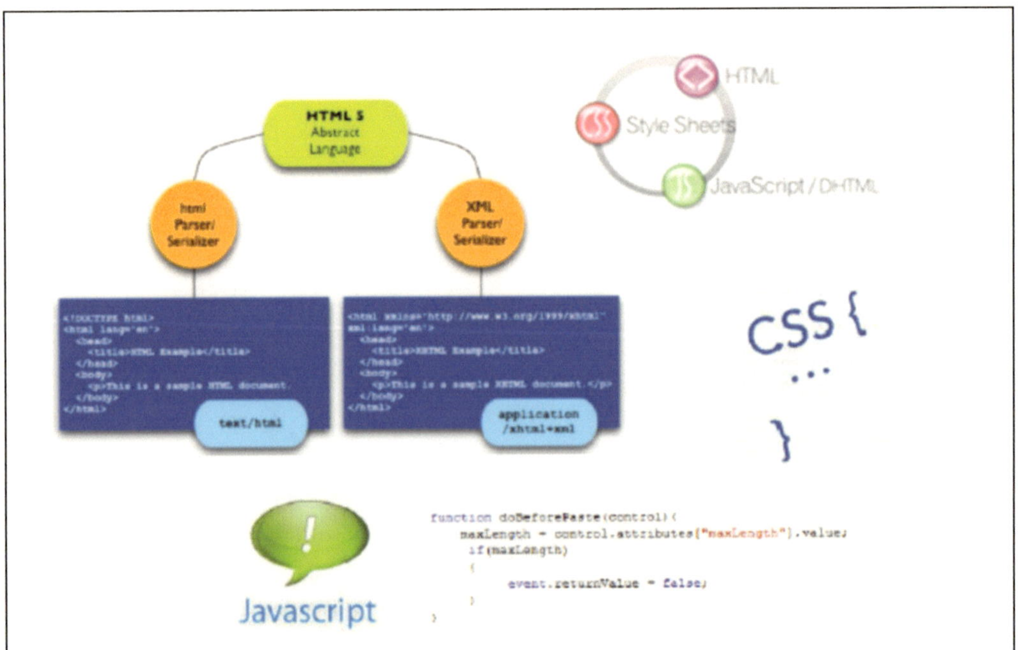

Fig. 6. Web apps standard languages.

A primary distinction about server-side and client-side programming language that characterizes the way the application is executed (on the server or on the browser) has always distinguished the different web applications. Many applications rely on a PHP platform even if in recent years languages such as Python, Ruby, etc. have taken the lead. Since every web application is executed through a web browser and there are a plethora of existent web client (i.e., Firefox, Internet Explorer, Safari, Opera, Chrome, etc.) besides the different versions found on mobile devices, each client software has different capabilities in executing and rendering an application. The main aspect is using languages that tend to be standard to support interoperability, which is becoming the main issue. However, standards help to create applications that allow other important goals such as accessibility, usability and multilingual to be reached. Two main visions when developing for applications are: one web ensuring that working within the architecture of the web and user intentions, meaning the difference in needs between users of desktop and mobile devices. Such objectives should be reached regardless of the type of organization considered. The solution is using markup and programming languages that comply with the standards.

4.1 The role of open web standards

With the advent of dynamic web and rich web applications (Preciado, 2005) introducing interactivity and multimedia features, languages for the web have proliferated requiring client browsers to have so-called external plug-ins to execute the website or application. Famous ones are Adobe Flash and Apple QuickTime, which are available freely but relate to commercial software to create such applications. This could generate an issue in execution on all browsers. The lack of interoperability is solved by trying to develop applications that follow standards, but the evolution of languages toward integrating of multimedia was slow compared to users' requests. This has contributed to the proliferation of Flash-based applications. Among the different versions of the languages, now we are approaching the HTML 5 specification, which combines the different efforts of the W3C and the Web Hypertext Application technology (WHATWG) Working group associations to create a language that could offer significant audio and video functionality including the advantages of the Document Object Model (DOM), ECMAScript language, the standard version of the Javascript client programming languages that evolved to include server-like requests. A web application developed with open standards makes effective use of an ecosystem of markup languages composed, as Fig. 7 shows, of different markup languages based on XML (such as SVG), style sheets and specific libraries (i.e., jQuery) allowing applications with different features to be developed.

This overcomes the need to develop different applications for different target devices, or operating systems. The new features of the HTML5 specification are that these applications can be packaged as standalone pieces of software, can run online or offline and include natively audio, video and graphics contexts. Equally, a web app can simply be a part of a website as an interactive functional web page where much of the processing is done on the client side using cross-platform standard web Application Programmig Interfaces (APIs) to access device features as necessary. Web applications are in some ways the opposite of so-called native applications that are applications that can also be downloaded through a website. Usually, applications are software designed to run directly on a specific platform and sometimes to work in vendor-specific environments, and thus with direct access to the

Fig. 7. HTML 5 and standard specifications ecosystem.

features of the underlying system. Open web applications indeed become installable websites that being built using standard web technologies with additional metadata that allow the user agent to discover, install, launch and grant additional privileges. Access to hardware features is made with APIs. Moreover, a web app can be downloaded as a standalone piece of software known as widget. A widget is standardized and operates entirely separately from any browser in a way like a native application. The most readily available widget engine is Opera. In this way, web standard technologies are opening the way for web-based applications including widgets with a target both the desktop and the mobile environment as targets.

4.2 Mobile web apps

An important field of work is the mobile environment, due the diffusion of such devices with increasing capabilities. Web applications developed specifically for mobile devices (Mahamoud et al., 2010) are transforming the software world with implications for the methods for developing, marketing and distributing software. The example of the mobile apps store is emblematic. As web apps, they are developed with reduced development cycles and distributed directly on the web without the need for installation, or, distribution and thus the need for a traditional marketing approach. Related to the different kinds of mobile devices, there are the Apple Store, the Google Android market, the OVI store and so on. The backdraw is that developing on mobile devices is a difficult due to the different types and features of mobile devices. There are many differences in hardware and software features, outlining the differences between old and newer devices. There are many variables to consider in such an environment that is rapidly changing and is fragmentary: diverse hardware and software, thin or fat client, carrier network or wireless, intermittent connectivity. There are so many challenges in supporting multiple devices on multiple networks for a highly variable business environment. There are many device platform choices, but looking at operating systems with enterprise capabilities, the only candidates are Apple iOS and Google's Android. However, limiting to one or two platforms is not the right solution even if it depends on the application given and specific market trends. Developing different applications according to different types of hardware is an expensive solution. A possible solution is the HTML5 browser delivery application for most products and native installed applications with a wrapper such as PhoneGap, but depends on the devices targeted and use cases (Stark, 2010a, 2010b).

A mobile web app differs from a mobile version of a website because the app is tailor-made for the mobile platform. The User Interface is generally more customized and includes more mobile device-centric user interfaces. And they differ from native apps for mobile devices since web apps make browsing a pleasurable experience but suffer from performance concerns. The choice of standards for developing mobile web applications could successfully reduce the time and cost of development aiming at reaching all kind of users. In addition, e-business and research institutes should look at enhancing their number of customers as a means to reach customer satisfaction in diversified market.

5. Ideas for future research

Future research should focus ton a research institute's aim to promote research and project outcomes as a core business and thus must follow the normal phases of selling a product with the added-value of ICT technologies, and distributed platforms, web applications and the wireless communication protocol. In this context, the research has to focus on the specific aspect related to market strategies and customer relationships. The market context is an important topic for e-business, but studies considering the typology of the market and the potential customers for different organizations such as research institutes could contribute to the vision of promoting, disseminating and transferring scientific and technological activities to the public and companies in order to realize a technological transfer. Identifying a market allows customers to be defined as in the perspective of a non-profit organization and a strategy for customer relationships, focusing on customer segments as the heart of the organization, grouping into distinct segments with common behaviors and requirements. The ideas should start from the assumption that adopting a business model is necessary regardless of the type of organization since a model helps to identify the key point of the business's activities and the resources needed. Especially for a business on the web, the points of convergence could push researchers into working on the same objective. Moreover, a research institute needs to model its organization on e-business optics to diversify the institute' activities in the perspective to reach the best result that also funds for the work of the employers.

6. Conclusion and further development

Research institutes and e-businesses even if they have different missions have some convergence points that make it possible to apply the same business model. We proposed a methodology that looks at the e-business environment, techniques and activities devoted to reach a specific value that could also be applied also in a not-profit organization and thus does not always see the economic aspect. The practical effect of our project in such an aim is the application to a marketing strategy, for example, using social media or tagging technologies to our products that are the results of researchers and projects. Working on products and services while taking into account the e-business perspective could contribute to an enhancement of the provided products and more attention to reach all kinds of potential users. In this perspective, great importance is placed on technologies and applications that play an essential role because the advances in ICT are dynamic and continue at an ever increasing rate. Further development will be the practical applications of such ideas in the context of disseminating information about the institute and its work as they are were a brand to promote, and real products to sell, highlighting the customer segments, enhancing the relationships and putting a value generator as the center of the work.

7. References

Chesbrough, H. (2007). Business model innovation: it's not just about technology anymore. Strategy and Leadership, Vol. 35 no. 6, 2007, pp.12-17. Emerald Group Publishing Limited, ISSN 1087-8572.

Smith, D.M. (2001). The E-Business Book: A Step-byStep Guide to E-Commerce and Beyond. ISBN 978-157-6600-90-0, Bloomerang Press, U.S.A.

Greenberg, P. (2009). CRM at the Speed of Light, Fourth Edition: Social CRM 2.0 Strategies, Tools and Techniques for Engaging your Customers. ISBN 978-007-1590-45-7. McGraw-Hill Osborne Media.

Hugos, M. H. (2011). Essentials of Supply Chain Management. 3rd edition. ISBN 978-047-0942-18-5. Wiley

Dutta, S., Mia, I. (2009). The Global Information Technology Report 2008-2009, Mobility in a Networked World. World Economic Forum, URL: https://members.weforum.org/pdf/gitr/2009/gitr09fullreport.pdf

Spencer, D. (2010). A Practical Guide to Information Architecture. Five Simple Steps LPP. ISBN: 978-0-9561740-6-2

Schewick van, B. (2010). Internet Architecture and Innovation. The MIT Press, New edition June 2010. ISBN 978-0-262-01397-0

Boccato, C., Benacchio, L., Nobili, L., Pastore S. (2005). "Cath the Stars in the Net!? Eight years of experiences in communicating astronomy via new technologies" Proceedings of In "Communicating Astronomy with the Public 2005": Proceedings from the ESO/ESA/IAU Conference ESO HQ, Garching, Munich, Germany , June 2005, eds. I. Robson & L.L. Christensed, pp. 242-250, ESA/Hubble.

Pastore, S., Benacchio, L., Boccato, C., Lazzaretto, E., Nobili, L. (2005). "The Learning from Starlight" project: experiencing mobile technologies to improve education and outreach of Astrophysics", Recent Research Developments in Learning technologies, Vol. 3, 2005, FORMATEX, Badojoz, Spain pp. 1138-1143.

Oreilly, T. (2007). What is Web 2.0: Design Patterns and Business Models for the Next Generation of Software. Communications & Strategies, No. 1, p. 17, First Quarter 2007. Available at SSRN: http://ssrn.com/abstract=1008839

Cox, B. (2003). Internet Marketing (NetEffect Series). Prentice Hall, 1 edition 2003. ISBN 978-010336286

Pastore, S., Boccato, C., Galliani, M., Nobili, L., Lazzaretto, E. (2008). "Implementations of the Web 2.0 Phenomenon and Its Technologies for Science Outreach and Communication in the Research Network". Proceedings of 3rd Int. Conference on Internet and Web Applications and Services, 2008. ICIW '08 (8-13 June 2008), IEEE Computer Society, pp. 547 - 551

Anthes, G. (2011). Invasion of the Mobile Apps. *Communication of the ACM,* Vol.54, No.9, (September 2011), pp. 16-18, DOI:10.1145/1995376.1995383

Leder K, Macdonald J. and Chris Speed (2010) Tagging technology: is future bright, A public workshop. ISBN 978-1-90443-43-8

Osterwalder, A. and Pigneur, Y. (2010). Business Model Generation. Self Published. ISBN 978-2-8399-0580-0

Myerson, J. (2009) Cloud computing versus grid computing. Service types, similarities and differences, and things to consider.IBM developerWorks technical library. IBM comporation 2009.

Cederholm, D. (2009). Web Standards Solutions, Second Edition. Apress. ISBN 978-1-4302-1920-0

O'Dell J. (2011). Which social sites are best for which marketing outcomes? Mashable business. Mashable.com. Retrieved 20 September 2011.

Meyerson, J.M. (2006). RFID in the Supply Chain: A Guide to Selection and Implementation (Resource Management) Auerbach Publications; 1 edition (November 20, 2006), ISBN-13: 978-0849330186

Reynolds, J. (2004). The complete e-commerce book, 2nd edition: design, build and maintain a successfull web-based business. CMP 2004. ISBN: 978-1578203123

Denso Wave, (2009). QR Code Standardization. QR Code.com. Denso-wave.com. Retrieved 23 April 2009.

Keahey, K., Tsugawa, M., Matsunugana, A., Fortes., J. (2009). Sky Computing, Internet Computing IEEE, vol. 13, no. 5, pp.43-51

Pastore, S. (2004). Using web services in a grid infrastructure: an early implementation of web services actors programming a grid application to access astronomical databases', LNCS -3270 Springer-Verlag Volumes, on "Grid Services Engineering and Management (GSEM'04)", 2004 pp.1-14

Pastore, S. (2008). The necessity of Semantic Tecnologies in Grid Discovery, *Journal of Networks (JNW),* Volume 3, Issue 4, April 2008, Academy Publisher, pp. 1-9.

Linthicum, D. S. (2009). Cloud Computing and SOA convergence in your enterprise: A step-by-step guide. Addison-Wesley Professional. ISBN: 978-0-321-65939-2

Erl, T. (2008). Service-Oriented Architecture: Concepts, Technology & Design. Prentice Hall/Pearson PTR. ISBN: 0131858580

Marshall, P., Keahey, K., Freeman, T. (2009). Elastic Site: Using Clouds to elastically Extend Site Resources.

Desoza, S. (2001). Web Application Development for Emerging Businesses. Technorati.

Preciado, J.C., Linaje, M., Sanchez, F., Comai, S. (2005). Necessity of methodologies to model Rich Internet Applications, Proceedings of the 2005 seventh IEEE International Symposium on Web Site Evolution, 2005

Mahamoud, Q.H. and Popowicz, P. (2010). Toward a framework for the discovery and acquisition of mobile applications, *Proceedings of 2010 9th International Conference on Mobile Business,* Athens, Greece, June 27-29, 2010

Stark, J. (2010a). Building iPhone Apps with HTML, CSS and Javascript. O'Reilly Media, Sebastopol, CA.

Stark, J. (2010b). Building Android Apps with HTML, CSS and Javascript. O'Reilly Media, Sebastopol, CA.

7

A Discourse on the Construction of a Service Innovation Model: Focus on the Cultural and Creative Industry Park

Rungtai Lin and Chun-Liang Chen
National Taiwan University of Art, Taiwan, R.O.C.

1. Introduction

As the growth of the service industry sector in developed economies increases, more and more researchers have turned their attention to examining recent trends in service innovation. This has included rising interest in the driving forces of innovation, models, strategies, and organizations, and has subsequently led to various well-known models on driving forces and service innovation (Gallouj and Sundbo, 1998). However, the role of the Internet and web-based services and the growth in high-technology environmental services indicate that certain types of knowledge-intensive business services (KIBS) industries are now taking a more proactive lead role in the economy (Wei, 2004). Service-dominant logic and service science are useful frameworks that emphasize a service perspective on innovation (Michel et al., 2008). Moreover, non-technological service innovation is an emerging and challenging issue in innovation studies (Gallouj, 2002). Innovation must be viewed in a broader technological context where social dimensions are also considered (Edvardsson et al., 2000; Gustafsson and Johnson, 2003).

According to UNESCO's definition, cultural industries are based on tangible or intangible cultures. These industries follow conceptual formulation, production and manufacturing processes to create commercial products or services in the market. They usually have patent or copyright protections (UNESCO, 2000), and their products often have multiple meanings and functions when examined for their cultural content, creativity, busines models, employment growth, and future potential viewpoints. The definition of cultural creative industries in Taiwan includes visual arts, music and performing arts, cultural exhibition and performance facilities, industrial craft, motion pictures, radio broadcasting and television, publishing, advertising, design, brand and fashion design, architectural design, creative living, digital gaming & entertainment, and so on. In Taiwan, cultural creative industry products are considered to be activities originating from creativity, culture, art and design. They undergo intellectual property operations with the potential to generate profit and employment opportunities. The Taiwanese culture industry consists of 16 business categories with an accumulative sales turnover of USD$ 17.2 billion in 2009, up from USD$ 14.5 billion in 2002 (MOEA, 2005). Given the immense size of Taiwan's culture industry, this article focuses specifically on cultural facilities for exhibitions and performances.

Consequently, this paper concerns itself with potential insights from theories of innovation in creative industries (Miles and Green, 2008).

"Culture" plays an important role in the design field, and "cross cultural design" will be a key design evaluation point in the future (Lin, 2007). While cross-cultural factors become important issues for product design in the global economy, the intersection of E-business and creative industries becomes a key issue making both local design and the global market worthy of further in-depth study (Osterwalder and Y. Pigneur, 2002). The globalization of the economy and innovations in technology has led to the cooperation of various small enterprises in strengthening their competitive capability and their ability to cope with rising business challenges (Chen and Jaw, 2009). Value networks are increasingly being recognized as a future business paradigm, since they are capable of linking various enterprises together (Haglind and Helander, 2003; Wu, Liu and Chen, 2009). Such value networks need to be periodically updated with service innovations, enabled by evolving technologies.

Cultural parks aim to expose visitors to the experiences of the living historical stories of a people or landscape, so that they may feel immersed within a given culture. There is never a boundary between a cultural park and the surrounding local community. Many communities exist either within or very near cultural parks, and as a result, a cultural park requires unconventional management techniques, such as deeper and more frequent communication with local residents. Cultural parks represent the cultural atmosphere chronologically inherited within a regional space. This area of space is developed in the context of a cultural environment. It connects established settlements in the context of history and space to form the concept and direction of developing a cultural park, which serves the purpose of familiarizing residents with local history and the development of local culture. Domestic research concerning cultural parks in Taiwan is conducted mostly on the reutilization of vacant space, operational management, marketing activities, formation and transformation park zoning, industry selection and assessment, and the local culture industry. Some attention is also paid to the innovative services of culture parks (Chiu and Chu, 2010).

The aim of this paper is to contribute to service innovation research with special attention to non-technological dimensions. We believe that this area—the "soft side" of service innovation—is largely neglected despite its enormous importance. The term "soft" is used to stress innovation that is specifically related to people and organizations, markets and relationships, knowledge and integration, and meanings and experiences (Roberta & Marco, 2010). These are established and emerging dimensions that our research indicates as crucial in building a sustainable competitive advantage. To this end, we identify the dimensions of service innovations that are necessary for the further development of the cultural creative industry, especially a cultural creative industry park. Therefore, this study analyzes the progress of innovation activities in such a park and explores the value transformation and value repositioning from the service science point of view. In doing so, this paper proposes a new cultural industrial service innovation model that examines service innovation at the firm level within a Taiwanese cultural creative industry park.

In addition to this conceptual framework, we also analyze the impact of information and communication technologies on service innovation activities. Thus, we attempt to fill gaps within the existing literature by answering the following questions: 1) how do information and communication technologies impact service innovations activities; 2) and what are the soft innovations in the proposed service innovation model?

2. Theoretical background

2.1 Connotation of service innovation

Service innovation can generally be divided into product innovation, process innovation, transfer innovation, market innovation, technological innovation, organizational innovation, structural innovation, specialization innovation, and so on (Yu and Lei, 2005). Among these, product innovation, process innovation and transfer innovation are based on the innovation of application technology, and they are closely related with the development of technological innovation. However, many innovations are non-technical in nature, such as organizational innovation, structural innovation, and specialization innovation. This article holds that the within the service processes of enterprises, the actual connotations of innovative services are as follows: apply new ideas and new technologies to reform and change existing service processes and products, improve existing service quality and service efficiency, create new value for customers, and ultimately form a competitive advantage for service activities. In one of the latest approaches—the "integrative" view (Gadrey and Gallouj, 1998; Gallouj, 2002)—technology is integrated with other aspects of innovation. This integrative approach represents a synthesis of prior approaches (Coombs and Miles, 2000) attempting to overcome the traditional dichotomy between manufacturing and services (Sundbo and Gallouj, 2000). As a result, innovation cannot be restricted to the adoption of new technologies, but must instead be conceived as a creative use of technology in order to interpret the market or integrate the knowledge of supply chains (Tether and Metcalfe, 2003).

2.2 Models of service innovation

As the importance of the service sector within economies has increased, so too have the number of models of service innovation. Bilderbeek and other scholars (Bilderbeek, Hrtog, Marklund, Miles, 1998) have put forward a well-known four-dimensional model of service innovation based on experiences of service innovation in Europe (Figure 1). These four dimensions—new service concept, new client interface, new service delivery system, and technological options—help offer a wider perspective on innovation within the services industry, fully describe the content of service innovation, and provide guidance on the actual development of new services. Various corporate functions link different dimensions together, and in essence the four-dimensional model serves as a framework aimed at service enterprises developing new products.

In addition, several recent theoretical and multidisciplinary developments have contributed to new perspectives on service innovation, emphasizing culture and organization (Normann, 2001; Kandampully, 2002; de Jong and Vermeulen, 2003; de Vries, 2006), experiential dimensions (Pine and Gilmore, 1999; Schmitt, 1999), customer knowledge integration in the value creation processes (Preissl, 2000; Prahalad and Ramaswamy, 2004; Zeithaml et al., 2006; Edvardsson et al., 2007; Gro¨nroos, 2007), and interrelations and networks among organizations (van der Aa and Elfring, 2002; Gummesson, 2004; Love and Mansury, 2007; Tether and Tajar, 2008). In this article, we will emphasize and integrate all of these above-mentioned dimensions.

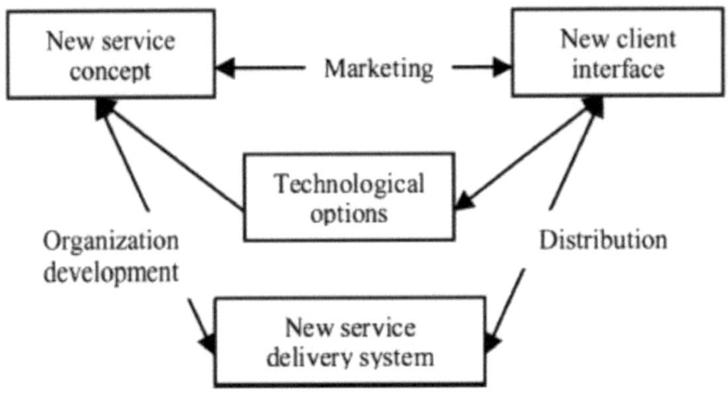

Fig. 1. The four dimensions model of the service innovation.
Figure 1: The four dimensions model of the service innovation

2.3 Cultural production system

Cultural production is the process by which cultural products (including goods, artifacts, visual and experiential objects, services, and art forms) are created, transformed, and diffused into the constitution of consumer culture (Lin, 2009; Lash and Urry, 1994/ 2002). A central premise of the cultural production process is that culture itself is constructed and negotiated by cultural actors (producers, intermediaries, consumers) through an interplay of symbolic and sensory modes of experience and the concomitant meaning systems in which the cultural actors are engaged (Venkatesh, Alladi and Laurie A. Meamber, 2006). According to the models set forth by Joy (1998, 2000), Kozinets (2001), McCracken (1988), and Solomon (1988), individuals and organizations involved in the production and diffusion of the arts and aesthetics contribute to the creation of symbolic meaning and the transfer of these meanings to cultural products.

Solomon (2003: 558–9) discusses a complementary conceptualization of the cultural production system (Figure 2). According to Solomon (2003), the set of individuals and organizations that create and market a cultural product is a cultural production system. The cultural production and distribution process entails relationships among a complex network of organizations that both facilitate and regulate the innovation process (Hirsch, 1972). A cultural industry system is comprised of all organizations engaged in the process of filtering new ideas as they flow from the creative subsystem to the managerial subsystem, communications subsystem, cultural gatekeepers, and lastly to consumers. The creative subsystem is responsible for generating new symbols or ideas. The managerial subsystem is responsible for selecting new ideas, making them tangible, mass producing these ideas, and then managing their distribution. The communications subsystem is responsible for giving meaning to the new ideas and providing them with symbolic sets of attributes that are communicated to consumers. Finally, cultural gatekeepers are responsible for filtering the overflow of information and materials intended for consumers (Solomon et al., 2002; Parsons, 1960; Solomon, 1988).

2.4 Service system

Creative industries are different from most other industries, in that their products are fundamentally intended to provoke particular kinds of responses from their users. To

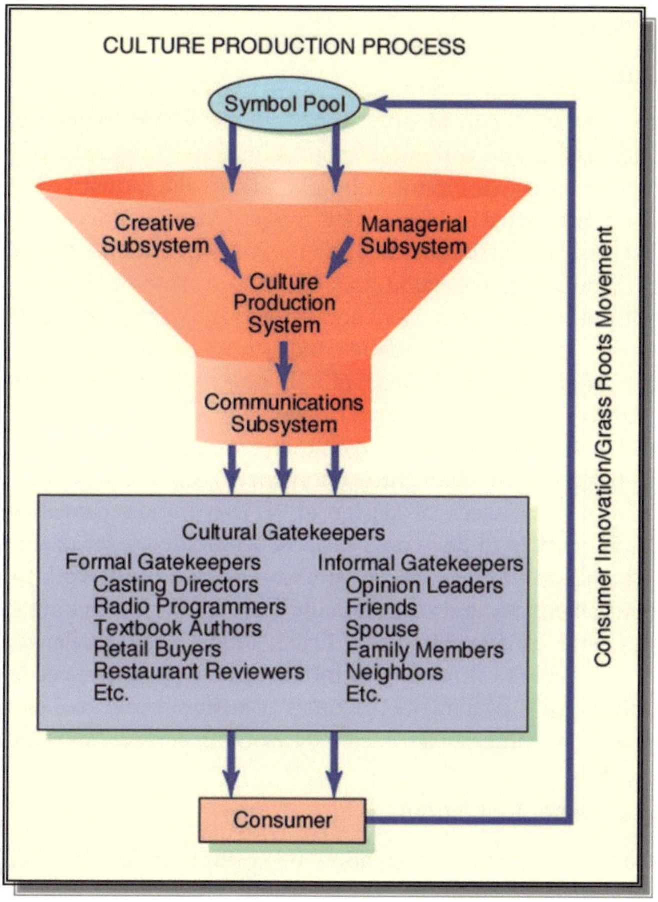

Fig. 2. The cultural production system.

varying degrees, these products enable experiences to be co-produced in tandem with consumers (Miles and Green, 2008). As a result, we seek to know how the theorization of the service system contributes to the understanding of cultural industrial park development. Service innovation is connected with changes in the service systems (Spohrer and Maglio, 2008). A service system is a value co-creation configuration (Maglio and Spohrer, 2008). It is an array of resources (including people, technology, organizations and shared information) connected to other systems by value propositions (Spohrer et al., 2007, 2008). Service systems include internal elements (e.g. employees), private systems and resources (friends and stockholders), and market systems and resources (suppliers and other economic exchanges). Suppliers and customers (together with other social and economic actors) compose "service systems," and are resource integrators on different levels. They interact through the mutual provision of services in order to co-produce (in the upstream value chain) and co-create value (downstream between the customer and the firm) in a "logic of togetherness" (Roberta & Marco, 2010). Value is co-created in service systems when resources are used. The role of the customers is not limited to consumption and merely being an operand resource as in mainstream marketing. Instead, customers are active (operant) resources in the value creation process and are always co-creators of value.

3. Model development

3.1 Data collection

The purpose of this research is to identify important constructs in service innovations, and understand the information and communication technology (ICT) roles of industrial services innovation management processes in the cultural and creative industry. Therefore, this paper evaluates research on innovative service models ranging from the more traditional technology model to modern service innovation models and the more recent integration model (Gallouj & Weinstein, 1997). Through the collection and integration of the literature related to service innovation, the cultural production system and the service system, we propose a new service innovation model for cultural and creative industries. We use in-depth interviews and secondary data analysis to assess the impact of ICTs on a cultural creative industry park at the National Taiwan University of Arts (NTUA). Two of our interviewers are industry experts who have worked for the IT professional institutions for more than 15 years and cooperated with NTUA on IT projects. The other three interviewers are teachers or experienced staff of related departments in the College of Design at NTUA. Building on these conceptual and theoretical roots, it is possible to develop a proposed framework for characterizing a service innovation model in cultural industries. To be useful, such a framework must be reasonably simple, logical, comprehensive, and operationally meaningful. In seeking generalization, the extant perspectives tend to oversimplify a firm's model. The challenge is to produce a framework that is applicable to firms in general but which serves the needs of the individual enterprise. Accordingly, the framework becomes a customizable tool that encourages the enterprise to focus on how value can be created by works of service innovation.

3.2 Constructing a conceptual model

The conceptual model of service innovation in cultural industries maps the following dimensions: new service concepts, new client interface, new service delivery system/organization, new services transformation system, and technological options. The five dimensions relate, respectively, to the knowledge of the characteristics of existing and competing services (business intelligence); the characteristics of actual and potential clients (market intelligence); the relationship with actors, co-production and the transformation of new services (management intelligence); the firm's capabilities, skills & attitudes with existing and competing service workers (human resource management); and available and supporting technological options (technological intelligence). These five dimensions are further explored below and in Figure 3.

1. New Service Concept : Some service innovations are highly visible, especially where delivery of the product is involved. However, frequently a new concept is not so much a physical product but a much more intangible characteristic like a new idea or concept on how to organize a solution to a problem. Although a particular service concept may already be familiar in other markets, the key thing is that it is novel in its application within a particular market.
2. New Client Interface : A second element of service innovations is the design of the interface between the service provider and its clients, and these interfaces are the focus of a good deal of service innovations. The communication between service suppliers and clients forms a major area for service innovation. Product offerings are increasingly

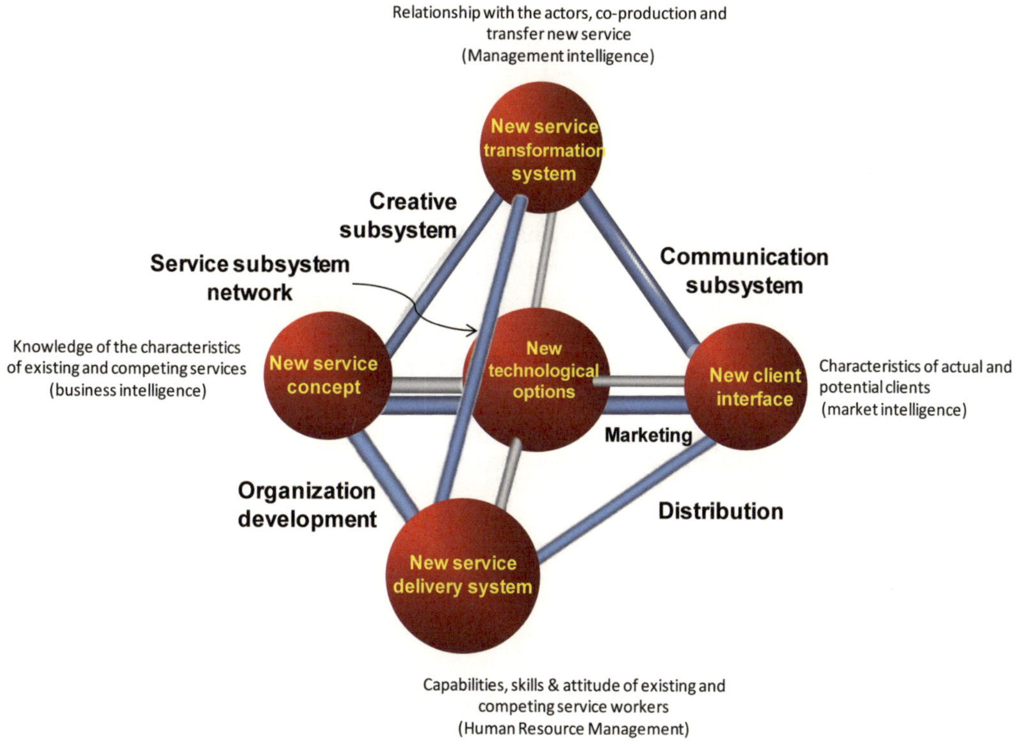

Fig. 3. The five-dimension model of service innovation.

marketed and delivered electronically as far as they have informational components. In business services in particular, clients are often part and parcel of the production of the service product. This is particularly true where the business service itself is offering support for innovation, as for example in R&D and design services.

3. New Service Delivery System/Organization：The third dimension refers to the internal organizational arrangements that must be managed to allow service workers to perform their job properly and to develop and offer innovative services. It is closely related to the question of how to empower employees to facilitate them so that they can perform their jobs and deliver service products adequately.
4. New Services Transformation System： Based on cultural production systems within cultural industries, the new services transformation system involves the ways in which cultural product producers, cultural intermediaries, and consumers of culture interact and collaborate toward the end of producing symbolic meaning. These actors operate within the domain of art and aesthetics in everyday life embedded within consumer culture. It is through service subsystem (production and consumption processes) network operations in the cultural industry that aesthetic symbols, meanings and creativity are integrated. A communication subsystem involves creating and directing marketing communications to cultural gatekeepers (such as the media, a formal gatekeeper, and opinion leaders) and foreign networks. The subsystem can finally transform these offerings into new services by co-production with the above-mentioned actors. In a creative subsystem, aesthetic symbols attached to the cultural product

operate as a code, or language, that contributes to the understanding of meaning. The meaning system includes abstract ideas, values and ethics, and material objects and services that are produced or valued by a group of people (Solomon, 2003). In the ultimate analysis this meaning system is the sum of shared meanings, rituals, norms, and traditions among people (Geertz, 1973). The goods derived from cultural industries have an aesthetic or semiotic content (Scott, 2000). They have "an influence on our understanding of the world," "drawing on and helping to constitute our inner, private lives and our public selves" (Hesmondhalgh 2007: 3).

5. Technological Options：The fifth dimension is the center of much analysis and debate, especially concerning the degree to which service firms themselves are giving shape to technology development. Clearly, service innovation is possible without technological innovation: technology is not always a dimension. In practice there is a wide range of relationships between "technology" and "service innovation," varying from technology mainly playing a role as a facilitating or enabling factor, to something much closer to supply-push, technology-driven innovation.

4. Case study and analysis

4.1 Background

The Cultural Creative Industry Park was established by NTUA in the Fu-Jhou suburb of Banciao District in New Taipei City, only ten minutes walk from the main campus. There are four craft companies that are incorporated with the Innovation and Incubation Center of NTUA. Inside are additional ceramic and metal studios, with each studio providing hands-on workshops using different craft materials. The public can physically understand and experience fascinating crafts from ceramic, glass, metal and fabric. The goal of the cultural creative industry park is to combine artistic craftsmanship and economy with service design, and ultimately establish NTUA as a distinctive trademark of the park. To accomplish the goal, the "ABCDE Plan" was initiated by NTUA. The "ABCDE Plan" refers to one of the park's slogans, referenced in Figure 4: to turn "Art" into "Business," we need "Creativity" and "Design" (Lin, 2007, 2009, 2010), which allows the creative products to be transformed into "E-business." NTUA has established this link between art and business and combined creativity and design through three divisions: Our Museum, Our Studio and Our Factory. In particular, NTUA tries to use E-business (ICTs) to integrate design, culture, artistic craftsmanship, creativity, service innovation and customer preferences at the NTUA Cultural Creative Industry Park.

4.2 The five-dimension model demonstration

Below, we present the five dimensions that we believe are helpful in describing and analyzing service innovations. This model is not statistically tested, but should be interpreted as a tool to map and characterize various service innovations.

1. New Service Concept：*Our (Art) Museum*. To implement the ABCDE plan, NTUA established an art museum in 2007, known as "Our Museum," for the purpose of linking professional teaching with the museum's research, education, and display functions. At the same time the museum presents cultural and aesthetic content about art and artifacts to the public.

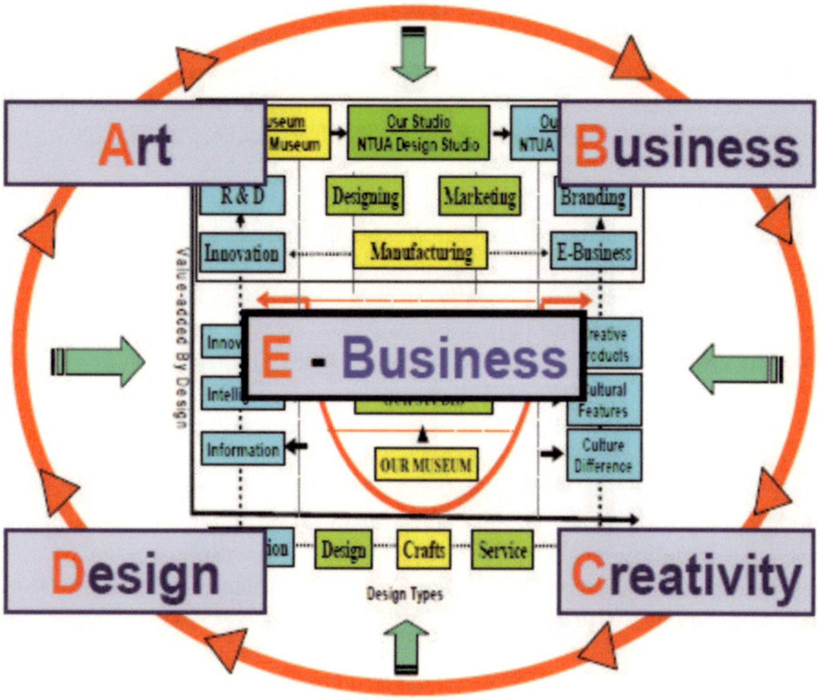

Fig. 4. The concept of the E-business model.

2. New Client Interfaces：*Our Factory*. Due to the challenging environment of cultural and creative industries, NTUA is devoted to developing its regional and international networks by operating a cultural creative industry park, known as "Our Factory." NTUA has established the link between "Art" and "Business." With this client interface, all small crafts, metal and ceramic companies can be incorporated into the Innovation and Incubation Center of NTUA.
3. New Service Delivery System/Organization：*Our (Design) Studio*. Developing craftsmanship and creativity as well as competences related to the arts are of strategic importance to NTUA. Therefore, a design studio, known as "Our Studio," was subsequently set up at the College of Design in NTUA with the purpose of providing innovative products. The college invests heavily in human resource management, including improving the capabilities and attitudes of both the students and craft workers.
4. New Services Transformation System：*Cultural production system*. Here, one example is the establishment of the NTUA Cultural Creative Industry Park with the cooperation of New Taipei City providing an innovative service through the *Holiday Cultural Bus Tour*. The *Holiday Cultural Bus Tour* is operated between NTUA main campus, the NTUA *Cultural Creative Industry Park,* and *the Lin Family Mansion and Garden*. The major purpose is to promote the cultural creative development of Banciao District, where the university is located. The tour journeys first to The Lin Family Mansion and Garden for experiencing cultural aesthetics. Then, based on the structure of *Our Museum, Our Studio* and *Our Factory* of NTUA, tour participants can appreciate the art of *Our*

Museum, experience crafts in *Our Studio*, and purchase creative products from *Our Factory*. The purpose of this customer journey is to showcase the aesthetic experience by connecting design and culture so as to synthesize humanity, creativity, cultural production creativities, and technology. In this way, it achieves the aim of service design promotion in public (Hekkert & Leder, 2008; Hekkert et. al., 2003; Helander & Tham, 2003).

5. New Technological Options : *Integrate all constructs to E-business.* Technology mainly plays a role as a facilitating or enabling factor in various innovations. Creativity and business are the elements for reaching an aesthetic economy, similar to the often-used concept of "Think Globally. Act Locally." These elements process the "Digital Archive" of Our Museum through the cultural creativities of Our Studio, producing cultural products in Our Factory in order to establish local industry-making aesthetic and economical products. The use of ICT channels could also reach a new factory, create new experiences for consumers and provide a co-production platform for designers and consumers. The majority of firms in NTUA Cultural Creative Industry Park become more effective by using technology-related techniques such as online access to art and knowledge databases, downloadable and streamed multimedia content (audio, video, podcasts), information systems (e.g. CAD, CAI, e-learning, co-design system, co-production system, and customer relationship management system), virtual museums, QR-code attachment for products, company dedicated websites, wireless connectivity enabling live feeding of information and tools, and so on. In the near future, the proposed ICT applications based on the digital archives at the NTUA Cultural Creative Industry Park will link to different dimensions, including: online exhibitions (text, image, audiovisual); virtual exhibitions (including 360-degree room views); real and imaginary exhibitions and gallery spaces; interactive gallery maps, games and play spaces for children and young people; multimedia tours; interactive kiosks; simulation and virtual reality experiences with sound, lasers and light shows; and IMAX presentations and "theme-park-like" attractions. Linking to these various dimensions will help NTUA reach new audiences and create new experiences for consumers.

To demonstrate the proposed five-dimension model, an integral example is the "cultural and creative fashion show" at the Cultural Creative Industry Park. This specific event combines aesthetics, creativity, fashion, technology, design, and commercial networks. Government officials are invited, and students, teachers, art personnel, and the cultural creative community are also involved. Students perform as the catwalk models to show their creative products, which are designed by themselves in Our Studio and supervised by professors and co-produced with Our Factory in the park. Moreover, students are able to communicate their inspiration and products to potential customers using this new style service. Through the creative stage and exhibition layout, the application of multimedia technology combined with creative products show that all participants can really feel involved in the aesthetics of art and life. As a result, the idea of turning "Art" into "Business" is realized, while the process is combined with "Creativity," "Design," and "E-business" to transform the aesthetic values into commerce by service innovation (Lin, 2007, 2009, 2010).

4.3 The roles of ICTs in service innovation

Although one of our foci is on non-technological innovation, we do not deny the importance of technology for innovation. It is important to understand the role technology plays in the different dimensions of service innovation. In our case, it plays the role of: 1) enhancing the effectiveness of a particular strategy, 2) virtually integrating and widening the boundaries of the physical environment, 3) a platform for information distribution, and 4) value co-creation within the service systems networks.

4.3.1 Enhancing the effectiveness of a particular strategy

1. Enabling the exploitation of reach and richness
   The elements linking the Cultural Creative Park that embark on the virtualization process at the operational level are quite rich. A client company could show more openness towards potential customers by new technologies, as one interviewer indicated, e.g. interactive gallery maps, dedicated sites, games and play spaces for children and young people; multimedia tours simulation and virtual reality experiences sound, laser and light shows; IMAX presentations and 'theme-park-like' attractions; etc.
2. Strategic vehicle for increased competitiveness
   The strategic interpretation of ICT as an integrated vehicle for increased competitiveness is its contextual acceptance of the two dimensions of differentiation and efficiency. The Cultural Creative Park constitutes another defining feature of the NTUA in Taiwan's cultural and creative industry. The Cultural Creative Park has dealt with ICTs in different ways, but applying technology remains a particularly incisive defining feature.

4.3.2 The virtual integration and widening of the physical environment boundaries

The virtual, as we have observed in the digital archive or on the website of *Our Museum*, neither substitutes nor opposes the physical environment. It integrates with the real and widens the park's boundaries, which then open up to the creation and reinterpretation of actual reality. As another interviewer indicated, "From the digital archives platform of Our Museum, students could visit the virtual art museum at any time, anywhere, and any device. This new service will enhance their incentives and abilities for them to create more delicate works of art." In this sense, we are witnessing concrete manifestations that stem from ICT and other technology (e.g. virtual museums; wireless connectivity enabling live feeding of information and tools; e-learning etc).

4.3.3 Platform for information distribution

1. Enabling the "dematerialization" of processes
   Our findings also draw attention more directly to the role that ICT can play in reconfiguring the supply chain structure. From our observations, we find ICT and other technologies play a central role, like a hub or platform, instead of in the industry supply chain structure. It is not just a facilitator to other drivers but also a starting point and link to other constructs for value creation. One of the interviewers stressed, "The CAD, CAI, e-learning systems in the Craft and Design Department are helpful for meeting the industrial demands of delicately designed products. This is especially because the design system can encourage industrial employees to work together with the student designers of NTUA".
2. Repository of shared information and knowledge
   In our case study, technology is not an innovative element in itself, but constitutes the driver that enables a company to activate co-design or co-production systems that

simultaneously explore and exploit knowledge from online access to art and knowledge databases. We also find development through a repository of the knowledge from the characteristics of existing and competing services, to form business intelligence at our proposed service innovation model (see Figure 4).

4.3.4 Value co-creation with the service systems networks

With the new service transformation system dimension, the customer experience could reflect much more about value integration and transformation, especially when joined with ICTs applications. Any organizations and individuals involved in the service innovation model will contribute to the creation and transfer of cultural products or a cultural journey experience. When the new service transformation is positive, it will develop a good client relationship network (e.g. CRM system), where it will integrate the whole service innovation's process. The new service transformation system can combine and transform creative ideas, technology application and consumer preferences from a global trend website or artwork and knowledge databases/virtual museum into service innovation operational reality. This is further supported by the service subsystem network, which is another important feature of our proposed service innovation model. As another interviewer said, "With all the infrastructure facilities settled, the NTUA Cultural and Creative Industry Park will have strong potential to become the most famous and unique cultural park in New Taipei City."

The relationship between the above-mentioned constructs of service innovation, the ABCDE model and the key findings (with italic type) of this paper are listed in Table 1. The new service transformation system is a combined process, and the linking of the four constructs should be exploited to improve organization development, creative sub-systems and communication sub-systems, so as to create better value for the customer. However, to ensure the success of the new services transformation system, companies need to be managed and coordinated with effective and efficient technological options. From these results, we can find the combination of technological management within an organization and human viewpoint that is responsible for increasing value co-creation, highlighting the emergence of a mostly neglected soft side of innovation. This perspective allows companies to shift their attention from innovation output to different ways to serve their market better (Vargo and Lusch, 2008).

4.4 Linking the various dimensions

The individual dimensions impact each other in both directions. From one perspective, all of the innovative works in cultural industries belong to a certain combination of the above five dimensions. Service innovation in cultural industries can only be consistently achieved through the development of each dimension and their connections and interactions. The proposed service innovation model is connected to five constructs by the following six value creation activities.

Often these cross-linkages are forged in practice by those responsible for 1) marketing, 2) organization development, and 3) distribution. Launching a new service concept or aesthetic content (for existing or new clients) requires marketing expertise e.g., the play spaces for children and young people in the Cultural Creative Industry Park. Similarly, creating an

	Art	Business	Creativity	Design	E-business
ABCDE Model Content	Our **Art** Museum	Our Factory & **Business**	**Cultural** production system.	Our **Design** Studio	ICT application and **E-business**
Revised Service Innovation Model	New service concept	New client interfaces	**New services transformation system**	New service delivery systems/ organization	Technology option
Activity/ Function	Knowledge of the characteristics of existing and competing services (Business intelligence)	Characteristics of actual and potential clients (Market intelligence)	Relationship with the actors, co-production and transfer of new service (Management intelligence)	Capabilities, skills & attitudes of existing and competing service workers (Human Resource Management)	Technology mainly playing a role as a facilitating or enabling factor in various innovation (Enabling technology)
Linkage					
New Service Concept		Marketing	*Creative subsystem*	Organization development	*The virtual integrates and widens the boundaries of the physical environment*
New Client Interfaces	Marketing		*Communication subsystem*	Distribution	*Enhancing the effectiveness of a particular strategy*
New Services Transformation System	*Creative subsystem*	*Communication subsystem*		*Service subsystem network*	*Value co-creation with the service systems networks*
New Service Delivery System/ Organization	Organization development	Distribution	*Service subsystem network*		*Platform for information distribution*
Technology Option	*The virtual integrates and widens the boundaries of the physical environment*	*Enhancing the effectiveness of a particular strategy*	*Value co-creation with the service systems networks*	*Platform for information distribution*	

Table 1. The relations of proposed constructs of service innovation, the ABCDE model and key findings.

adequate interface with clients, and adapting the service delivery system requires knowledge of how services are distributed (both in terms of where they are produced and of how they are delivered). Below, we briefly introduce three additional activities in the pathways between specific dimensions.

1. Service Subsystem Network
   The service subsystem network includes internal employees, private friends and other cultural gatekeepers (e.g. opinion leaders, family members, etc). The pathway emphasizes the opportunity to select people with relational and/or specific technical capabilities in order to support interaction in an industrial domain. Moreover, it is important for managers or staff in particular to have specific competencies that constitute defining co-workers for the organization. These resources allow them to take an active part in the guidance and advancement of a cultural organization.
2. Creative Subsystem
   The creative subsystem is responsible for generating new symbols or ideas. In this pathway, where Our Art Museum dematerializes their offerings, the social and

economic actors (e.g. sophisticated museum guides, college professors, etc.) play a key role in knowledge transfer within the creative subsystem. Our results clearly show that attention paid to the creation of creativity from a widespread culture. Some actors must become genuine knowledge integrators and combine the knowledge generated from the interactions of the cultural creative activities.

3. Communication Subsystem
   The communication subsystem has dual objectives. First, the subsystem strives to make vital processes specific to the design sectors they have decided to operate in more efficient. Second, it is responsible for giving meaning to new ideas, and providing them with symbolism to increase the added value of their services. In this approach, in which firms are involved in a process of replication of a school's niche strategy, factory staff, artisans and craft professors can also become genuine knowledge integrators, and include the information generated from their interactions with customers.

5. Conclusions

Based on Bilderbeek's four-dimension service innovation model and service system and cultural production system, we added a fifth "new services transformation system" dimension that plays an important role in the service innovation model for cultural creative industries. It expresses the new service concept synthetically, supported by factories and organizations, and maintains a relationship with the new client interface. On this dimension, the customer experience reflects much more about value integration and transformation, especially when joined with ICT applications. Any organizations and individuals involved in the service innovation model will contribute to the value creation and the transfer of cultural products/services. When the new service transformation is positive, it will develop a healthy client relationship network and integrate the whole service innovation process. This article allows the specificity of each construct to be emphasized, especially in terms of new services transformation systems and the role of technology. We found the convergence of cultural production systems and service science on the study of service systems to be particularly helpful in establishing a basis for systematic service innovation. The services transformation system dimension identifies the relationship with actors, value co-creation and transforms new service in enhancing management intelligence. We do not only see the generation of new service models but also perceive previous models increasing their efficiency and flexibility. From the service science perspective, we reinterpret the "ABCDE" model. We turn "Art" into "Business," while the process is combined with "Creativity," "Design," and "E-business" to transform the aesthetic values to commerce by service innovation.

This is a starting point for better understanding the role of ICT and soft innovation in supporting the redefinition of service innovation models and the conditions that enable their business development. The next step is more in-depth analysis. The proposed framework for service innovation management provides practitioners with a structured approach to manage the service innovations of the Cultural Creative Industry Park. We also anticipate that the paper will yield results of interest and usefulness to cultural parks that are developing new innovation service models around information and communication technologies. Future research efforts might be both qualitative and quantitative, and deepen the practical implications of the different roles played in service innovation in cultural and creative industries. The sample size should also be increased in future research, adding selected organizations that represent different cultural industries and different countries. Such a future study would avoid the argument that the case studies are too specific to be relevant to other organizations in culture-related businesses.

6. References

A. Osterwalder and Y. Pigneur, (2002) "An E-business Model Ontology for Modeling E-business," presented at the 15th Bled Electronic Commerce Conference e-Reality: Constructing the e-Economy, Bled, Slovenia.

Alladi Venkatesh and Laurie A. Meamber, (2006), "Arts and Aesthetics: Marketing and Cultural Production," Marketing Theory, Vol. 6 (1), pp. 11-39.

Chen Chun-Liang, Jaw Yi-Long, (2009). "Building global dynamic capabilities through innovation: A case study of Taiwan's cultural organizations ", Journal of Engineering and Technology Management, Vol. 26(4), pp. 247-263.

Coombs, R., Miles, I. (2000), "Innovation, Measurement and Services: the new problematique", in Metcalfe, J. S. and Miles, I. (eds.), Innovation Systems in the Service Economy, Kluwer Academic Publishers, Boston, pp. 85-103.

de Jong, J., Vermeulen, P. (2003), "Organizing successful new service development: a literature review", Management decision, Vol. 41 No. 9, pp. 844-858.

de Vries, E. J. (2006), "Innovation in services in networks of organizations and in the distribution of services", Research Policy, Vol. 25, pp. 1037-1051.

Edvardsson, B., Gustafsson, A., Johnson, M. D., Sandén, B. (2000), New Service Development and Innovation in the New Economy, Studentlitteratur, Lund.

Edvardsson, B., Gustafsson, A., Enquist, B. (2007), "Success factors in new service development and value creation through services", in Spath, D. and Fähnrich, K. P. (Eds.), Advances in Services Innovations, Springer, Berlin, pp. 165-185.

Gallouj, F. (1998), Innovating in reverse: services and the reverse product. European Journal of Innovation Management, Vol.13, p123–138.

Gallouj, F. & O. Weinstein, (1997), Innovation in services, in Research Policy, 26, pp. 537-556.

Gallouj, F. (2002), Innovation in the Service Economy: The New Wealth of Nations, Edward Elgar, Cheltenham.

Geertz, C. (1973), The Interpretation of Cultures. New York: Basic Books.

Grönroos, C. (2007), In Search of a New Logic for Marketing: Foundations of Contemporary Theory, John Wiley & Sons.

Gustafsson, A. and Johnson, M. (2003), Competing in a Service Economy: How to Create a Competitive Advantage through Service Development and Innovation, Jossey-Bass, San Francisco, CA.

Gummesson, E. (2004), "Return on relationship (ROR): the value of relationship marketing and CRM in business-to-business contexts", Journal of Business & Industrial Marketing, Vol. 19 No. 2, pp. 136-148.

Gummesson, E. (2006), "Many-to-many marketing as grand theory: A Nordic School contribution". In Lusch, R. F. and Vargo, S. L. (Eds.), Toward a Service-Dominant Logic of Marketing: Dialog, Debate, and Directions. New York.

Hesmondhalgh, D. (2007). The Cultural Industries, Sage, London.

Hirsch, P.M. 1972. Processing Fads and Fashions: An Organization-Set Analysis of Cultural Industry Systems. The American Journal of Sociology, Vol. 77(4), pp. 639 – 659.

Joy, A. (1998), "Framing Art: The Role of Galleries in the Circulation of Art", in J.F. Sherry, Jr. (ed.) Servicescapes, pp. 259–303. Chicago, IL: American Marketing Association.

Joy, A. (2000), "Art, Works of Art, and the Discourse of Fine Art: Between Art Worlds and Art Markets", in R.W. Belk, J. Costa and J. Schouten (eds) Research in Consumer Behavior, pp. 71–102. Stamford, CT: JAI Press.

Kozinets, R. V. (2001), "Utopian experience: Articulating the Meanings of Star Trek's Culture of Consumption", Journal of Consumer Research, Vol. 28(1), pp. 67–88.

Lash, S. and Urry, J., (1994/ 2002) Economies of Sign and Space. London: Sage.

Lin, R. (2007), "Transforming Taiwan Aboriginal Cultural Features Into Modern Product Design – A Case Study of Cross Cultural Product Design Model," International Journal of Design, vol. 1, pp. 45-53.

Lin, R. M.-X. Sun, Y.-P. Chang, Y.-C. Chan, Y.-C. Hsieh, and Y.-C. Huang, (2007), "Designing "Culture" into Modern Product: A Case Study of Cultural Product Design," ed., pp. 146-153.

Lin, R. (2009)，Designing Friendship into Modern Products. In: Friendships: Types, Cultural, Psychological and Social, Editor: Joan C. Toller, NY: Nova Science Publishers, Inc. (ISBN: 978-1-61668-008-4)

Lin, R. & Lin, C. L. (2010). "From Digital Archive to E-Business - A Case Study of Turning "Art" to "E-Business". Proceedings of 2010 International Conference on E-Business, Athens, Greece.

Love, J. H., Mansury, M. A. (2007), "External linkages, R&D and innovation performance in US business services", Industry and Innovation, Vol. 14 No. 5, pp. 477-496.

McCracken, G. (1986), "Culture and Consumption: A Theoretical Account of the Structure and Movement of the Cultural Meaning of Goods", Journal of Consumer Research Vol. 13(1), pp. 71–84.

M. Dubosson-Torbay, A. Osterwalder, and Y. Pigneur, (2002), "E-business model design, classification, and measurements," Thunderbird International Business Review, vol. 44, pp. 5-23.

MOEA (2005), Taiwan annual report: Cultural and creative industries, Ministry of Economic Affairs, Taiwan, Republic of China.

M. Haglind and J. Helander,(1998), "Development of Value Networks -an Empirical Study of Networking in Swedish Manufacturing Industries," In the proceedings of IEMC'98 conference, Puerto Rico, USA, pp. 350-358.

Michel, S., Brown, S.W. and Gallan, A.S. (2008), "An expanded and strategic view of discontinuous innovations: deploying a service-dominant logic", Journal of the Academy of Marketing Science, Vol. 36 No. 1, pp. 54-66.

Miles I. and Green L., (2008), Hidden Innovation in the Creative Industries, NESTA: London.

Miles, I., Kastrinos, N., Flanagan, K., Bilderbeek R., Den Hertog P., Huntik, W., Bouman, M. (1995), Knowledge-Intensive Business Services: Users, Carriers and Sources of Innovation[R]. Rapport pours DG13 SPRINT-EIMS, March, 1995.

Normann, R. (2001), Reframing business - When the Map changes the Landscape, Wiley, UK. Kandampully, J., (2002), "Innovation as the core competency of a service organization: the role of technology, knowledge and networks", European Journal of Innovation Management, Vol. 5, No. 1, pp. 18-26.

Parsons, T. (1960). Structure and Process in Modern Societies. Glencoe, Ill.: Free Press.

P. Hekkert, D. Snelders, and P. C. W. van Wieringen, (2003), "Most advanced, yet acceptable: Typicality and novelty as joint predictors of aesthetic preference in industrial design," British Journal of Psychology, vol. 94, pp. 111-124.

Pine, II, B. J., Gilmore J. H. (1999), The Experience Economy_ Work Is Theatre and Every Business a Stage, Harvard Business School Press, Cambridge, MA.

Prahalad, C. K. and Ramaswamy, V . (2004), The Future of Competition: Co-creating Unique Value with Customers, Harvard Business School Press, Boston, MA.

Preissl, B. (2000), "Service Innovation: What Makes It Different? Empirical Evidence from Germany", in Metcalfe, J.S. and Miles, I. (eds.), Innovation Systems in the Service Economy, Measurement and Case Study Analysis, Kluwer Academic Publishers, Dordrecht, pp. 125–148.

Roberta Sebastiani , Marco Paiola (2010), "Rethinking service innovation: four pathways to evolution", International Journal of Quality and Service Sciences, Vol. 2 No. 1, pp. 79-94.

Schmitt B. (1999), "Experiential marketing", Journal of Marketing Management, Vol. 15, pp. 53-67.

Scott, A. J. (2000), The Cultural Economy of Cities, London: Sage.

Solomon, M. R. (1986). The Missing Link: Surrogate Consumers in the Marketing Chain. Journal of Marketing, Vol. 50 (October), pp. 208 - 218.

Solomon, M.R. (1988), "Building Up and Breaking Down: The Impact of Cultural Sorting on Symbolic Consumption", in J. Sheth and E.C. Hirschman (eds) Research in Consumer Behavior, pp. 325–51. Greenwich, CT: JAI Press.

Solomon, M. R. (1992). Consumer Behavior. Boston: Allyn&Bacon.

Solomon, M.; Bamossy, G.; Askegaard, S. (2002). Consumer Behavior - A European Perspective, 2nd edition. Upper Saddle River, NJ: Prentice-Hall. pp. 471 - 475.

Solomon, M.R. (2003) Consumer Behavior: Buying, Having and Being. Saddleback, NJ: Prentice Hall.

Spohrer, J. and Maglio, P. P. (2008), "The emergence of service science: toward systematic service innovations to accelerate co-creation of value", Production and Operations Management, Vol. 17 No. 3, pp. 238-46.

Sundbo, J., Gallouj, F. (2000), "Innovation as a Loosely Coupled Systems in Services", in Metcalfe, J. S. and Miles, I. (eds.), Innovation Systems in the Service Economy: Measurement and Case Study Analysis, Kluwer Academic Publishers, Boston, pp. 43-68.

Tether, B. S. and Metcalfe, J. S. (2003), Services and Systems of Innovation. CRIC Discussion Paper n. 58, February.

Tether, B. S. and Tajar A. (2008), "The organizational-cooperation mode of innovation and its prominence 1 amongst European service firms", Research Policy, Vol. 37, pp. 720–739.

UNESCO (2000). What do we understand by Culture Industries? In "Culture Trade and Globalization". United Nations Educational, Scientific and Cultural Organization. Retrieved March 1, 2005, from http://www.unesco.org/culture/industries/trade/html_eng/question1.shtml

Vargo, S. L. and Lusch, R. F. (2008), "Service-dominant logic: continuing the evolution", Journal of the Academy of Marketing Science, Vol. 36 No 1, pp.1-10.

Wei Jiang, Mark Boden, (2004), "Knowledge-intensive Business Service & Innovation." Beijing: Science Press, pp. 15–16.

Wen-Hong Chiu, Li-Sheng Chu, (2010), "Exploring Service Innovation of Culture Parks in Taiwan: A Perspective of Cultural Value", Service Systems and Service Management (ICSSSM), 2010 7th International Conference, Tokyo

Wu Ching-Sung, Liu Su-Houn, Chen Chun-Liang, (2009). "The Asymmetries Alliances of E-Business MNE Subsidiaries in Taiwan ", International Journal of Technology Management, Vol. 48(3), pp. 336-357.

Zhang Yu, Lin Lei, Wu Gui-sheng. (2005), Research on the type of corporate service innovation. Technology Management Research, 9. p130-133 (in Chinese)

Zeithaml, V.A., Bitner, M. J., and Gremler, D. D. (2006), Services marketing: Integrating customer focus across the firm (4th ed.), McGraw-Hill, New York.